W9-BGE-435

Popular Cinema as Political Theory

Popular Cinema as Political Theory

Idealism and Realism in Epics, Noirs, and Satires

John S. Nelson

First published in 2013 by
PALGRAVE MACMILLAN®
in the United States—a division of St. Martin's Press LLC,
175 Fifth Avenue, New York, NY 10010.

Where this book is distributed in the UK, Europe and the rest of the world,
this is by Palgrave Macmillan, a division of Macmillan Publishers Limited,
registered in England, company number 785998, of Houndmills,
Basingstoke, Hampshire RG21 6XS.

Palgrave Macmillan is the global academic imprint of the above companies
and has companies and representatives throughout the world.

Palgrave® and Macmillan® are registered trademarks in the United States,
the United Kingdom, Europe and other countries.

ISBN: 978–1–137–37470–7

Library of Congress Cataloging-in-Publication Data

Nelson, John S., 1950–
    Popular cinema as political theory : idealism and realism in epics,
noirs, and satires / John S. Nelson.
        pages cm
    Includes index.
    ISBN 978–1–137–37470–7 (alk. paper)
        1. Motion pictures—Political aspects—United States. 2. Politics in
motion pictures. I. Title.

PN1995.9.P6N46 2013
791.43'6581—dc23   2013024783

A catalogue record of the book is available from the British Library.

Design by Newgen Knowledge Works (P) Ltd., Chennai, India.

First edition: December 2013

10 9 8 7 6 5 4 3 2 1

For Anna Lorien,
whose conversations encourage
and whose suggestions enhance

Contents

Tables

Acknowledgments

The first time I taught political theory to university students, we found ourselves debating the virtues and advantages of idealism versus realism in political action. When do people of high principle improve our lives with politics of grand vision? When do we fare better with strategies of clear-eyed calculation and practices of hardball enforcement? This wasn't a focus I'd planned for the course, but it emerged unmistakably in our vigorous conversations. I've seen since that it comes often to the fore when analyzing political action, especially for the familiar venues of our everyday lives. I hope that this makes a book on political idealism and realism in popular cinema a good way to thank the generations of students who've been helping me learn politics, especially in popular culture. The book emphasizes movies that are epics, noirs, and satires because they are three of the popular forms most conventionally connected to politics of idealism versus realism.

Popular genres of film, television, and literature are more recent preoccupations of mine. To explore their politics is a telling way to carry out my long-standing fascination with inquiries that feature analysis of rhetoric in facing how certainties and necessities lie mostly beyond the horizons of the human sciences. Popular cinema turns out to be a special joy to explore with students in their teens and twenties. Sometimes it delves into complications of our everyday situations. Sometimes it summons elements from our diverse pasts. Sometimes it leaps toward possibilities for our distant futures. But always, it taps an impressive sophistication that young people in our culture develop early for making sense of moving pictures. This extends to their recurrent forms—from comedies, fantasies, and mysteries to romances, thrillers, and westerns.

The pages to come examine politics in many movies and a few television series. It also attends to several of the popular novels that have helped inspire these entertainments. All these are popular in every sense. They are the kinds of films and shows that rerun almost continually on cable, and they are the sorts of best sellers or cult classics that linger year after year in book stores. You're likely to know lots of them already, and you're apt to enjoy most of the rest.

The essays in this volume spring primarily from discussions with students, and that's why the main acknowledgment must go to them. All the movies and shows analyzed here also have been discussed in great detail with family members. Especially they have been addressed with Connie Nelson, who's been my movie companion for many decades. Without her help, this book would have been inconceivable.

Colleagues have contributed too. Even though movies are not his thing, Bob Boynton is a fine and faithful sounding board for the "unusual" ideas about politics that inform my takes on popular cinema in particular and popular culture in general. Early versions of the chapters ahead have gained from suggestions at several professional meetings as well. The American Political Science Association accommodated discussion of one chapter; the Midwestern Political Science Association hosted examination of a second; the Western Political Science Association made time for talking through a third; and the Foundations of Political Theory Annual Workshop on Political Myth, Rhetoric, and Symbolism addressed a fourth. The University of Iowa Project on Rhetoric of Inquiry has helped improve my writing for more than three decades, and this book owes a lot to it. Colleagues in its Rhetoric Seminar have provided useful feedback on one of the essays to follow, then vetted another with an even wider audience. Likewise friends in the Foundations Workshop on Political Myth, Rhetoric, and Symbolism have sustained two decades of provocative essays, terrific commentaries, and otherwise wonderful conversations. I thank all these scholars for their intellectual curiosity, political wisdom, and generosity in sharing their own work as well as engaging mine.

INTRODUCTION

Doing Political Theory with Popular Films: Styles in Action in Everyday Life

(Featuring *Star Trek Into Darkness*)

Americans don't read books;
Americans don't read newspapers;
Americans go to the movies.[1]

—Stephen Colbert

Popular movies, novels, and television series help make our politics by making our myths. These are the symbolic stories that shape and make sense of what people do.[2] It's easy to see political mythmaking in movies like *Argo* (2012), *Lincoln* (2012), and *Zero Dark Thirty* (2012). Each concerns historical figures in the official, if sometimes secret, politics of government.[3] When we see Tony Mendez (Ben Affleck) of the CIA rescuing American diplomats from a hostile Iran, or we see "Maya" (Jessica Chastain) of the CIA tracking Osama bin Laden to his death in Pakistan, we need not see James Bond (Daniel Craig) resurrected in *Skyfall* (2012) to know that covert operations are back in heroic vogue. When we watch President Lincoln (Daniel Day-Lewis) shaving truths, trading jobs for votes, or otherwise playing gutter-ball to outlaw slavery, none of us misses that the current occupant of the Oval Office has a mighty model for stooping to compromise—and "get things done."

Yet it's not always easy to say what our myths of governing might mean for everyday politics in the mundane lives of ordinary people. Nor is it always clear how a popular movie presents any political stories, whether for presidents or nonvoters. Why consider that potent myths of politics might lurk in a run-of-the-mill romantic comedy?[4] Why seek politics for us regular folks in a radically unrealistic thriller?[5] Or why think that the politics in watching prime-time television preoccupy many a vampire movie?[6] And if movie politics often seem elusive, how can carefully combined and refined ideas about those politics—in other words, how can political theories—be developed in movies, TV, or novels, whether mythically or otherwise?

Political Mythmaking in Popular Genres

Even people prominently linked to popular literature and cinema go so far as to deny that movies can be vehicles for ideas of any kind. Author and provocateur Gore Vidal contended that "a moving picture, because it moves, is the one form of narrative that cannot convey an idea of any kind, as opposed to a generalized emotion."[7] Vidal knew all too well the major political figures of his day, he ran twice for public office, he wrote highly respected novels of politics and ideas, he even created screenplays for popular cinema and television.[8] So he was well-positioned to know. And yet...and yet...Vidal also acted in two movies with myths of popular politics that can speak instructively to political theory. He played Senator Brickley Paiste in *Bob Roberts* (1992), which surpasses even *A Face in the Crowd* (1957) at showing the everyday dynamics of right-wing populism in the United States. Then in *Shadow Conspiracy* (1997), Vidal played Congressman Page in a movie developed enough in its political ideas to name an entire subgenre of conspiracy thrillers for purposes of analysis by political theorists.[9]

That does not make *Shadow Conspiracy* particularly good as a movie, and maybe Vidal would have taken this to concede his claim. (Surely he wouldn't have acceded without some acerbic reply.) On the other hand, *Bob Roberts* is an engaging and enduring movie, analyzed later in this book. Moreover many of our most intriguing, powerful, and practical myths of politics for citizens in their daily lives are the symbolic stories captured by the conventions that define individual genres for novels, movies, television, and other popular media.[10] The ambition of this book is to show how we can learn from the political theories in these myths.

The mythic figures in popular genres are the characters, settings, and events familiar from many works in the genre. The myth of St. George and the dragon is conventional for epics. This means that, in many epics, a hero defeats a monster in its lair to rescue a damsel in distress. For all its feminism, *Titanic* (1997) articulates that pattern. Other epics enact an odyssey, as in *Cold Mountain* (2003), where a hero confronts diverse dangers in coming home. Still other epics lay a hero low before he rises again to liberate his community, as in *Braveheart* (1995), *Gladiator* (2000), and *The Dark Knight* trilogy (2005, 2008, and 2012).[11] Further templates of myth have also become conventional for popular epics, but then most popular genres are sprawling and varied.

We also need to recognize that stray figures from any of these epic myths can appear in particular works that are not epics. By popular genre, *Hannibal* (2001) is horror and noir rather than epic. Still it features a female St. George in Clarice Starling (Julianne Moore). From a human monster, Mason Verger (Gary Oldman), Clarice rescues Hannibal Lecter (Anthony Hopkins) as a male in distress, although admittedly monstrous himself. Of course, Hannibal contrives to be saved by Clarice from Mason and his mafia minions, so that she might learn to protect Hannibal. He even hopes that she might come to love him or at least emulate his strange, perfectionist leap beyond the movie's focal clash between her moral idealism and the political realism of an FBI that employs but harasses and scapegoats her. (This book's final chapter returns to perfectionism as peculiar politics that sometimes unsettle Western dilemmas of idealism versus realism.) But at a minimum, Hannibal wants to rescue Clarice from the predatory sexism and other aspects of patriarchy that she suffers in the Department of Justice. Then, more conventionally, he's St. George; and she's the damsel in distress—even as their movie remains horror and noir, not epic.

Therefore no individual convention of a popular genre can be a necessary or a sufficient condition for a movie to manifest that genre. Instead a popular genre is a somewhat ragged and changeable network of conventions. These recur much of the time and in various mythic permutations throughout the genre's many works. To identify the popular genre(s) of a particular work, we need to notice the conventions that predominate in making it meaningful. Mostly this is a quick, easy, consensual call. Popular forms help us cognitively as we ascertain and communicate meanings for politics or anything else.[12] And when there is uncertainty or controversy about the genre of a work, the resulting investigations can spur the sorts of productive discussions that improve our political theories.

My project here is to appreciate the political mythmaking in popular genres as especially practical and accessible theorizing about politics. In popular movies, novels, and television series, the politics are mostly in settings outside the modern institutions of government. To make sense of politics in popular genres is to do political theory with the myths that surface in the uses of genre conventions by specific stories or dramas. This requires resisting our academic and cultural assumption that myths are mistakes somehow embraced by many people, past or present. The mythic politics in popular cultures are not outdated beliefs, widespread falsehoods, or appealing exaggerations.[13] Actually myths vary in purpose, power, and truth.[14] To understand the mythic politics in popular genres and to assess their implications for political theory, as our explanations of politics, we do especially well to compare genres and particular works within them.[15] Here the focus falls on epic movies, political satires, and neo-noir films.

Like all popular genres in our cultures, these are modes of political action. They remake the political myths we learn and live as citizens. The mythic accounts of politics we find in works for popular genres can refine and extend our academic accounts of politics. These popular theories of politics often pay more attention to the cultural, social, and psychological textures of our lives.[16] These popular theories of politics are sometimes more imaginative than our academic theories in choosing cases, configuring causes, and conceiving alternatives. In addition, the aesthetics of popular media such as cinema and television typically enable their accounts of politics to be more vivid in presenting political characters, actions, situations, and prospects. Such lessons spring from discussing hundreds and hundreds of movies with college students, graduate students, colleagues, and friends. Yet many of them would have me tell the story of this book in a more personal way.

Political Styles in Everyday Action

The chapters to come feature three popular genres that almost everybody knows, although not necessarily by the names I favor: epics, noirs, and satires. Popular movies and novels have prospered in all three of these genres in recent decades, although the story of popular television is more mixed. Yet by academic reputation, none of the three genres seems strongly tied to the others, to the lives of ordinary people in electronic times, or to their everyday politics. Each of the genre studies ahead contributes to correcting those misimpressions. I conceived each as a separate, stand-alone study; and any of them can be read that way by anybody particularly interested in its focal genre or featured films. Yet in analyzing the films, I started to learn how strikingly the different studies can complement each other—for all address the Western antinomy of idealism versus realism.

In Western civilization, the antagonism between political realism and political idealism is at least as old as Niccolò Machiavelli's realist advice that *The Prince* "must learn how not to be good"—in part by turning away from ideal societies and principles.[17] Within a few years of Machiavelli's writing, Thomas More ventured a classic idealist counter in his *Utopia*.[18] But the dispute arguably goes back to the West's beginnings in ancient Greece, which pitted Sophists (often realists in a rough sense) against Platonists (idealists, if not exactly of a modern kind).[19]

There are many dimensions and dynamics of idealism, and the same goes for realism. By now, their running disputes have become convoluted in theory and complicated in practice. If we start simply, though, we can say that idealists guide political action by applying principles, thus shaping realities to principles and ideals far more than the reverse. Realists guide political action by calculating consequences, thereby letting recent results and current complications inform ideals and principles far more than the other way around.

On this basis, the respective criticisms are familiar.[20] Realists complain that, since ends must justify means, idealists confuse ends sought (ideals) with ends attained (results). This leads idealists to miss what's actually happening and why, typically at a terrible cost, all too often to others. The road to hell is paved with good intentions, say the realists. Idealists lament that, because means must constitute ends, realists let themselves assume that any means—however awful—can be redeemed by great enough ends. That induces realists to overreach in their aims and brutalize by their means, while excusing bad results now as steps toward better results later. Doing whatever it takes is a recipe for going disastrously overboard, answer the idealists. Bryan Cranston's Walter White in *Breaking Bad* (2008–2013) is a case in point.

Idealists pride themselves on high standards and deep sympathies, realists on hard heads and harder hearts. Realists also celebrate their capacities for success, and their insistence on this seems persuasive to most Americans. Isn't it most moral to get the best results practical? That's what realists promote; and they're right not to cede morality or virtue by definition to idealists. Realism deserves to be respected as political morality and not just as political strategy. The trouble is that realist claims to monopolize practical success or even strategy merely turn the definitional tables on idealists, who also can make good cases for practical as well as moral efficacy.

Philosophers go to town with idealism and realism. There are ontological idealists, such as Plato on *eidoi* (ideas, forms) as the true beings behind the shadowy appearances that are the ordinary things in our everyday lives; and there are ontological realists, such as the scientists who take the detailed subsistence of the world that they study to be completely independent of their inquiry. There are aesthetic realists, epistemic realists, ethnographic realists, legal realists, literary realists, photorealists, theatrical realists, and more.[21] In counterpoint, there are absolute idealists, actual idealists, linguistic idealists, musical idealists, objective idealists, transcendental idealists, and others. The twentieth century invented magical realism as a popular genre of fiction and film to explore the strange extremities of mundane existence in our oxymoronic conditions of partial totalitarianism, routinized terror, and creeping catastrophe.[22] Recent decades propose practical utopianism as a form of theory-in-action for persistent radicals who refuse despair.[23] Eventually, almost inevitably, idealists scramble for the resources taken to distinguish realists, and vice versa.

Across their many fields and inflections, we may suspect, idealism and realism remain in some part projects of politics.[24] In the pages at hand, idealism and realism are political styles.[25] They are sensibilities for experiencing community affairs. Especially they are distinctive ways for doing community business—which is to say, for engaging people who share significant aspects of their lives. Often we analyze styles in terms similar to genres. Thus political styles distinguish themselves in part by the typical characters, settings, and performances they recognize and enact. So these aspects of idealism and realism dominate the detailed takes on popular movies to come.

Still we should pause to notice that politics are plastic and energetic enough to evolve simultaneously in several forms: as styles, structures, movements, ideologies, and more. At any given time, to be sure, different politics feature different forms. At present, monarchism and totalitarianism are principally politics of structure, featuring distinctive forms of government. Feminism and environmentalism are primarily movements, coalescing from diverse angles to move against patriarchal oppressions and industrial developments, respectively, more than toward some characteristic institutions or creeds. Socialism and libertarianism are currently articulated as ideologies. In other words, they specify social sciences and diagram ideal communities, which they use by contrast to diagnose current maladies. Then such ideologies offer prognoses; and if they project further ills along current trajectories, the ideologies prescribe therapies to cure political diseases and pursue political ideals. For a century, political theory has emphasized ideologies.

But these days, at least, neither idealism nor realism aspires to be an ideology of politics. Neither tries for the detail needed by a social science or a policy platform. If idealism or realism promotes a form of government at present, it sounds the same for both: "democracy." But for both, it remains a diffuse gesture more than a specific structure. In fact, the two use the same word for contrary structures. Idealism seeks direct or popular democracies; while realism wants elite, pluralist, or representative democracies. Neither faces well enough the practical and theoretical troubles with "democracy" as a form of government to proceed mainly in that mode.[26]

It's clear that idealists criticize realism, and realists contest idealism; but it's not clear that either kind of politics coheres tightly enough to specify government programs. Idealists show family resemblances in their political sensibilities and gestures, but idealists are too diverse in their priorities and methods to look much like a political movement. The same goes for realists. Therefore we do better to appreciate idealism and realism as political styles for personal action, especially in everyday life.[27] Popular movies, novels, and TV are good at exploring such politics; and these media attend most acutely to political idealism and political realism via popular genres.

Political Forms in Cinema Analysis

Political idealism is especially at home in popular epics. Therefore the first chapter considers the implications for political theory of a recent resurgence in epic movies from Hollywood.[28] It notices the role of computer graphics in accommodating affordably the vast scale and ambitious imagination conventional for epics. Nevertheless it shows how these resources support epic responses to challenges of imperial politics faced by the United States. The result is an idealist repertoire of political devices for liberating communities from dynamics of empire. To augment these epic lessons for political theory, a coda considers how the political preoccupations of epic movies also surface in the academic call for "epic political theory" as a mode of political action.

Satires ironize our hopes, fears, and realities, our standards and practices. They doubt, debunk, deconstruct, ridicule, and otherwise run riot with politics. Their motley styles often alternate between idealism and realism. The second chapter features three movies that satirize populism as campaign and movement politics, for populism also has become especially prominent in American politics in the last quarter-century. The three share a playful emphasis on popular songs, and this helps them explore rhythms of political action that scholarly theories of populism neglect. The three films also share the motley, episodic plots of epics. That helps them spotlight the political mythmaking in popular entertainments like movies. It enables them to demonstrate the acumen of some political theories apparent in popular cinema. And in a coda, it lets the three films contribute to our theories of political truth.

For several decades, the film noir that coalesced with the Second World War has become a popular genre often called neo noir. As a cluster of films, classic noir has been celebrated for its realism in aesthetics and politics. As a popular genre starting to reach beyond movies to literature and television, neo noir remains fascinated by realism; but it's becoming more open to idealism. The third chapter analyzes realist and idealist politics in three neo noirs of great cinematic power. Along the way, it refines the political theory of realism as a political style. Next it explicates a trenchant criticism of realism in everyday life, one that needs to inform more academic theories of politics. Then its coda sketches a theory of idealist style as an alternative for action in public and private endeavors.

The fourth chapter engages the political debate between realism and idealism in a series of eight movies made annually of late for television. Individually and overall, these movies meld the popular genres of epic and noir. Hence they provide occasions for articulating the political theories of epic and noir that have been emerging in the earlier studies, while doing the same for the accounts that have been coalescing for idealism and realism as political styles. These eight movies provide a rare and provocative experiment in everyday encounters of (epic) idealism with (noir) realism. As epic noir, each movie gives us a keen sense of idealism and realism as political styles in everyday action. Yet because the eight movies also work together as a dramatic series on television, a coda for the fourth chapter can explore several intriguing inferences about the political inclinations of American television by comparison with Hollywood cinema.

Idealism and realism are far from the only political styles prominent in our times. Among the many others is perfectionism after the fashion of Friedrich Nietzsche. Of late, it's coalesced as the style that distinguishes some of Hollywood's most striking characters. In confrontations, perfectionists often defeat idealists and realists, left and right; and perfectionist politics even unsettle Western oppositions between idealism and realism. The concluding chapter analyzes two recent classics of neo noir to identify key characteristics and consequences of perfectionism as a style of personal action. It also connects these to perspectivism in doing political theory. In turn, this enables a coda to acknowledge several kinds of formalism—on the way to answering worries that a formal analysis of political styles tends to favor idealism.

Each chapter—save, arguably, for this one—concludes with a coda. As a device, the coda is familiar to most people from music. In music, a coda is a passage that suits a composition enough to end it in style—yet differs from it enough (in pace, register, rhythm, or the like) to seem somewhat independent, to accomplish something further, and thus to expand its horizons. That's exactly the contribution from each coda to come.

As the next chapter explains, codas are conventional for popular epics. Rather than an argumentative chain of premises and conclusions or a historical line of causes and effects, an epic stitches several episodes into a loose series that need not follow or produce a linear logic. Each episode is an emblem of the epic's focal tale, hero, or community; each is a somewhat independent moment that evokes aspects of the whole. Accordingly an epic coda is a concluding emblem that shifts register to evoke the whole in a somewhat different way, adding to our awareness of what's at stake. It also reminds us that the exposition is not linear overall.

As a paradigm for political mythmaking, epic is an abiding concern here. That holds even when a different genre such as noir or satire takes center stage for the moment, and the codas can remind us of the continuing interest in epic. Moreover this entire effort has an epic—which is to say, episodic—structure. Composed somewhat separately, each chapter has been stitched loosely to the others, providing an account of adventures in doing political theory as analysis of popular cinema. The codas help us reach for the greater horizons possible in such a project.

Perhaps paradoxically, though, this introduction ends with a proem for the whole book ahead—more than with a coda for the few pages already behind. In general, a proem is a preamble, an introductory discourse. In epics, a proem is an introductory emblem of the whole work. An epic proem is an opening episode that encapsulates and previews the principal pattern that helps the epic cohere. As literary theorists say, it evokes the figure in the carpet. It starts the epic with a sample moment that engages the audience, and it imparts an initial sense of how to receive the rest of the story. In this respect, a proem launches the epic in the midst of its action, with an exemplar of what's to come.

A rough equivalent for this appreciation of popular cinema as political theory is to start by analyzing idealism and realism in a movie of interest to prospective readers. For some readers, though, such a beginning could seem like starting in midstream. To entice, not confuse, the opening has been conventional for the human sciences. Yet we needn't miss all the advantages of leaping early into the political analysis of a popular film. We can end this introductory discourse with a proem for the book as a whole; and by epic convention, it can turn the sections so far into our invocation of the muse.

A Proem on the Prime Directive

Through midyear, at this writing, one of the highest-grossing movies of 2013 has been *Star Trek Into Darkness*. By popular genre, it's not exactly epic; and it's far from noir or satire. But its genre of science fiction suits political theory especially well and often resembles epic.[29] In fact, there's outright overlap in stately works of cinema such as Stanley Kubrick's *2001: A Space Odyssey* (1969), *Dune* (1984), and *Cloud Atlas* (2012). Literary science fiction from Olaf Stapledon and Doris Lessing partakes too.[30] And *Star Trek: The Motion Picture* (1979), the first of the many movies set in the *Star Trek* universe, is itself an epic. Yes, its sequels instead fit an action-adventure template that makes room for modern histories and individuals while keeping many conventions of epic.[31] And yes, a big part of the J. J. Abrams job as director in launching the latest series of *Star Trek* films, of which *Star Trek Into Darkness* is the second, seems to be adjusting the franchise further into thrillers. Yet more chases, fights, and surprises still leave thrillers recognizable as epic offshoots, and *Star Trek Into Darkness* focuses on idealism versus realism.[32]

To clinch the case, *Star Trek Into Darkness* begins with its own proem on perplexities of political idealism and realism. The movie opens in the midst of a chase scene. A legend on the screen locates it on the Planet Nibiru. Known to viewers from a prequel and lots of predecessors, the captain and medical officer of the Federation Starship USS Enterprise sprint through something like a cornfield. Robes and cosmetics disguise them as Nibiruns, who race after Kirk (Chris Pine) and McCoy (Karl Urban) from a primitive city at the foot of a massive volcano. Suddenly a fierce creature looms before the two, but a phaser blast from Kirk knocks it down and out. Bones grouses that Kirk has just stopped their rescue. Kirk has been running with a scroll. Possibly to slow pursuit, he puts it high on a plant, where it unrolls to show a diagram with text. The Nibiruns pause before it. Kirk and McCoy run past more plants, reach a cliff, leap into an ocean, and board their submerged starship.

Meanwhile Spock (Zachary Quinto) places bombs in the volcano, to dampen its impending eruption and save the Nibiruns from extinction. The Enterprise can't link to Spock well enough to beam him back, but he's ready to sacrifice himself to save Nibiru, and he completes placing the explosives. To follow "the Prime Directive," the Enterprise and its mission must stay unnoticed by the Nibiruns, to keep from changing their nascent civilization. "If Spock were here and I were there," Kirk asks, "what would he do?" The matter-of-fact answer is, "He'd let you die." But Kirk is not willing for Spock to sacrifice himself. Against arguments from Spock and others, Kirk has the Enterprise rise from the sea and fly over the mouth of the volcano. This enables it to beam up Spock, then power toward the stars. The spectacle is breathtaking! Standing over the scroll, the Nibiruns see the Enterprise soar from the sea to loom over the volcano, see the volcano start to explode but sputter to a stop, then see the ship streak beyond the clouds.

This beginning is the film in a nutshell. Kirk reports the mission as a success, and arguably it is: saving Nibiru, the Enterprise, McCoy, Kirk, and Spock. But the Prime Directive—to explore and observe but not interfere—has been violated. By proem's end, the Nibiruns are already sketching the starship and debating what they've seen. And that's the account sent separately to headquarters by First Officer Spock.

Cut to Starfleet Command in San Francisco, on Earth. For trashing the Prime Directive against interference in a planet's early evolution and civilization, Kirk is stripped of his starship. His career continues only because Captain Pike (Bruce Greenwood), who'd induced Kirk to enlist, lobbies to reeducate him as first officer on another ship. Pike fumes that Kirk doesn't recognize how the rules apply to him even when he disagrees with them.

Lacking humility, Kirk thinks that rules are for other people. He doesn't comply with them, doesn't take responsibility for that or anything else, and doesn't "respect the chair" of a starship captain. Instead, says Pike, Kirk uses "blind luck to justify playing God." In this last complaint, though, is a telling observation. Kirk's audacity as a realist, who breaks rules so that he—but especially others—might live long and prosper, somehow keeps winning him and them the favor of an otherwise fickle Lady Luck. In other words, Kirk as a realist shows striking skill at courting *fortuna*, as theorized in *The Prince* by Niccolò Machiavelli to be crucial for modern political leaders who go boldly where no one has gone before.[33]

The Prime Directive is a focal convention of *Star Trek* shows, video games, and feature-length films. It's a wonderful figure for thought-provoking movies. Taken literally, however, it's a strange way to run a Starfleet, as the proem for *Star Trek Into Darkness* suggests. How could the initial mission to save Nibiru from extinction by a volcano sidestep a verdict of interference? By staying secret from the Nibiruns? Isn't interference undetected still interference? *Could* it make no difference to their culture? Have they no ideas to be affected by making the volcano implode rather than explode? How could Starfleet know? As a philosophical axiom of action, the Prime Directive is an exercise in perplexity: either an intervention has no unintended effects because it makes no differences at all, or it makes differences big enough for side effects to be inevitable. After all, intended differences have to be big enough to be worth the huge expenses, risks, and sacrifices involved in Starfleet missions.

Whether to reveal the ship in saving Spock arises as a challenge in the midst of a mission to interfere, with Kirk and McCoy already chased from the city, the scroll already unfurled, and the mountain already showing signs of eruption. Spock's readiness to sacrifice himself to keep the starship unseen is inspiring, if no less than we'd expect from such a renowned and rational idealist. But it's hard to see how Kirk is wrong to save Spock, and it's even harder to see how Spock or Starfleet Command can cite the Prime Directive as a reason to let Spock die.

Nonetheless Kirk goes down without any real resistance. He snaps at Spock for correcting the misleading report on Nibiru; but Kirk doesn't contest anybody's reasoning, let alone the directive's coherence. The brash young talent who beat the unwinnable Kobayashi Maru simulation in the previous movie had plenty to say to Starfleet about the incoherence of that test and his integrity in defying its intended lessons from defeat. Yet he doesn't contest the directive, the mission, or his punishment even though he'd surely handle them the same a second time around. Why?

My sense is that, even as a realist, Kirk recognizes the integrity of the Prime Directive as a prudential trope—an idealistic figure—for effecting noninterference. Thus he knows to take the Prime Directive as a Starfleet way to do good by its human standards while keeping interference with others to a minimum. He accepts and agrees with it, but as a realist. A legalist might literalize the rule to dispute it, as I just did. A militarist might enforce a standard interpretation, as Starfleet does with Kirk. A bureaucrat might apply the rule, to abide by it for its sake or his own.[34] As Spock shows, an idealist might make the rule's spirit into a commitment to self-sacrifice for its fullest possible observance, not to vindicate the rule but to serve the Federation and the worlds it would explore. Yes, imploding the volcano interferes; but there wouldn't be a future for the Nibiruns without it, whereas showing them a starship won't serve them in any way but to spur their civilization onto paths otherwise unlikely. Taking the Starfleet oath, Spock pledges to practice the Prime Directive in all ways that make decent sense for the Federation and beings beyond. He promises to put this principle before his career, his life, even the lives of his family and friends.

For Spock as an idealist, the Prime Directive is a highly admirable and demanding ideal. For Spock as a Starfleet officer, the Prime Directive is the cardinal rule: possibly to observe above all others. But for Kirk as a realist and a Starfleet captain, the Prime Directive is a highly admirable and demanding rule of thumb.[35] It's one among several handfuls of major precepts that Kirk must attune to his situations and harmonize in his actions through his second-nature capacity of political judgment and good fortune. This judgment has been Kirk's lifetime in the making. It's been cultivated by his family, friends, foes, educators, entertainments, and other experiences. It's been refined by his reflections and his sense of new situations. Kirk's rules of thumb are more flexible than Starfleet's rules or Spock's ideals. Ironically it's not just Kirk's dawning sense of Spock as a fellow officer and a fast friend but particularly Kirk's feeling for Spock's potential importance to Starfleet and the Federation that we see in what Kirk does. He recognizes that he's already interfered with Nibirun development, and he judges that a further sensation is worth suffering to save Spock. But Kirk doesn't argue his perspective to Spock, Pike, or the rest of Starfleet Command because he sees as a realist that it wouldn't do him or them any good. They have styles and perspectives of their own, and the time isn't ripe for persuasion.

For Kirk as realist and Spock as idealist, the Prime Directive is the primary convention of action for all members of Starfleet. This doesn't make it absolute. No-interference of any kind under any circumstances with the internal development of alien civilizations is neither possible nor desirable, at least for Starfleet. Accordingly, realists, idealists, and many others respect such conventions as tropes—as figures—with meanings that are nonetheless clear and useful. Here we analyze idealism and realism as styles of political action in popular movies. Political styles are networks of conventions for action, and popular movies use networks of conventions for meaning. Thus popular styles such as idealism and realism are genres of political action, just as epic, noir, and satire are genres of popular cinema, literature, and television. In the pages to come, we even start to appreciate popular genres of movies as popular forms of political action.

The rest of *Star Trek Into Darkness* pursues some of its politics of idealism versus realism by adapting recent headlines and history. Its most radical and fearsome realist is Admiral Marcus (Peter Weller), who schemes to use special Starfleet torpedoes to spark a war between the Federation and the Klingons. The film rehearses idealist *and* realist condemnations of American strikes by cruise missiles and drones in Afghanistan, Pakistan, Libya, and Sudan. By this point, Kirk is back as Enterprise Captain. Spock as an idealist talks Kirk as a realist out of using the Marcus torpedoes to bombard the Klingon planet safely and indiscriminately from afar. Spock appeals to Kirk's sense of honor, alive in him as it is in most realists, and Kirk beams down a landing party to accomplish their mission in person and more peacefully. (Realists no more lack all honor than idealists lack all calculation: the challenge for political theorists is to do better than the caricatures that such styles provide of themselves and others.) This headline contest between idealism and realism is meant to stay as obvious as can be. Therefore it calls little on conventions of *Star Trek*, let alone conventions of science fiction as a genre.

But that's not the way most of the movie works. Instead it echoes and develops this overt confrontation with many others between idealism and realism. These are sometimes less blatant but often more detailed. They emerge mainly in the film's clever use of conventions from the *Star Trek* complex or science fiction in general. Some literary critics define science fiction as "the literature of change," "the literature of cognitive estrangement," "a form of the fantastic that denies it is fantastic," or fictional "events that have not happened."[36] For our purposes, however, the popular genre of science fiction just is the use of conventions such as teleportation, faster-than-light (FTL) travel, time travel, space aliens, sentient robots, invented cultures, imaginary ecologies, and futuristic technologies.[37] Like the rest of the franchise, *Star Trek Into Darkness* makes ample use of many: its transporter beam teleports; its warp drive is FTL travel; Spock can be advised by Spock Prime (Leonard Nimoy) because the elder version has traveled back in time; and Klingons and Nibiruns are space aliens. Various *Star Trek* works abound in sentient robots (Data) and the rest.

An early, realist convention of science fiction is sometimes called "the cold equations," after a story of that name.[38] To respect knowledge of natural constraints, science fictions sometimes feature situations where scientific analysis says that survival (or something else desperately desired) isn't possible. These challenge characters to adjust to the cold, hard facts. Toward the end of *Star Trek II: The Wrath of Kahn* (1982), radiation floods the compartment where Spock (Leonard Nimoy) is fixing the warp drive. To save others, he stays to complete the repair. As he dies, Kirk (William Shatner) arrives on the safe side of a transparent radiation barrier. Their fingers can't quite touch through the "glass." Kirk is horrified at Spock's sacrifice, but Spock gasps his famous refrain that "The needs of the many outweigh the needs of the few... or the one." This is the cold-equations scene (even though the film's sequel recreates Spock).

At an earlier time, *Star Trek Into Darkness* faces the same super-villain. Reworking the earlier movie with Kahn, it reverses roles to reprise the cold-equations scene: Kirk braves radiation to save the ship and possibly the world; Spock finds him, but they can't quite touch; Kirk speaks the famous words; then he dies. (McCoy brings Kirk back from the dead toward this movie's end.) Such striking use of a realist convention from science fiction enables the more recent film to climax its political education of Kirk. He remains a realist, but one scene after another has been teaching him some of the humility and self-sacrifice in many idealist politics. The dialogue that leads into Kirk's death scene shows him coming to humility and a capacity for self-sacrifice by a largely realist route, rather than simply converting to a kind of idealism. And the realist structure of the cold-equations scene helps the movie show that an impressively honorable realist is what Kirk remains.

The Abrams movies seem interested in getting little jokes from the impudent violation of minor conventions. The *Star Trek* reboot in 2009 plays with a corollary convention of science fiction that disasters ensue if people meet other versions of themselves through time travel. Spock Prime lets Kirk infer this corollary; but on the sly, the older Spock advises the younger—and ridicules the convention. *Star Trek Into Darkness* continues the counseling and the play with this corollary. It has Spock Prime warn that Kahn will try to manipulate Spock, enabling Spock to make a tricky but idealist plan for Kahn's defeat.

Star Trek Into Darkness also has Spock Prime suggest that he's learned over the years a more sophisticated version of the corollary convention of time-travel. It's exactly parallel to a more sophisticated take on the Prime Directive than the younger Spock had seemed to embrace. Asked for advice by Spock when he seeks to defeat Kahn, Spock Prime first says his "vow is never to give you information that could alter your destiny. That being said..." Spock Prime appears to recognize that never-alter-your-destiny can be just as perplexing and dubious a guide to action as never-interfere-with-your-development. So he proceeds to advise Spock on how to save the Enterprise from Kahn.

To set up a key confrontation, this Abrams sequel also makes a cheeky change to the *Star Trek* convention that operating warp drives prevent starships from catching and battling each other. Expressly so that the Marcus starship can't continue its attack on the Kirk starship near Klingon, the Enterprise warps toward Earth. But we pause only a beat until the daughter of Marcus (Alice Eve), aboard the Enterprise under false pretenses because she distrusts its mission from her father, blithely announces as a near afterthought that research for Marcus has equipped his ship with a way of catching others that also are warping the space-time continuum in order to travel faster than light. Earlier action and dialogue have suggested that idealists would prefer to sidestep or postpone some kinds of fights, including the one that Marcus is picking with the Enterprise. Under the previous convention, warping away from the confrontation offers that option. But the "new technology"—that is, the amended convention—takes it away. This is what realists such as Kirk, let alone Marcus, might expect and prefer.

Throughout *Star Trek Into Darkness*, we see Kirk as a realist who bends and breaks rules to do what needs (in his excellent and lucky judgment) to be done. Throughout the movie, we see Spock as an idealist who discerns the best reasons for rules then abides by these ideals. The film shows us one clash after another between Kirk's realism and Spock's idealism. It adds a lot of clashes, too, with the more extreme "realism" of Marcus and the more extreme "idealism" of Kahn. (As we see in later chapters, another word for the Marcus style might be "cynicism"; and a better word for the Kahn style is definitely "perfectionism.") All along, though, the movie also has us see Kirk refining his realism by learning from Spock—and Marcus and Kahn. And it has us watch Spock making his idealism more sophisticated through attention to Kirk, Marcus, Kahn, and especially Spock Prime.

Therefore the film as a whole features confrontations *and* collaborations of realists with idealists. As an episode on Kirk violating the Prime Directive in order to save Spock from the Nibiru volcano, the proem for *Star Trek Into Darkness* is an emblem of the film's overall focus. By starting the film with an episode that contrasts Kirk's realism to Spock's idealism, moreover, the proem helps give that focus to the full film. The hope is that this introductory discussion of idealism and realism will work the same way for the full book in hand. The treatment of idealism and realism in the proem for *Star Trek Into Darkness* is meant to exemplify *and* focus this book's analysis of the two political styles as they appear in popular works of epic, noir, and satire.

What follows, then, are cinematic case studies in the politics of idealism and realism. The emphasis is on encountering these styles in everyday life as well as in government. The goals are to show how to view and do popular cinema as political theory, but there's attention to novels and television too. The main method is to analyze several films from popular genres that persistently pit idealism against realism, in order to theorize the everyday, popular politics of idealism and realism in our times. But of course, my discussion of the proem for *Star Trek Into Darkness* is meant merely as an emblem of what's to follow, since much more could be said about such a carefully detailed film if *it* were to focus the analysis to come.

CHAPTER 1

An Epic Comeback? Postwestern Politics in Film and Theory

(Featuring *Alexander, King Arthur,* and *The Lord of the Rings*)

The Homeric journey, grounded in the wish to return home, is at once the most venerable of all narrative templates and, as *The Way Back* demonstrates, one of the trickiest to dramatize. Anthony Minghella hit the same problem in *Cold Mountain*: an odyssey, when you get down to it, is just one damn thing after another.[1]

—Anthony Lane

In the beginning, epic is not a popular genre as much as epic is the whole of popular, orally based literature.[2] When is "the beginning?" Different in historical times for distinct peoples, it comes when a community can recognize itself. Usually this occurs in looking back on its origins, although not all early epics are origin myths in the strictest senses.[3] For ancient Greeks, the epic period happened more than two-and-a-half millennia ago; for current Finns, it transpired less than two centuries ago. By contrast, no popular genres start to take shape as conventional families of dramas and narratives until the eve of electronic times. Horror, thriller, romance, science fiction, and the rest typically sprawl across mass-disseminated literature plus electronic media such as cinema and television. In consequence, it is not surprising that epic long remained an impulse across many other genres more than a popular form in its own right for electronic cultures. Still epic has been consolidating itself as a specific genre for the better part of a century now, even as it functions also as something of an Ur genre to inspirit most of our other popular forms.

Early epics in literature show a strong elective affinity for "warrior politics." These are the politics of warlords, from barbarian hordes and nomadic tribes to territorial clans and urban gangs. By accounts since the ancient Greeks, warrior politics persist where people lack the settled places and special languages for politics in a specifically Western sense.[4] (From the perspective of the republican-rhetorical tradition of politics in Western civilization, "warrior politics" are arguably oxymoronic, because they are "violent politics" rather than peaceful politics as speech-in-action-in-public.[5]) Warrior politics usually come with cultures of honor and anger.[6] Across diverse settings and sizable swaths of historical time, early epics participate in the generic interest of epics in community identity and direction. They address such political questions as who we are, what time it is, who will lead us, where, how, and why.

As a popular genre in our times, especially in cinema, epic conventionally stands out for its story structure and vast scale. Most epics are episodic, with each of the movie's scenes, acts, or other dramatic elements relating to the others less as historically or chronologically progressive times than as emblems of the whole tale, the whole hero, or the whole community. This need not chase out historical drama or chronological narrative, but it often results in moments that step aside from any modern march of time. *Places in the Heart* might seem to provide a line of causes and effects for a small town in the Great Depression. But then it culminates in surveying a service in the local church to show a full and "timeless" array of the drama's community members, living *and* dead. Throughout, the movie shows all its people and episodes as enduring "places in the heart." Thus it mimics how early epics stitch together loose patchworks of lore and legend into sequences of moments that depart in many ways from chronological norms of consistency and historical connections of cause-and-effect. As the mythos of Arthur, the Arthuriad is a collection of tales that share characters, settings, and sometimes even deeds that can reach from *The Death of Arthur* to *The Once and Future King*.[7] Similarly *The Song of Roland* and the mythos of Robin Hood each repeat their characters and supplement their motifs rather than follow a strictly linear chronology.

These emblematic moments—with their featured characters, deeds, scenes, and codes of conduct—evoke the enduring, somewhat "timeless" ideals of the community. They are how the popular genre of epic becomes one of our preeminent forms for dramas of political idealism. The offshoot genres of action-adventure and thriller often constrict the epic array of a community's characters to a hero, a love, and a villain. They spike adrenaline rather than explore endurance. They pursue mystery and suspense rather than review community commitments. Each courts an intense personal connection with a viewpoint character rather than surveying a vast trajectory of events and company of characters to show how their ideals—our ideals—cohere and prevail.

Often in an epic, the cast ("of thousands") is immense. The times traversed in the story and in the screening are extraordinarily long. Epic spaces are enormous, whether measured in settings spanned, vistas grand, or the cinema's scope. Moreover the politics characteristically are earthshaking or world-making in importance. Accordingly epic cinema has become the premier genre for spectacle.[8] Likewise epic continues to concern the qualities, heroes, and ideals that define particular communities. And perhaps less clearly, but no less significantly, epic features politics of liberation—or at least resistance—most often in reaction against specifically imperial powers, whether at home or abroad. These are the main claims about epic politics advanced in these pages.

Generic Politics

Before we explore epic politics and their implications further, though, we do well to clarify further what it can mean to analyze the politics of a popular genre. We borrow from French to refer to persistent forms of popular culture as genres.[9] These are durable networks of conventions. Across media such as cinema, literature, radio, and video, specific works cluster into popular genres by family resemblance.[10] Their stock settings, scenes, and characters cohere mostly by elective affinity rather than any stronger necessity. Thus they stay familiar to us even as we inflect them through further versions. Most politics in popular movies take shape less in officially political settings or overtly political events than in the quiet symbolism of subtexts. In turn, subtexts arise in important part from particular uses of conventions from popular genres.[11] Hence specific genres (or subgenres) often display conventional, elective affinities for distinctive kinds of politics. These political implications are not simple curiosities or accidental facts; instead our popular genres weave their politics deeply, pervasively into their myths and aesthetics. Still we *are* talking about Hollywood, and therefore American politics; so specifically socialist and conservative politics familiar from Europe stay few and far between in America's genre movies.

In a ramshackle network of studies, I've been exploring politics of popular movies across many genres. To draw on some of the wider analysis to date can be to provide a useful context for individuating epic as a popular genre as well as appreciating the politics implied by its conventions. For example, epic is not alone in its affinities for warrior and especially republican politics. Yet epic is the popular genre that concentrates most clearly on how these politics tend to generate empires even as they also try to resist them. Other kinds of politics occasionally surface in particular epics, yet these alternatives are more conventional for genres that contrast with epic.

No single convention can guarantee the overall operation of any genre that it helps to characterize. Thus length alone is not enough to make a film epic. Ready examples include such long, long documentaries as *The Sorrow and the Pity* (1969) or most Ken Burns contributions to PBS, for these are documentaries rather than epics in genre—even though great length is not conventional for the documentary as a genre. Could extraordinary length or any other epic convention help make *The Sorry and the Pity* or *The War* (2007) an epic documentary? Yes, sometimes, depending on what networks of conventions the movie includes and how. Much of our popular experience is generic, and we make meanings generically from the ways particular conventions appear and implicate others in their culturally sustained families.[12]

As a family of conventions, a popular genre accommodates some politics more readily than others. Thrillers feature republican politics of heroism. To take a specific example, conspiracy thrillers pit such heroism against authoritarian systems.[13] Pausing on occasion for spectacular moments of environmental politics, westerns insistently compare republican to liberal politics.[14] Vengeance movies, too, are mainly republican and liberal.[15] Martial arts movies typically feed republican virtues into perfectionist action: "Just Do It," as the Nike slogan says after the fashion of Friedrich Nietzsche.[16] War movies show generically that war is hell; and since the Vietnam War, they make the martial standards of warrior and republican politics into arguments for lessons to be drawn from particular wars that they dramatize.[17] Yet fantasies favor the versions of republicanism associated with (European) feudalism, even as they challenge the modern priority for political and other branches of realism.[18]

The dark fantasies of horror, however, are existentialist (ghosts, mummies, zombies) or perfectionist (vampires, werewolves, witches).[19] When it comes to morality, especially, science fiction sustains a generic interest in the politics of perspectivism; whereas detective fiction and horror would deliver us from sharply defined evils.[20] As the fourth chapter details, neo-noir movies pursue the existentialist politics of awakening to resistance of corrupt systems; and those systems often present incipiently totalitarian versions of perfectionist politics as their dangers—from fascist or Marxist ideologies, from celebrity cultures, from Ayn Rand capitalists, from powers of surpassingly beautiful or wealthy people, even from consumer societies. Neo noir (roughly 1980 onward) also shows strong interest in idealist criticisms of realist politics. Classical noir (1941–1958) is misogynist, its continuations (1959–1979) and neo noir remain at least masculinist, yet neo noir has been developing an effectively feminist subgenre. From *Batman* (1989) forward, an additional subgenre of neo noir overlaps with superhero movies, sharing their fascination with perfectionist politics. To these we could add the possibility of an emerging genre of "fractal films." These films are beginning to probe the politics of nonlinear systems that arguably dominate our increasingly globalized era.[21]

To discern distinctive politics in a popular genre is to contrast the genre and its typical politics to others. It is not to say that every work in the genre must manifest politics standard for that popular form. Nor is it to say that the genre's distinctive politics never appear in other genres, at times, or even that these politics may not prove similarly prominent in some other genres. It is rather to explore how a form of popular culture coheres, distinguishing itself from many others, and how it helps people experience the dynamics of its characteristic politics. A surge in epic films from Hollywood idealistically calls into question the recent disposition toward imperial politics evident in America's assertive state, economy, and culture.

Epic Movies

Why say that epic has been making a comeback lately as a popular form of American movies? By my count, Hollywood issued several epic films a year in the 1960s and into the 1970s. Then, by consensual account, the success of *Star Wars* blew away the old Hollywood. The ensuing saga is itself something of an epic or two (or six, with more to come) depending on which boundaries make most sense for a specific analysis: the *Star Wars* movies feature every major convention of epic cinema. Yet the first of these films taught Hollywood to turn its would-be blockbusters into thrillers or action-adventure movies more than epics. Thus this "oldest" genre slid into a cinematic eclipse that lasted until the new century.

Only with the end of the twentieth century did individual epics rev back to a high pace of production. The analysis at hand arises from attention to nearly a hundred epic movies—individual films or three-film arcs—from 1950 through 2008. Unsystematic as it remains, their enumeration suggests a recent acceleration in the appearance of epics from Hollywood. Some of these films have more than one version, explaining their two different running times listed below. Later influence urges that two earlier, especially famous epics deserve mention—*The Birth of a Nation* and *Gone with the Wind*—although they do not figure in any of the counting (table 1.1).

Table 1.1 Recent Hollywood epics

Sl. no.	Epic films	Minutes	Full epics	Their directors
	The Birth of a Nation (1915)	159		D. W. Griffith
	Gone with the Wind (1939)	238		Victor Fleming
1.	Quo Vadis (1951)	171	1.	Mervyn LeRoy
2.	The Ten Commandments (1956)	220	2.	Cecil B. DeMille
3.	Ben-Hur (1959)	212	3.	William Wyler
4.	Spartacus (1960)	184	4.	Stanley Kubrick
5.	El Cid (1961)	182	5.	Anthony Mann
6.	King of Kings (1961)	168	6.	Nicholas Ray
7.	How the West Was Won (1962)	155	7.	John Ford
8.	Lawrence of Arabia (1962)	216	8.	David Lean
9.	The Longest Day (1962)	180	9.	Ken Annakin andAndrew Marton Fox
10.	Cleopatra (1963)	192, 320	10.	Joseph L. Mankiewicz
11.	The Fall of the Roman Empire (1964)	188	11.	Anthony Mann
12.	Doctor Zhivago (1965)	197	12.	David Lean
13.	The Greatest Story Ever Told (1965)	225	13.	George Stevens
14.	The Bible (1966)	174	14.	John Huston
15.	Camelot (1967)	179	15.	Joshua Logan
16.	2001: A Space Odyssey (1968)	139, 148	16.	Stanley Kubrick
17.	Little Big Man (1970)	150	17.	Arthur Penn
18.	Godfather (1972)	175	18.	Francis Ford Coppola
19.	Godfather: Part II (1974)	200	19.	Francis Ford Coppola
20.	King Kong (1976)	134		John Guillermin

continued

No.	Film	Page(s)	Ref	Director
21.	Star Wars (two three-film epics, 1977–2005)	794		George Lucas (et alia)
22.	Apocalypse Now (1979)	153, 202	22.	Francis Ford Coppola
23.	Star Trek: The Motion Picture (1979)	132		Robert Wise
24.	Mad Max (1979, 1981, 1985)	291		George Miller
25.	Chariots of Fire (1981)	123	23.	Hugh Hudson Fox
26.	Excalibur (1981)	140	24.	John Boorman
27.	Gandhi (1982)	188	25.	Richard Attenborough
28.	The Right Stuff (1983)	193	26.	Philip Kaufman
29.	Dune (1984)	137, 190	27.	David Lynch
30.	The Natural (1984)	134		Barry Levinson
31.	Places in the Heart (1984)	111	28.	Robert Benton
32.	Back to the Future (1985, 1989, 1990)	341		Robert Zemeckis
33.	Braveheart (1985)	177	29.	Mel Gibson
34.	Dances with Wolves (1990)	180, 224	30.	Kevin Costner
35.	Godfather: Part III (1990)	162	31.	Francis Ford Coppola
36.	Robin Hood (1991)	104, 116		John Irvin
37.	Robin Hood: Prince of Thieves (1991)	143, 155	32.	Kevin Reynolds
38.	1492: The Conquest of Paradise (1992)	154	33.	Ridley Scott
39.	Forrest Gump (1994)	142	34.	Robert Zemeckis
40.	Heat (1995)	171	35.	Michael Mann
41.	Rob Roy (1995)	139	36.	Michael Caton-Jones
42.	Waterworld (1995)	136, 176	37.	Kevin Reynolds
43.	The Postman (1997)	177	38.	Kevin Costner
44.	Titanic (1997)	194	39.	James Cameron
45.	Magnolia (1999)	188	40.	Paul Thomas Anderson

Table 1.1 Continued

Sl. no.	Epic films	Minutes	Full epics	Their directors
46.	*The Matrix* (1999, 2003, 2003)	403		Andy and Lana Wachowski
47.	*The 13th Warrior* (1999)	102		John McTiernan
48.	*Crouching Tiger, Hidden Dragon* (2000)	120		Ang Lee
49.	*Gladiator* (2000)	155	41.	Ridley Scott
50.	*O Brother, Where Art Thou?* (2000)	103		Joel Coen
51.	*LOTR: The Fellowship of the Ring* (2001)	178, 208	42.	Peter Jackson
52.	*The Four Feathers* (2002)	131		Shekhar Kapur
53.	*Gangs of New York* (2002)	166	43.	Martin Scorsese
54.	*Hero* (2002)	96		Zhang Yimou
55.	*LOTR: The Two Towers* (2002)	179, 223	44.	Peter Jackson
56.	*Big Fish* (2003)	125		Tim Burton
57.	*Cold Mountain* (2003)	152	45.	Anthony Minghella
58.	*The Last Samurai* (2003)	154	46.	Edward Zwick
59.	*LOTR: The Return of the King* (2003)	201, 251	47.	Peter Jackson
60.	*Love Actually* (2003)	135	48.	Richard Curtis
61.	*Alexander* (2004)	175, 214	49.	Oliver Stone
62.	*The Aviator* (2004)	170	50.	Martin Scorsese
63.	*King Arthur* (2004)	126, 140	51.	Antoine Fuqua
64.	*Ladder 49* (2004)	115		Jay Russell
65.	*Troy* (2004)	163	52.	Wolfgang Petersen
66.	*Beowulf & Grendel* (2005)	103		Sturla Gunnarsson
67.	*King Kong* (2005)	187	53.	Peter Jackson
68.	*Kingdom of Heaven* (2005)	145	54.	Ridley Scott
69.	*The New World* (2005)	135	55.	Terrence Malick

No.	Film (Year)		Director No.	Director
70.	Apocalypto (2006)	139	56.	Mel Gibson
71.	Bobby (2006)	120		Emilio Estevez
72.	Curse of the Golden Flower (2006)	114		Zhang Yimou
73.	Flags of Our Fathers (2006)	132		Clint Eastwood
74.	The Fountain (2006)	96		Darren Aronofsky
75.	Letters from Iwo Jima (2006)	142	57.	Clint Eastwood
76.	Across the Universe (2007)	131		Julie Taymore
77.	Beowulf (2007)	113		Robert Zemeckis
78.	I'm Not There (2007)	135	58.	Todd Haynes
79.	The Last Legion (2007)	110		Doug Lefler
80.	Pathfinder (2007)	99		Marcus Nispel
81.	There Will Be Blood (2007)	158	59.	Paul Thomas Anderson
82.	300 (2007)	117		Zack Snyder
83.	Australia (2008)	165	60.	Baz Luhrman
84.	The Curious Case of Benjamin Button (2008)	159	61.	David Fincher
85.	Outlander (2008)	115		Howard McCain
86.	Avatar (2009)	162	62.	James Cameron
87.	Day of the Falcon (2011)	130		Jean-Jacques Annaud
88.	The Tree of Life (2011)	139	63.	Terrence Malick
89.	The Way Back (2011)	133		Peter Weir
90.	Cloud Atlas (2012)	172	64.	Tom Tykwer plus Andyand Lana Wachowski
91.	Django Unchained (2012)	165	65.	Quentin Tarantino
92.	The Hobbit: An Unexpected Journey (2012)	169	66.	Peter Jackson
93.	The Hunger Games (2012)	142	67.	Gary Ross
94.	Les Misérables (2012)	157	68.	Tom Hooper
95.	Life of Pi (2012)	127	69.	Ang Lee
96.	Lincoln (2012)	150		Steven Spielberg

Arguably it is only with *Gladiator* in 2000 that epic movies have resumed their rapid rate of production from the 1960s. Throughout the last half-century, even so, epics continued to be for Hollywood *the* prestige pictures. Of the 69 longest epics in Hollywood cinema between 1950 and 2013, only nine gained no Academy Award nominations. Each running 135 minutes or more, these long films are the fullest-fledged epics; and all are stand-alone films: we're not counting any *Star Wars* sets here. From the 69, 12 won Academy Awards for Best Picture or Best Foreign-Language Film, and another 21 received one of these two crowning nominations. Together the 69 epics won an astounding 141 Oscars along with an additional 214 nominations: a mean of more than five nominations per epic. This holds despite the way that the recent surge in epic movies must work against a high average when more epics compete for largely the same number of movie awards each year. It is a safe bet that no other movie genre comes close to such a record in this or in any other comparable period. Yet Hollywood prestige differs from prominence in numbers and popularity, and epic cinema was not especially telling in American mythmaking for the last two decades of the twentieth century.

Classifications and counts here can be subject to big complications. Keep in mind that our focus is epic as a popular genre of movies. The form is more specific, more limited, than the use of "epic" as a reviewer's adjective might suggest. With epic arguably the oral form at the beginning of drama and literature, many "big" movies can seem "epic" without featuring the conventions that distinguish popular epics in the last century and more. Ready examples are action-adventure blockbusters and thriller franchises as well as similar movies made from ancient myths, such as *Clash of the Titans* (1981 and 2010) or the two *Percy Jackson* films (2010 and 2013) to date. Because these share some epic conventions for heroes, especially, these films share some politics with epics; but conventions specifically for thrillers and action-adventure movies differ enough from epics to inflect the implicit politics in different directions. Thus the roster above of recent movie epics doesn't include such neighboring films.

The same goes for mock epics. To ironize and ridicule, satires of any genre play with its conventions. This can clarify the conventions along with their implicit politics.[22] Thus mock epics are good places to see caricatures of the epic hero, his stock mentor, the usual prophecy, the epic battle, the rally or conference or syzygy episodes, and other conventions explained below. Satirical exaggeration can make the politics hard to miss for epic scenes like single combats, enemy misdirections, or early weddings. Almost by definition, though, mock epics lack the sense of portent—of high and sustained seriousness—that typifies epic as a popular genre. Satires delight in lampooning such pretensions. And with brevity the soul of wit, mock epics almost never reach epic proportions either. So the epics analyzed here omit the pseudo-epic romps especially associated with Mel Brooks and Monty Python.[23]

Popular tastes and marketplace realities might suggest of late that the most numerous and often the most prominent "epics" in cinema have become the loose strings of box-office induced "sequels." These often reprise characters, settings, and plots in one movie after another—until audiences lose interest, at least for a while, yet also until the focal figures in these films have made lasting impacts on the popular imaginations that just are America's vital myths. Such movies present themselves as continuations by contrast with remakes or takeoffs from the likes *Hamlet* or *Romeo and Juliet*, which each have more than ten extant movie versions. More systematically than with remakes or takeoffs, Hollywood strings of sequels make modest attempts (or more) to update each appearance of their recurrent plots, settings, and characters in specifically chronological, even historical terms. Nonetheless there is little interest in "realistic" (aka, "modern") historical development of these ingredients across the resulting chain of movies, and there is seldom significant psychological development of any key characters. In fact, these figures seldom display fully modern, individuated psyches in their first appearances, let alone the later ones. At least incipiently, they are types from the outset.

The beginning-middle-end (past-present-future) template so emphatically available for stories in Western civilization implies that sets of movies seldom would start taking the episodic shape of epics until each reaches at least four films. Even by this relatively adventurous standard, episodic clusters of Hollywood films abound. Just name the focal heroes or (less frequently) the signal villains, and viewers of a certain age will know these franchises of four movies or more (as reckoned by 2013) in table 1.2.

Figures such as Zorro, She, and the Lone Ranger seem to receive repeated remakes of the same movie (or two or three) more than they get extended series of sequels that form the virtual epics momentarily at issue here from largely American cinema. By further contrast, notice that the main cinematic arc of the eight Harry Potter movies predated those movies. Moreover J. K. Rowling made the three youths at its heart develop psychologically as they mature physically. Their component dramas, film by film, are less episodes in the strict, fully epic sense than they are historical progressions of events that produce important changes in the characters. And the only individual film even close to epical is the eighth.

The counts above for virtual epics in the movies do not include animated sequels, which can seem increasingly common. When there is more than

Table 1.2   Epic series of Hollywood movies

Cinematic series of episodes	Characters	Films to date	Earliest	Latest
Tarzan	Hero	41	1928	1999
James Bond	Hero	24	1962	2012
Jason in Friday the 13th	Villain	11–12	1980	2003
Michael Myers in Halloween	Villain	8–10	1978	2009
Freddie Kruger on Elm Street	Villain	8–9	1984	2003
Star Trek with Kirk and Spock	Heroes	7–9	1979	2013
Alien	Villain	8	1979	2012
Batman	Hero	7	1989	2012
Superman	Hero	7	1978	2013
Damien	Villain	3–7	1976	2006
Rocky	Hero	6	1976	2006
Death Wish	Hero	5	1974	1994
Die Hard	Hero	5	1988	2013
Dirty Harry	Hero	5	1971	1988
The Exorcist	Hero	5	1973	2005
Predator	Villain	5	1987	2007
X-Men	Heroes	5	2000	2011
Bourne	Hero	4–5	1988	2012
Hannibal Lecter	Villain	4–5	1991	2007
Indiana Jones	Hero	4	1981	2008
The Karate Kid	Hero	4	1984	1994
The Terminator	Villain, hero	4	1984	2009
The Crow	Hero	4	1994	2005
Star Trek with Picard and Data	Heroes	4	1994	2002
The Hulk	Hero	3–4	1977	2008

one count for an epic set, the higher number counts every film in the set, whereas the lower number does not count any remakes. The lower number tells how many episodes differ by basic plots—and thus how many episodes the set has according to the most cautious of counts.

Before we sideline these virtual epics, however, let us notice that remakes complicate the counting and the classification. Not the first but the second version of *The Bourne Identity* is the one on its way to going (virtually) epic.

Does this mean there are four films about Jason Bourne so far or only three, and should we count *The Bourne Legacy* too? 'Twas *The Silence of the Lambs* with Anthony Hopkins that did well enough to spur the remaking of *Red Dragon* (initially done as *Manhunter*, with Brian Cox as Lecter) as well as the making of *Hannibal* and the attempt to go beyond Hopkins with the key role for *Hannibal Rising*. Does that mean there are five Hannibal movies to date or just four? Either way, it seems (to me) right to say at this point that the Hannibal films together approximate a cinematic epic; while it is less clear (at least to me) that the Bourne films do, even though a case could be made for them. Likewise the Hulk has done his origin story at least twice in the four potential installments to date. So maybe we do not yet have an epic in the making? And what of the many movie series with sequels that go straight to TV or DVD? The first series of Damien movies reaches four only if we count the fourth, made for TV, before the fifth remakes the first— then other television episodes appear.

Another issue is whether we should count the animated offspring of such virtual epics in live-action modes, especially when there are tons of computer-generated imagery (CGI) in the non-animated movies. Superhero series often come to include feature-length animations, although those typically go direct to DVD. And how about the epic cinematic sets supported by TV series too: Batman, Superman, the Hulk, and so on? (Cartoon spin-offs on television are legion, and the "adult swim" shows that they are not just for children anymore.) And what ought we do with films that show leagues or alliances of superheroes: should we treat the whole Marvel universe of *The Avengers* (2012) as one epic tapestry or more? Already it includes scores of feature-length films, remakes, sequels and prequels, animations, made-for-television movies, and TV series. When it comes to mythmaking through moving pictures, or even cinema by contrast with television and computer games, complications for classifying and counting can overwhelm the sophisticated methods that might yield subtle but powerful correlations—not to mention the multiple linear regressions that came to define several social sciences in the twentieth century. Suffice it to say that epic politics are now prominent aspects of political mythmaking through moving pictures.[24]

When we get rich enough variations of what seems in retrospect to have become an originary movie, such as *Mr. Smith Goes to Washington* (1939), we can start to get dynamics of a distinct subgenre or even a popular genre.[25] In movies as in literature, subgenres have formed for the likes of King Arthur, Robin Hood, and other epic figures—in much the same fashion as for the archetypal figures of horror: ghosts, mummies, vampires, werewolves, and many more.

No doubt, some recent icons are missing from this roster; it aspires to illustration rather than completion. These epic characters from cinema can also make a claim on generalizations about political mythmaking through moving images, and they might adjust some of the lessons drawn here. For the most part, though, these virtual epics have conventions that we see in the individual films that count as epics, making it permissible to leave sets to the side for now. Yet we should acknowledge too the towering characters that escape confinement in any such series. They can come to appear with so many inflections in so many films with so many lineages that we probably do best to acclaim them as "mythic," maybe even "archetypal." Easy examples of this include Dracula, Frankenstein and the Monster, plus Dr. Jekyll and Mr. Hyde. Of course, this may have happened even earlier with the literary likes of Hercules.

Virtual epics all reach beyond trilogies. By popular genre, their individual episodes are predominantly thrillers or superhero sagas. Mostly they mark a generation (yes, mine); and for its popular cultures and perhaps ensuing ones, they become virtual epics. Some, like the Bond and Batman series, have managed many times over the daunting transition to new actors in the leads. Some, like the Terminator flicks, might not survive it; and a few, such as the Rocky films, seem disinclined to attempt it. I do not try to display, but we should try not to forget, the many marginal franchises—especially in horror—that want to become as long-running as Jason in the *Friday the 13th* flicks, Michael Myers in the *Halloween* movies, or Freddie Kruger in the *Elm Street* series. The *Howling, Saw,* and *Subspecies* series come immediately to mind. For the rest of the present analysis, nonetheless, let us turn back entirely to more individually complete films.

Neighboring Genres

A last complication with classifications and counts reveals another argument for saying that epic is making a comeback in Hollywood's new century. Several movie genres that we do well to distinguish from epic are nonetheless such close neighbors that they often overlap. Their prominence in a particular period can indicate further interest in epic politics even when the specific works of cinema are not entirely or even exactly epics. This holds for eight popular genres of long standing plus a possible new one only now forming next door.

We should expect many close companions for epic as a popular genre. It parallels the ways in which warrior and especially republican politics provide the main Western stems for subsequently differentiated politics. Thus republican politics arise in taming warrior politics. Then republican politics provide some of the trapping and much of the opposition to imperial politics after the fashion of ancient Rome. Republican virtues inform feudalism in the middle ages. Beyond that, the first two modern ideologies spring more or less directly from politics of republics. Authoritarianism (in the mode of Thomas Hobbes) tries to scientize and otherwise systematize the specifically republican invention of authority.[26] Then liberalism (along the lines of John Locke) attempts the same for the pointedly republican principle of liberty.[27] Populism (after the fashion of Robert La Follette) as a postmodern movement develops the republican celebration of the people.[28] Revving republican action and radicalizing populist champions, perfectionism (on the model of Friedrich Nietzsche) as a postwestern impulse leaps beyond public founders to culture creators.[29] For Western civilization, the politics of republics are the principal politics from which most of the others emerge. By now, variants of all these politics related to republicanism coexist and interact as neighbors in our popular cultures.[30]

The situation is much the same for epic. In loosely historical terms, its earliest offshoot in ancient Greece is tragedy. Like epic, tragedy has been so basic and protean a form that it becomes a meta-genre as much as a popular one; yet each shapes Hollywood films as truly popular forms. A good test for other neighboring genres is whether their names sometimes seem synonymous with "epic" or at least make "epic" a ready descriptor. We often talk in terms of "epic fantasy," "epic science fiction," and "epic romance," especially for historical romances.[31] We often hear of "superhero epics" and "war epics." Likewise "operatic" almost says "epic"—as "vast" or even "overdone."[32] It might not be an accident of timing that opera is recently making for itself a secondary home in movie theaters, adding to its primary venue in concert halls. By extension, movie musicals are another "epic genre" of Hollywood cinema. Their earlier heyday coincided substantially with the earlier prominence of film epics from Hollywood, and signs of their current resurgence could be compared to the pattern already identified for current epics. To the extent that these generic neighbors come to the fore when epic reasserts itself in cinema, they strengthen the sociological arguments for expecting salience of epic sensibilities, and even specifically epic politics.

Still more telling is the continuing emergence of a family of films possibly on the way to becoming a popular genre. In the largest, almost metageneric sense, we may think of these as "fractal films," for their interest in fracturing (or at least fractioning) the pat linearity of time and space in most movies from Hollywood. Some fractal films are experiments by auteurs who seek high art or personal edification rather than political mythmaking. But many seem to cultivate the kinds of audiences that popular genres engage, and a few continuing streams of fractal films spring from genres as old as moviemaking. Thus tales of time travel typically disrupt usual cinematic continuities of time and space, while nonlinear conspiracies deploy devilish discontinuities of plot and other complications of scene and sense. The proliferation of neo-noir movies in the last three decades is adding substantially to the corpus of fractal films from Hollywood, because many neo noirs pursue nonlinear patterns of plot or even character. Of course, new genres often form as new configurations of previous forms that cohere because we see them differently, perhaps in adjusting to further works that focus us differently.

With fractal films, the further works amount to a specific candidate for a new and neighboring popular genre that resembles epic. They delight some viewers (and confound others) by piecing together in pointedly disjointed ways some ragtag complexes of character and happenstance. These present our postmodern unto postwestern situations as "chaotic" in the mathematical sense.[33] That is, they show people involved in fractal, nonlinear, self-similar systems that spur disproportionate effects at great distances and surprising times. From *Abandon* (2002) and *Babel* (2006) to *Syriana* (2005) and *Synecdoche, New York* (2008) or to *Vantage Point* (2008) and *Where the Truth Lies* (2005), fractal films conventionally lack the impersonal heroes and sometimes the grand scale of epic movies. By contrast with epics, many fractal films are strikingly intimate in their scopes and personalities: *The Butterfly Effect* (2004) and its sequels (2006 and 2009), *The Dead Girl* (2006), *Jacob's Ladder* (1990), *The Lookout* (2007), *The Prestige* (2006), and *Vanilla Sky* (2001) are good examples.

What might we learn from fractal films that can inform an exploration of epic politics? We can experience the strange suitability of epic's conventional patchwork, nonlinear, episodic narratives to the small-scale and personal politics of everyday lives in our current—increasingly postmodern? incipiently postwestern?—conditions. That fractal films might be coalescing into a popular genre roughly at the same time as the popular genre of epic films is reasserting its relevance reinforces our reasons to see in epic a sustained attention to resisting systems that viewers experience as unduly limiting or outright oppressive. We might learn how the nonlinear social systems that existentialists find pervasive these days in the lives of ordinary people can work in imperious (if not exactly imperial) ways. Although we ordinary folks might have no specific prospect of epic heroism, we might learn to pattern our plights and opportunities to take advantage of actions that epics show as successful in response to imperium at many levels. We might learn useful moments of impersonality, magnanimity, honor, strength, and other virtues from epic heroes. These moves and moments are evident, even if sometimes in minor-league ways, on the part of effective protagonists in fractal films.

Impersonal Heroes

But let us not get too far ahead of the story. Instead let us attend in more detail at this point to epic virtues as ways into epic politics. They can help us understand how epic politics—and movies—attune us to recognizing and resisting imperial politics. Especially revealing is the epic virtue of heroic impersonality. It can seem especially surprising in popular movies, where it runs against the modern psychological grain of subjective individualism popular in America. To make sense of this impersonality, particularly in response to imperial politics, we do well to step back for a moment to situate epic more amply in the history of cinema and Western civilization.

The recent resurgence of epic in cinema traces in part to CGI technology that makes vast spectacles "affordable" to produce. By Hollywood standards early in the twenty-first century, this prices epics from $100 million each to several times that. When *Troy* shows us in glorious panorama not only the beautiful face of Helen that launched them but more or less literally the "thousand ships" that awed the ancient world, we can thank the special effects from computer graphics more than the miniatures made by the model builders for earlier eras of film. Yet the argument here is that this latest epic comeback owes as much to anxieties of American empire. Or more carefully put, whatever the conscious intentions of moviemakers in this century, their many epic films enact a persistent, generic preoccupation with resisting imperial politics.

In our Western "citylization," anti-imperial politics are originally the politics of republics.[34] Epic in cinema, even recent cinema, features heroes who are peculiarly republican—at least by Hollywood standards. Warrior heroes do not disappear from epics; instead they become more civilized. They become reluctant leaders who are uncomfortable with normal politics but who can come to the fore in revolutionary times. This is because they enact great honor, strength, and vision—yet also personal reserve—along with their superlative prowess in combat and strategy. These men (mostly, since their republican-rhetorical tradition has been deeply masculinist) show a striking "objectivity" about themselves. Their perceptions and judgments seem peculiarly "impersonal."

Adapted from warrior politics, this epic objectivity of the hero is more psychological than methodological. It is a lack of modern ego, a stylistic more than a critical distance from personal ambitions and deeds. This does not preempt personal pride or gritty endurance—far from it—but epic impersonality grounds pride and endurance in loyal family and friends more than resourceful selves. Such objectivity equips epic heroes to face times and causes more premodern than modern. Possibly as a result, it also fits epic heroes to times and causes less modern (individual, industrial, and developmental) than postmodern (eclectic and electronic) or even postwestern (globalized or apocalyptic), at least in their politics.[35] The impersonality of these imposing, epic personas is a big part of what makes epic heroes emblems for their communities—even more than it makes them individuals who meet modern tests of historical, psychological, and literary realism.

A pervasive defect of *Alexander*, becoming more pronounced from one version to the next, is that Oliver Stone's epic tries hard to psychologize its hero.[36] Such a modern, "inner" sense of character is antithetical to the generic interest of epic in ethos: that is, in character as a community and public construct.[37] Epical attention to virtues and vices is typically not a concern for desires and motives. By contrast, *Troy* enacts key characters and events invoked by the title character in *Alexander*; yet *Troy* does not much psychologize Achilles, Hector, or its other figures. To be sure, this probably is why *Troy* was not particularly popular with American critics and audiences little accustomed to the formality and externality of epic: people tried to view it as a thriller and found it wanting in those terms. Still it is why *Troy* works well as a Hollywood performance of a Greek epic. *Hero*, too, refrains from psychology in much of a modern sense. As a martial-arts epic, it appropriates instead the formality of stylized gesture that echoes earlier epics such as *Ivan the Terrible* (1944 and 1958) and *Dune*.

In *A Connecticut Yankee in King Arthur's Court*, Mark Twain tries to show us moderns, insistently dichotomizing ourselves into subjects and objects, the unfamiliar "psychology" of King Arthur and his knights.[38] Maybe it would be better to talk in terms of the absence of inner psyche for politics in the middle ages. Like the public characters of ancient Greece and Rome, medieval politics featured standing, face, reputation. Their largely republican devices of politics cope better than Hank Morgan, the Connecticut Yankee, expects with the cultures of anger and honor that can result in offense, vengeance, vendetta, and other aspects of mostly tribal life. As Twain tells, the relative absence of self-concern and reflection leaves these public characters like oversized boys. The acute interest in how others might see them puts precarious chips of honor on their shoulders, and they are inclined to strike out in momentary offense then fight until their energy flags. Yet with anger dissipated in physical exertion, they move quickly back into full and comfortable comradery. They toss away their weapons and throw their arms over each others' shoulders, where the chips—in a sense, their epaulets as martial signs of specific honors earned—had sat before being dislodged.

An epic hero generally shows (even *is*) more outside than inside. This can be an aspect of the republican emphasis on ethos as character-in-action-as-seen by other participants.[39] Success in public life depends, importantly, on seeing yourself as others see you. Garry Wills argues that George Washington showed real genius for this.[40] In much the same way that epic heroes can seem to stand somewhat outside themselves, turning back on their characters as behavioral patterns seen from public perspectives, epics can begin to make their communities "objects" to themselves. This can help polities accomplish an incipient kind of community consciousness, a dawning self-recognition. In itself, this is not a fully self-conscious and self-critical practice of community; yet it can prove a strong step in such directions. Epics can help their communities recognize who they have (started to) become and what they are doing. From the hero's perch of the ultimate insider, epics can reach outward toward a kind of "objectivity" about communal identities and projects, often with the hope of helping to liberate peoples from some oppressive or otherwise obnoxious practices that they have not yet recognized in what they are doing.

Political Mentors

In epics, as "everybody knows," heroes generally have mentors. Because the heroes are mostly male and begin their sagas mostly young, the mentors are mostly male and much older. (Mentoring differs from mothering.) And because the heroes make marks far beyond their fathers, those fathers seldom are the principal mentors. When Godfrey the father (Liam Neeson) mentors Balian the son (Orlando Bloom) in *Kingdom of Heaven*, an exception is supporting the rule, because Godfrey has not raised Balian to adulthood but instead enters his life later. Godfrey belatedly schools Balian in combat and diplomacy, before Godfrey dies from their journey to Jerusalem. And when Marlon Brando's Godfather mentors Al Pacino as the next Godfather, as father to son, we do well to remember that their attainments seem loosely equal. In martial-arts movies, the comparable figures are the masters who teach apprentices the arts of war. But in epics, the prowess of heroes is even more political and characterological than it is martial. In terms of Jungian archetypes, accordingly, the epic mentor is the Wise Old Man.[41]

Examples are legion. Almost offscreen, but even so the crucial mentor for *Braveheart*'s liberator of Scotland, is the uncle (Brian Cox) who adopts the orphaned hero as a boy. Notice that he apparently provides the young man Continental culture and learning more than combat practice or strategy. Ben Obi-Wan Kenobi (Alec Guinness) and Yoda (Frank Oz) mentor Luke Skywalker (Mark Hamill) in *Star Wars*: his tutelage in becoming a Jedi Knight covers much more than the military. In *Gladiator*, Marcus Aurelius (Richard Harris) mentors Maximus in virtue and possibly politics, then Proximo (Oliver Reed) teaches him the politics and rhetoric of winning the crowd more than the contest. In *Australia*, King George (David Gulpilil) takes Nullah (Brandon Walters) walkabout, mentoring him in crafts of cultural and personal survival that have little to do with fighting. Adoptive brothers teach Arthur to fight in many of the related epics, but Merlin mentors *The Once and Future King* in civilization and diplomacy. In *The Lord of the Rings*, Gandalf (Ian McKellan) mentors Frodo (Elijah Wood) in resisting the lure of imperial-unto-totalitarian power. Lieutenant Dan (Gary Sinise) might mentor Forrest Gump (Tom Hanks) in combat; but if so, we don't see that. What we do see is mutual mentoring in adulthood. Alexander (Colin Farrell) learns fighting from others, but philosophy, civilization, and politics from his mentor, Old Ptolemy (Anthony Hopkins). In *The Matrix*, martial arts are part of the Morpheus (Laurence Fishburne) mentoring for Neo (Keanu Reeves); but a larger part is his mentoring in revolutionary arts. Old Lodge Skins (Chief Dan George) mentors the Little Big Man (Dustin Hoffman) in living and resisting rather than fighting. And so on.

When we do get an epic heroine, there is also apt to be mentoring, but not necessarily by a Wise Old Man or a Wise Old Woman. Instead the mentoring can come from someone closer to the heroine's cohort. Thus Ruby Thewes (Renée Zellwegger) mentors Ada Monroe (Nicole Kidman) in *Cold Mountain*. This makes the "mentor" closer to a sister, and it might even move epic mentoring toward feminist sisterhood.[42] If female mentoring comes from an older woman, should we worry? *Crouching Tiger, Hidden Dragon* shows why we might have some concern in such a case, especially if the mentoring is more martial than political.

When we do not get a mentor at all, the hero becomes all the more "impersonal" and "exterior." Many scenes show how Mad Max (Mel Gibson) goes mad and eventually becomes a new founder fit for apocalyptically new times. Yet the absence of a mentor in any of the *Mad Max* movies leaves the title figure's crazy, creative prowess basically inscrutable. This holds somewhat for the descent into insanity of Howard Hughes (Leonardo DiCaprio) in *The Aviator*. It even has resonance for the title character (Peter O'Toole) in *Lawrence of Arabia*, whom the movie psychologizes extensively yet leaves largely mysterious as a leader for revolution in an adopted land where he never fully finds a home. What of the mentorless title figure played by Elizabeth Taylor in *Cleopatra*? This epic presents her as a nearly natural conniver unable to prevail for herself or her people against long odds produced by competing conquerors from Rome.

This epic emphasis on experienced men mentoring the hero in political arts reinforces the form's concerns for community identity and liberation, especially from imperial power. An interesting convention of epic movies is that excellent mentors for virtuoso leadership need not themselves be community leaders. They also come from such reflective pursuits as philosophy (Ptolemy) and magic (Merlin), so they sometimes observe from the sidelines more than they enter frontally into the political fray. There can be ambiguity about this, of course. There is reason to argue that prominent mentors are mostly former greats or near-greats now past their prime. There is room to recognize that some mentors are great politicians in semi-separate arenas for advisors, academicians, and the like. Yet the Wise Old Man who mentors the young Hero often differs from the Hero's father. These hold especially when the father is a brutal or distracted warlord: a king, a prince, or a knight who lacks the time or the political talent to raise the Hero to liberate and lead a community free from imperial ambitions. From Alexander to Luke Skywalker, in fact, epic fathers often embody the aspiration to empire that the epic hero eventually must confront and defeat on behalf of his people.

Liberated Communities

So the politics that Hollywood cinema pairs with the impersonal but mentored heroes of epics are the loosely republican politics of community identity and liberty. This is not by mere accident or generalization but by generic convention. Most popular epics in literature, cinema, and television feature politics of community identity: their heroes embody who we are at root then enact what we do at best. In recent movies, more specifically, this means liberating us from powers imperial or imperious. Such epic heroes conventionally sacrifice themselves to free (us) others from colony, tyranny, or their everyday counterparts. Who we are as a community is an unmistakable preoccupation of three-fourths of the numerous post-1950 epics that I have analyzed, and the same holds for the epics from 2000 onward.

Moreover liberation from empire or its functional equivalents is the hero's main project in more than half the epics studied prior to 2000, and a similar portion of the epic films after 1999 feature the same sorts of politics. Let me say again that this seems all the more remarkable because epic cinema so clearly suits politics of grand display and massive spectacle. It would be plausible to expect that conventions of lavish display in epics would favor empires rather than oppose them.[43] Yet epic politics are principally republican. For all their fascination with spectacle, epics link it to empire and liberation far more than ensuing publics.

Vaguely comparable counts for the predominant politics in other genres suggest that these portions are decently impressive. They leave little doubt that epic movies since the middle of the twentieth century sustain a conventional affinity for the classic interest of epic in defining our communities.

They also show that epics from Hollywood promote more the specific politics of combatting empire, even as the epic embrace of scale and spectacle
might seem more likely to celebrate empire. The closest that other genres
come to such anti-imperial politics probably is the anti-totalitarianism of
dystopias—leaving anti-imperial politics rare, for example, in thrillers. So
strong is the conventional drive of epic movies toward liberation from empire
that *Alexander* and *300* warp their "histories" in many ways to make two
epics of free-Greek resistance (in the West) to Persian empire (in the East).

In epic movies at the middle of the twentieth century, another big use
of spectacle is to display the majesty of monotheism. Religious epics cluster in that era, as the first table suggests. Strictly speaking, *The Passion of
the Christ* (2004) from Mel Gibson is a passion play rather than an epic—
although both these popular forms love pageantry. Similarly *Jesus Christ
Superstar* (1973) is a musical much more than an epic. Such cases leave *The
Last Temptation of Christ* (1988) as the outstanding outlier by era, and it
is the signal exception that highlights the rule. With epic spectacle used
repeatedly to glorify religion, especially in the West, we might expect epic
spectacle to glorify empire; and recent epics do deploy spectacle to evoke
or explain the seductions of empire. Still the principal politics in cinematic
epics of late drive principally in an opposite direction: resisting, attacking,
and overthrowing empire.

Three Epochs for Epics

To see how these politics arise from the genre conventions of epic movies, let
us specify some of the major figures of epic in general for three loose subsets
that follow familiar contrasts in the field of political theory among premodern, modern, and postmodern epochs. Yes, these periods are Eurocentric,
except for the increasing prominence of America in postmodern times.
Premodern times stretch from the "barbarisms" before Western civilization through the classical periods of ancient Greece and Rome, their collapse, then the middle (allegedly "dark") ages of the Holy Roman Empire.
Modern times take shape with the Renaissance and the Reformation, reach
new highs with the Enlightenment, then march through the twentieth century. The postmodern period overlaps the modern age but still distinguishes
itself as an eclectic collection of electronic cultures that begin by the nineteenth century and gain so much momentum by the twenty-first that they
might be carrying us on beyond the Western world.[44]

General conventions of epic receive telling inflections for movies focused
on each of these periods of Western civilization, so a quick tour of these
three kinds of epics can clarify the politics at issue. By "general conventions

of epic," across all three kinds, I mean stock figures from the popular genre across media, but with special attention to movies. Since genre conventions are usually loose and flexible, the room for variation ranges from ample to enormous. The resulting talk is categorical and taxonomic, sometimes to a fault. Virtually by definition, the "authors" of popular epics are for the most part "popular," which is to say, historical figures who typically seem to have intended to contribute to the vernacular cultures of their eras and whose success depends on approval by the populace in their times.

Premodern Epics

In general, premodern epics feature magnitude. They show souls great with daring, success, acclaim, or folly. Their stakes are great, often with whole worlds hanging in the balance. They portray great loves, distinguished by deep passions—yet conventionally with mere moments of earthly fulfill-ment. These epics have vast populations on call, with the "cast of thou-sands" a standard slogan for epic movies in the middle of the twentieth century. They present vast vistas on the screen (or at least reference distant horizons). They evoke vast scales in space (moving among many, far-flung locales) as well as vast scopes in time (reaching across years and generations). Prominent among their spectacles are towering cities, terrible battles, and threatening wilds.

Epic heroes quest for identity, community, responsibility, or redemp-tion.[45] The resulting plots usually turn on sacrifice or salvation. Often these heroes sacrifice the present to the past (in vengeance) or future (in faith). Heroes characterize themselves in deeds, establishing ethos through a code of honor. The pervasive pathos of these epics is awe. Their kind of time is destiny, and their unit of time is the episode. Notable twists pit such epic styles against more historical sensibilities, as in *Lonesome Dove* or *The Thirteenth Warrior*. Other movies show epical declines or catastrophes: for example, *Lawrence of Arabia* and *Legends of the Fall*.

Epics that foreground premodern figures shape these conventions in dis-tinctive ways. "Authors" for tales about Achilles, Alexander, Jesus, Arthur, El Cid, and other premoderns are the traditional bards, divine inspirations, or other sources that contribute to our popular cultures without exactly enter-ing into them. Often the premodern heroes are founders. Because many antedate the realms founded, the ethos they enact is often a warrior code of worth. ("Onward Christian Soldiers" notwithstanding, Jesus is an obvious outlier in inverting pagan virtues even as He still founds or at least opens a new realm for others.[46]) Premodern spectacles display their focal com-bats in ample arenas separated by daunting distances: witness *Gladiator* and

Alexander but also *Crouching Tiger, Hidden Dragon*. Yet the magnitude of premodern epics springs even more from their heroes: figures of astounding audacity, courage, hubris, and especially sacrifice.

Usually in a premodern epic, the sacrifice is of the human to the community. This favors plots of tragedy or comedy, with a pervasive pathos of astonishment and admiration. The pathetic strategy standard for premodern epics is formalism.[47] The conventional time is fate; and the episodes are principally emblems of the heroic leaders, whom premodern epics characterize more through their gestures than their effects. A few of these films, including *Alexander*, twist instead toward hollow triumphs; and Christian epics sometimes turn the hero away from this world, as in *Ben-Hur*. More often, though, epic movies have premodern heroes found lasting and beneficial communities that foreshadow later people and polities.

Epic creation of a people might seem irrelevant to liberation from empire: if there were no community yet, how could there be an empire to oppress them? It is telling that most of these Hollywood epics feature Western civilization. They share its disposition to treat supposedly uncivilized tribes or barbarian hordes as materials for the formation of a civilized people even as it also fears them as Eastern (or southern or northern) empires of primitive, sybaritic, brutal, even idolatrous warlords. Think of Egypt and Persia in the eyes of ancient Greeks, or of India and China as beheld by ancient Macedonians, or of Gaul and Germania as seen by ancient Romans. However dubious the historical warrant, the mythic commitment of Hollywood epics is clear: "we" emerge as a full and free people in liberation from imperial powers synonymous with the absence of truly adequate civilization, which is to say, "our" civilization of the West. Not every movie epic on premodern times works this way, but most of them do.

Modern Epics

Modern epics have historically specific authors, and these films often treat themselves as historically based biographies of earlier heroes. The heroes are typically developers: rather than create a community from whole cloth, they take away the oppressions or other limits that have kept it from becoming all it could and should be. Neither William Wallace (Mel Gibson) nor Mahatma Gandhi (Ben Kingsley) invented his people, the Scots or the Indians, respectively; instead each led beyond the oppression, English or British, that had prevented his people from coming fully into their own freedom and community. So go *Braveheart* and *Gandhi*, respectively. Nor in *Titanic* did Jack Dawson (Leonardo DiCaprio) create Rose Dewitt Bukater (Kate Winslet); instead he helped free her from imperious "rule" by her mother (Frances

Fisher) and her fiancé (Billy Zane), enabling her to develop into a self-ruled and deeply fulfilled woman.

Linear history is the kind of time that dominates modern epics, making their episodes into historical stages of community growth or psychological stages of character development. Accordingly modern epics characterize their heroes through events and their consequences. Often their sacrifice is of the loved to the cause. Their magnitude shows in ambition, fortune, and virtue-osity, encouraging plots of romance or criticism. The usual ethos is a gentlemanly code of honor. The pathetic strategy is most often one of realism, of course, with the attendant pathos oscillating between wonder and horror at spectacles that favor forbidding wilds, big buildings, and military engagements.

Yet the "modern subgenre" of movie epics makes room for several standard twists. It includes many a Faust story.[48] Often these are antirealist, anti-hardball epics. They caution against despairing idealisms, showing how these too readily become realisms where the ends are all that could have any hope of justifying intrinsically evil means that get too outrageous for any apology. Here the great cinematic examples are the *Godfather* movies. There also has been room for antimodern epics. These attack development as dishonorable and disastrous: *Dances with Wolves* and *The Last Samurai* are cases in point. Movie epics focused on modern times can even become anti-epical, turning the genre against itself. But by this point, they typically shade over into the subgenre of movie epics attentive to postmodern times.

Postmodern Epics

Two instances of antimodern unto postmodern epics are *Little Big Man* and *Forrest Gump*. As they show, postmodern epics twist toward undoing epic as a project. In different ways, these two movies turn apparent celebrations of American values and events into portraits of Americans as holy or at least fortunate fools. Each film takes epic form while deflating our polity's epic, imperial pretensions. This enables each to pursue ironically the epic politics of liberation from empire. Through each, we meet the empire, only to learn that it is us. *Little Big Man* shows how imperial we Americans have become without knowing it, whereas *Forrest Gump* more slyly suggests how mindless but imperious the mass publics and popular cultures in the United States have become since the Second World War.

The preeminent comparison in political theory, we may pause to note, is Thomas Hobbes's myth of the State of Nature as a State of War. It is antiwar in portraying anarchy (absence of modern sovereignty) as political hell on earth—that is, the worst possible condition. It is anti-heroism in notoriously depicting life without sovereignty as "solitary, poore, nasty, brutish, and short." It is anti-community in promoting individual rationality for dissolving gangs. It is anti-foundation in favoring hypothetical consent to establish political obligation over the historical—actual—act of consent that would amount to a specific founding. Yet it is pro-imperialism in recommending expansive sovereignty as the crucial cure for natural chaos. These inversions of epic conventions and their affinities for politics are central to the political theory from Hobbes. To recognize this can be to ironize the arguments by Sheldon S. Wolin "that the intentions which inform Hobbes's political theory were epical in nature and that his theory can be understood as having an epical aim."[49] The last part of the present chapter returns to this topic, after more about postmodern epics especially.

Echoing premodern epics, postmodern epics usually have collective authors. Made intentionally (if oxymoronically) as myths, specifically epic treatments of events already familiar from current cultures and personalities typically get shaped by too many people—including their audiences, consumers, viewers, publics, or the like—to individuate the contributions. Among the best cases in point, actually, are Hollywood movies themselves: famously resistant to analysis that would find in some singular cinematic "auteur" an equivalent for the individuated historical author of, say, a novel.[50] Likewise the largely postmodern studies of anthropologists, next door to folklorists and classicists, maintain that myths are made collectively over long periods by whole societies rather than individually by specific writers who can be localized in modern space and time.[51]

With quasi-imperial powers exercised by social systems, the magnetic figures who rebel against everyday authorities in order to liberate us little guys become candidates for migrating from thrillers to epics. Consequently postmodern epics often have maverick heroes.[52] Personal codes of fidelity are their ethics; and they conventionally sacrifice self to principle, even though the resulting idealism is more ironic than pure.[53] In postmodern epics, the heroes demonstrate magnitude of self through moments of despair coupled with strategies of resistance and taking personal stands against corrupt systems.[54] This complexity of character is categorically greater than epics conventionally provide for their premodern and modern heroes.

To handle such complexity of character, epics in a postmodern mode have distinctive recourse to characterization through composites. They present collaborative companies of heroes, with each of the company's figures characterizing an important aspect of a collective hero. An easy example is *The Fellowship of the Ring*, based on the first part of *The Lord of the Rings* by J. R. R. Tolkien.[55] At times, each of the ten fellowship members (including Gollum) is an archetype; so that the epic can construct an unusually intricate psychology for the overall hero that emerges from the company as a whole. This device sustains the usual exteriority and simplicity of the epic hero while providing even more complicated protagonists overall than the somewhat individualized heroes available in modern epics.

In the movies, at least, postmodern epics favor plots full of fantasy or irony. The kind of time that emerges is more inventive than fated or historical. Sometimes episodes even come across overtly as fragments. A pathos of fascination frequently is sufficient to unify them; and the playful, self-aware use of figures fits into a pathetic strategy of symbolism.[56] Spectacles in postmodern epics incline toward military campaigns, fantastic structures, and exotic locales. Epic movies with postmodern settings can enjoy making epic an overt theme, as in *O Brother, Where Art Thou?* Their composite characterization can yield nonpersonal (in continuity but also contrast with impersonal) heroes, as in *Love Actually*. Postmodern twists can wring epics from conventionally anti-epical genres such as neo noir: note *Magnolia*, *Crash*, and *All the King's Men*. Their postmodern eclecticism can even link the timeless moments of community that conventionally close or open epic movies to an otherwise (seemingly) historical narrative—as in *Places in the Heart* plus several of the *Star Wars* movies.

Conventional Scenes

Those timeless moments of community in epics bring together all the main characters or other components. When the gatherings are regular, they are rites; when they are surprising and little precedented, they are syzygies: strange, tense, temporary alignments of the main elements that help define the community but that it mostly connects indirectly and over greater reaches of space and time.[57] Among the stock scenes for movie epics, syzygy scenes are among the most distinctive. This is to say that syzygy scenes are among the least likely to appear in films genred primarily in another way. But it is not to say that all epics include a syzygy scene, not by a long shot, especially since ritual gatherings can serve most of the same epic purposes. The convention of gathering members is clearly a device for evoking the identity of a specific community while affirming its past contribution, future promise, and present endurance (or end).

Premodern epics seem a little more inclined to do such a scene early as a feast (*Alexander*), modern epics as a wedding (*Godfather*), and postmodern epics as a festival (*The Fellowship of the Ring*). When performed more in closing, this scene of community gathering generally provides a coda of commemoration. Premodern and modern epics might be more likely to stage a final celebration (*King Arthur* and *The Natural*) or a late lamentation (*El Cid* and *Ladder 49*), with the event markedly organized. Postmodern epics just might favor in conclusion a less planned, more fortuitous collection (*Love Actually*). We *are* talking about cinema, so montage is another familiar way for epics to commemorate, particularly toward a film's end (*Titanic*). Yet the inclinations are weak, if they persist at all, and counterinstances abound. The main pattern is that movie epics include a scene or two of community gathering by rite or syzygy.

Other scenes standard for movie epics similarly help them concentrate on the politics of community identity and liberation. A prophecy unites the community across epic stretches of time by giving it a trajectory appreciated, at least in part, from the outset. In premodern epics, scenes of prophecy presage what is to come by providing obliquely symbolical hints. These can be dire portents (*Apocalypto*) or redeeming promises (*King of Kings*). Modern epics, unsurprisingly, are more partial to predictions informed by science or specific experience (*1492*). The prefiguring leap of "proception" or, since the context is cinema, perhaps I should say "projection," is more at home in postmodern epics.[58] Thus the *Matrix* movies are notably interested in how Neo has been proceived or projected as "the One."

According to Hollywood, at least, the epic challenge is to subdue the evil empire and free our own community by martial prowess or political virtuosity. Of course, battle is more prominent by far than formal politicking. Even so, movie epics can include one or another kind of conference to fulfill the community's defining ambitions or at least its urgent needs. In premodern epics, this scene tends toward the parley, on or near the battlefield, where what a community usually seeks is recognition enough to continue beyond the battle. The title figure in *Alexander* perplexes his men at arms by repeatedly defeating other tribes only to extend them the political recognition usually gained by conquest or negotiation—and in exchange for only a limited sort of subjugation to Alexander's empire. The modern epic is more likely to stage a full-fledged negotiation, typically done apart from a field of battle, where the stock aim is some greater realization of the community's sense of itself, including its liberty. This is what William Wallace pursues in negotiations with English powers, even as Robert the Bruce (Angus MacFadyen) initially uses similar negotiations to betray the Scottish people in exchange for privileging the Scottish "nobles." A postmodern epic is more likely to frame a less formal facing among adversaries, often bringing the epic to a somewhat mixed culmination. Having sailed to England, Pocahontas (Q'orianka Kilcher) faces King James (Jonathan Pryce) and Queen Anne (Alexandra Malick), but also Captain John Smith (Colin Farrell) and John Rolfe (Christian Bale), on behalf of *The New World* that she both enacts and encounters in Terrence Malick's strangely poetic epic of that name.

In epic films, the hero meets prophesied obstacles, enemies, and especially arch nemeses in battle. Generally the foes stage confrontations mano a mano, with the hero fighting long odds. Premodern epics might prefer single combats, where the community's champion defeats the representative of the opposition (David over Goliath) in a contest of man against virtual beast or barbarian. In *King Arthur*, the title figure (Clive Owen) begins a last stand against barbarians almost single-handedly and finally kills his grizzled foe, Cerdic (Stellan Skarsgård), one-on-one. Modern epics might favor more regulated duels for their heroes that turn into battles of our one or few against their many (*The Last Samurai*). Or they show epic villains on the other side of these loaded confrontations by subverting honorable combat through assassinations (all *The Godfather* films). Postmodern epics could incline toward face-offs, where human heroes must best villainous machines, monsters, or more (*Star Wars*).

Epics conventionally have the hero rally his people with a stirring speech that moves the men to arms, but especially clarifies the moment as a great turning point in the tale. Epic heroes also display verbal skills in misdirecting the enemy's attention. Because community *is* communication, it is not surprising that epic heroes in movies mostly outdo their enemies in communication skills—and not just in speaking but also in listening, including openness to hearing bad news and disagreements from comrades. Reluctance by fearful or resentful subordinates to share bad tidings with their superiors is a recurrent reason that epic opponents fail to prevail. The Hollywood lesson from epics is that community freedom requires free communication.

A corollary is that movies which show strong respect for both sides in an epic conflict typically pay sustained attention to communication on both sides. Thus *The Longest Day* gives many scenes to the Axis powers, especially the Germans, as well as the Allies. There is a decent balance for both sides also in *Hero*, *Troy*, and *The Godfather* films. Clint Eastwood's epic couple of 2006, *Flags of Our Fathers* and *Letters from Iwo Jima*, has earned lavish praise for this.[59] Yet other epic movies, including some great ones, resolutely deprive the enemy side of much realism, sympathy, or even attention. *The Lord of the Rings* offers some sense of what Saruman is doing but little of what transpires with Sauron. Some epics with ample access to the enemy are running away from balance toward impressing viewers with the perfidy and perversity of the villain: take Emperor Commodus (Joaquin Phoenix) in *Gladiator*. Few epics provide much of a third perspective, stepping to the sidelines of the focal confrontation for a different view; perhaps they would not manage to become or remain epics if they did not really root for the hero or rue the villain. *The Thirteenth Warrior might* help us experience *Beowulf* from an Arab standpoint; but Ahmed Ibn Fahdlan (Antonio Banderas) ends up fighting for Beowulf, just as British journalist Simon Graham (Timothy Spall) ends up siding with *The Last Samurai*. Epic politics from Hollywood almost always take sides—without hesitation or equivocation.

A Coda on Epic Theory

In Hollywood movies, epics conventionally *climax* with victory or defeat. They liberate the people from confusion over who they are and where they are bound. And they liberate the people from oppression by imperial powers within or without. But they often *conclude* with a coda. Mainly it turns away from confronting our enemies toward embracing our communities. This chapter is an exercise in appreciating movies as political mythmaking. Yet making political myths for our communities is also what some of our most impressive political theorists attempt. With political theories offered as their political deeds, they try to do politics in popular realms.

Rarely do recent theories come close to the mythic potency of popular movies or stories. These popular works benefit from more vivid settings, colorful characters, and overt dramas or narratives.[60] That is how Stephen King and company can outdo the imposing Frankfurt School at its own project of "crisis theory," bringing home to us in everyday life a sense of civilizational catastrophe coming over the horizon.[61] This holds even when we allow generously for the ways that academic theories sometimes inspire authors and screenwriters. To close this account of epic as political mythmaking, let us shift from movies to theories by considering the proclamation, collapse, and putative resurrection of "epic political theory." As a coda, accordingly, this exercise in political theory ends by turning back to its own community, in order to consider what epics might teach political theorists about their own cause and craft.

Culminating arguments that he had been refining throughout the 1960s, Sheldon S. Wolin published in 1970 a brief book.[62] It had begun as lectures delivered on several occasions to appreciate Thomas Hobbes and "the epic tradition of political theory." In 1960, Wolin had advanced a version of what Hannah Arendt and many others were then terming "the western tradition of political thought and action."[63] Wolin's treatment, in *Politics and Vision*, helped to define what came at times to be called "the Berkeley School" of political theory.[64] This developed in contrast to the "Straussians" centered at the University of Chicago, the separable approaches of such other European émigrés as Arendt and Eric Voegelin, and the Harvard cluster of stars that came eventually to feature Judith Shklar and Michael Walzer in Government. (This came before John Rawls gained even greater attention in Philosophy at Harvard, leading swiftly to a "Rawls industry" that piped the main tune for political theory as an academic field for the next decade or two.[65])

By the end of the 1960s, Wolin was invoking *The Structure of Scientific Revolutions* by Thomas Kuhn to argue for political theory as potentially and properly revolutionary, in action as well as thought.[66] This made Wolin part of a mad scramble across many disciplines to claim mantles that Kuhn had made invitingly vague while endowing them with prestige from philosophy of science.[67] The contrast for Wolin and his colleagues was between political theory and political science. Self-professed political scientists dismissed political theorists as armchair speculators or intellectual historians rather than objective and systematic scientists. In response, many self-identified theorists denied that any true or practical science of politics could be desirable or even possible, at least after the fashions of physics, chemistry, or biology. Wolin made part of this argument in a prominent article in the *American Political Science Review*.[68]

'Twas a time for manifestoes on the scientific study of politics to appear as presidential addresses to the American Political Science Association.[69] The ambition of self-identified political behavioralists was to secure recognition of "their" discipline as the genuine science of politics. Several had seized on Kuhn's work to specify criteria for "normal science" that could be met by behavioralists—and so could justify the elimination of unscientific projects left over from the pre-paradigmatic days of the discipline. Kuhn's case for normal science could echo the hardball realism already entrenched among political scholars by their battles against the naïve idealism of the "classical democratic theory" that ignored evidence of popular inattention to politics. Within the emerging research multiversity, this hardball would break eggheads (or at least their careers) to make scientists (or at least their grants from the National Science Foundation).[70]

For years, Wolin had been suggesting that political theory, perhaps even in its academic forms, could and should remake politics.[71] His book on Hobbes as an epic theorist for modern times could be said to have responded bravely to behavioralist attempts to marginalize political theory as sheer speculation or normative stipulation outside the normal, admirable scope of objective science. Certainly it tried to liberate political theory as a field of scholarship from imperial subjugation by brands of "political science" that defined themselves as categorically superior. To be sure, Wolin never issued an epic political theory of his own.[72] At least twice, however, he went qualitatively farther than just calling on others to act as political world-makers.

The first time was when the leading would-be liberators of political theory at the University of California in Berkeley tried to secede from their academic department of political science. Their ambition was to (re?)form a department of political theory at Berkeley that could show their colleagues around the world how to proceed. But they failed even at Berkeley. A few stayed there, some fled down the road to the University of California at Santa Cruz, and some went eventually to other places more hospitable to political theory (yet still mostly within the imperium of political science). Their successors in spirit have included the Caucus for a New Political Science that long operated on the margins of the American Political Science Association, the seemingly coöpted "Perestroika" movement for greater "openness" and "diversity" in political science, and lately the "qualitative methods" subfield that has aspired in part to legitimate at least some humanistic inquiries in a discipline of political science probably as hegemonically scientistic as before.

The second time was when Wolin founded *democracy*. It was a progressive response to *The Public Interest* as a vehicle for political theorists and other intellectuals to address a more popular readership with more practical proposals for political reforms. It, too, failed. Most of the articles lacked imaginative ideas and popular appeal, leading the publisher and financier to pull the plug after a few years. Have other magazines taken up the proposed enterprise? There are many candidates: *The Atlantic Monthly, Harper's, The Nation, The New American Prospect, The New Republic, The New York Review of Books*, maybe even the *New Yorker* and *The Washington Monthly*. Yet most antedate the Wolin effort, and there is little reason to trace their present formats to its influence. Nor have blogs so far filled this void.

Neither of these Wolin initiatives drove in a direct way toward epic political theory. Still they were partial steps into practicing politics. Probably they were full steps into doing political theory in its own right, by contrast with analyzing political theory by others in the mode of intellectual history. Better to have tried and failed than never to have tried at all? Yes, but this also implies that somebody ought to be trying epic political theory: to do political theory in ways that can remake our politics, and not just to study calls or attempts by others. Make no mistake: Wolin framed his call as a manifesto, maybe, but even more as a history of Hobbes's ideas—rather than an epic contribution of Wolin's own to remaking present politics:

> Briefly, my argument will be that the intentions which inform Hobbes's political theory were epical in nature and that his theory can be understood as having an epical aim. I shall also suggest, without supplying exhaustive proof, that from Plato to modern times an epic tradition in political theory has existed and that Hobbes is one of its ornaments. The phrase "epic tradition" refers to a type of political theory which is inspired mainly by the hope of achieving a great and memorable deed

through the medium of thought. Other aims that it may have, such as contributing to the existing state of knowledge, formulating a system of logically consistent propositions, or establishing a set of hypotheses for scientific investigation, are distinctly secondary.[73]

What follows in the Wolin lectures is an exposition in tandem of Hobbes's political theory and epic political theory as a genre. Wolin settles for interpreting Hobbes as an epic theorist who helped make our political world into one that Wolin has found deeply objectionable in one work of criticism after another.

The irony in timing is intriguing. Throughout the 1950s and 1960s, as Wolin worked toward his call for epic political theory, Hollywood was contributing scores of what it regarded as epic films. These are mostly Biblical, classical, national, and western epics. In 1970, as Wolin published his call, *Little Big Man* marked a more ironical sensibility for epic that ushered the genre momentarily toward the margins while impugning epic ambitions as imperial. From *Star Wars* onward, what might have been epic adventures turned mostly into thrillers. In moving pictures, intended epics found a more economical outlet through the television miniseries. Is it any wonder that Wolin's summons to epic political theory elicited little response in the United States? Epic did not disappear from the repertoire of Hollywood or popular culture in America, but it did diminish and turn significantly parodic for a while. Ambient conditions for epic in America may not have been hospitable for Wolin's project.

Yet there was wisdom and daring in the Wolin call. Self-defined behavioralist scientists of politics portrayed their (former?) colleagues in the unscientific field of political theory as inherently inferior in method and indefensible in practice. To rally theorists to a more engaged and powerful calling, epic political theory was to trump the science of politics, conducted from a fairly impotent distance, with an actual practice of politics. Moreover it was to make (at least a few) political theorists into practical masters of politics by motivating and appreciating them as the true architects of political realms and possibly whole civilizations. Of course, this raises the generic question of whether epic ambitions long escape imperial inclinations: leaving "their" empire in order to make our own, if only to defend ourselves securely against their ambitions?[74] On the other hand, it is equally to the point to notice that the imperialist subordination or exile of political theory by self-proclaimed scientists of politics continues largely unabated today.

Epic movies evoke some of the advantages of "epic political theory" as a way to liberate a self-consciously unscientific field from oppressive regulation by putatively scientific projects. Notice that epics conventionally encourage a certain objectivity on the part of their heroes, who would be political theorists in response to the Wolin call. This can help political theorists reply to claims and practices of scientific objectivity: themselves more about psychology than method when done well. Furthermore epic political theory can participate in this historical moment's reach for objective leverage. This is like Malcolm Gladwell trying to turn the nonlinear chaos of movements into specific levers for social policy and political practice.[75] Instead why not go with the flow: why not go even farther through the radicalism and responsiveness of politics in styles, stances, and movements?[76] These contrast in figure and practice with the reach and rigidity of completely predictable effects-at-a-distance through the pretense of a fixed foundation for a governmental fulcrum plus the social exertion of leverage through idealogics. To construct worlds by words and to constitute them by deeds is to engage, interact, immerse, and penetrate—rather than to leave objects to be moved by (but separately from) ourselves. Surely movies have some elective affinities to movements.

Epic movies also show how retrospection (re-presenting the hero's feats) can become construction (remaking the community's character). This is exactly what a practice of political theory long centered in intellectual history needs to learn in order to make new politics. Epic devices for responding to imperial moves continue all too salient for political theorists, and the abiding concern of epics with the identities of their own communities might help political theorists invent professional practices with greater political reach and power.[77]

Political theorists have reason to love the ambition, the scope, of this project to (re)make the world or at least its politics by truly *doing* political theory. Wolin's epic theory recognizes that doing political theory can be doing politics. Especially it aspires to do new politics, adventurous politics, politics that few—if any—have done before. At least by form and self-conception, this epic theory aspires actually to do political theory: new, plain, and unapologetic. It writes *theory* directly: without the false humility, effacement, or confusion that mistakes theory for the mere history of others' more original ideas or for the sheer inventory of propositions left for testing by other means somehow more fully scientific.

Yet political theorists also have reason to distrust the arrogance, the pretension, the self-congratulation in scholars who pronounce their writings or teachings as legislative—possibly even constitutive—for what we do and who we are. What an insult this can be to politicians, pundits, staffers, journalists, or other potent practitioners! They sometimes take arms against our sea of troubles, and they often suffer frontally the slings and arrows of outrageous fortune. We academicians should take care when claiming to trump such efforts by contending instead with one another. Often we merely author arguments from virtual lighthouses lodged safely along the shore.

Did books or articles by Wolin redo American politics, let alone Western civilization? Did his public journal of *democracy* make any dent in the politics that Wolin opposed or any notable addition to the politics he supported? Let us credit completely the intention in the effort. But not even the Berkeley School in full seems to have much affected, let alone entered, our practical politics. Showing this has become the career of one of the Berkeley School's most distinguished but heretical members, John G. Gunnell. In book after book, he reminds political theorists that most of their work leaves untouched the actual, practical politics of our public and even private lives. To speak from the sidelines is seldom to affect the spectacle, since refined words get lost in the ruckus.[78] Cheerleading can have an impact; but in our times, the pundits are the people with bullhorns and gymnastics to inflame spectators and energize their teams on the fields of play. For the most part, as Judith Shklar suggested with sad eloquence, it has been a long, long time since political theorists have had significant readerships, real audiences, true publics.[79]

When Quentin Skinner and company announced a belated return to "grand theory," the altered name gave away the academic game at issue.[80] We get from grand theory almost pure pretension with scant performance, at least in practically political terms. There is none of epic's generic structure, its specificity, or its capacity for contributions to who we are and what we do. There are theorists such John Dunn and John Dryzek who continue to connect macro and micro with sufficient skill and vision to start re(con)figuring our styles as sensibilities for experience and strategies for action.[81] But as their work becomes more concretely and creatively political, it generally gets less "grand." Of course, it is no accident that Dryzek in particular engages green politics. The environmentalists who promote "ecopoeisis" write their political theory, like their poetry and science fiction, to refigure our economies and everyday lives.[82] They join feminists, Nietzschean perfectionists, and other postmodernists or postwesternizers in redoing everyday styles as politics and pursuing the "chaos" of nonlinear movements.

In postmodern unto postwestern settings, the impressive magnitude of epics in cinema can link in distinctive ways to kinds of community that are differently fragmentary and flexible than modern political theory readily accommodates with its Hobbesian turn to sovereign states. In the West, these kinds of community and devices of connection have surfaced at times in the politics of republics, which helps explain their long affiliation with epic movies.[83] So the current resurgence of epic films can track the (re)emergence of "republican" politics with postmodern or even postwestern inflections. Similarly the conventions that are taking shape to distinguish many epic films of late from their predecessors can point to forms and politics of importance to political theory in the new century.

In something of the spirit of epic political theory, we might be more ready than before to recognize various genres of popular literature and cinema as making political myths. This is to recognize popular movies and popular genres as doing political theory, yes, but especially it is to recognize them as doing politics. Sometimes epic movies *are* epic political theory, in that they help re(con)figure our political worlds, and so are other genres of popular movies. When *2001: A Space Odyssey* shows travel to the Moon as similar to a two-stop airplane trip from my own city to another, doesn't this projection of a near future start configuring our present senses of everyday life, including familiar politics? When movies have such popular, public, political ambitions and effects, how can political theorists not at least study them? And when movies have epic effects on our politics, how can political theorists not venture at times to make them?

CHAPTER 2

Rhythms of Political Satire: Postmodern Politics in Words, Musics, and Movies

(Featuring *Bulworth, Bob Roberts,* and *O Brother, Where Art Thou?*)

We need a song. You got to sing, Bulworth.
You can't be no ghost, 'cause you got to be a spirit, boy.
You got to be a spirit, and a spirit would not descend without song.
We need a spirit, Bulworth, not a ghost.

—The Rastaman

S atire counters the chorus of conventional wisdom when the world becomes corrupt.[1] In tone and outlook, satire is often among the most realist of popular genres. Yet it could not fault realities so resoundingly without appealing at times to idealist sensibilities and standards. Nor could it provoke vital alternatives without inspiring people through contrasting tunes, engaging rhythms, and fulfilling harmonies that reach beyond our corrupt realities. The idealism implicit in at least some satire coordinates people's actions against the target system, and they help satire turn savage criticism into civilized invention. Consequently the Rastaman played by Amiri Baraka tells the title character in *Bulworth* (1998) not merely to haunt the American memory with what might have been, but more to quicken the American muse with the empowering shape of song.

'Tis an awesome power that bards bring to politics. Song makers are mythmakers, since myths are musical words as much as they are symbolic stories.[2] Popular songs work as political myths.[3] They attune us to realities and rhythm our responses.[4] Musics that meld with words in song can move us to dance, to act in time with one another in modes of cooperation that become armies, ceremonies, communities, and more.[5] Accordingly movies animate us as much through their musics as their images or words.[6] The sounds of films help make them full-bodied, giving viewers virtual as well as vicarious experiences of politics.[7] When movie images are surfaces on screens, no matter how big, the cinema's surrounding sounds can be crucial for endowing them with depth and texture. In the sounds as well as the sights of satire, its rhythms of realism and idealism slip into our everyday experiences and deeds.

Movies produce politics by making myths. Hollywood appreciates how myths can be musical words, as well as memorable images, that rhythm our lives. Hence popular films about the politics of campaigns do some of their most effective work through devices that link words to sounds. This principle accounts for the distinctive strategies of *Bulworth* and *Bob Roberts* (1992): two campaign satires that rely crucially on genres of popular music to criticize recent politics—and hint at constructive courses to take in their stead.

The two films also share satirical devices of plot, setting, and character. Both turn on the plot trope of conspiracy that Hollywood uses to evoke our troubles in recognizing and resisting whole systems of oppression.[8] Both set themselves in the midst of news documentary coverage of nineties-style campaigns for the US Senate. These are the kinds of campaigns that continue to dominate major elections in the twenty-first century. They are replete with debates, telespots, stump speeches, church appearances, photo opportunities, and other commonplaces of big-money elections for the national stage. Both pit peculiar truth-tellers against a wily establishment that pulls strings of government from behind the official scenes. Both incorporate into senatorial campaigns the dynamics of assassination that burdened presidential politics in the second half of the twentieth century. Perhaps unsurprisingly, since movies about official politics are not taken to do well at the box office, both films are the creations of actors turned directors, who act as closely to authors as Hollywood productions can manage. Both these "auteurs" are known for left-liberal causes, and both star in the vehicles at issue: Warren Beatty in *Bulworth* and Tim Robbins in *Bob Roberts*.

What puts *Bulworth* and *Bob Roberts* in a class nearly by themselves, though, is a shared interest in how popular musics can be appropriated for political uses largely alien to their early affinities. *Bulworth* puts rap rhythms into the mouth of an establishment WASP. Then he uses them to drama-tize a long litany of lies and exploitations attributed to electoral politics in America. *Bob Roberts* focuses on a new son of the military-industrial com-plex in the national-security state. Its title character borrows folk melodies, harmonies, rhythms, and other figures to promote a ruthless, Ayn Rand individualism of entrepreneurial success over the welfare populism that it tries to caricature, discredit, and defeat.[9] By analyzing these devices for poli-tics in words and musics, we can learn how these satirical films make politi-cal myths and inspirit political acts.

Myths into Politics

To follow arguments about details of particular movies, let alone assess them, there is no substitute for viewing the films before and after reading the analyses. If you are yet to see *Bulworth* and *Bob Roberts*, this is the point to push the pause button for the prose at hand and watch two enjoyable movies. Back already? Even when the viewings are recent, analysts often do well next to synopsize the focal films. The purpose is to put readers on the same page as analysts for background aspects of the plot, settings, and char-acters. These provide context for the arguments and observations to come. They help locate readers in the same communication space as analysts, so that telling details of the focal films can be addressed in a situation of more or less mutual understanding.

Bulworth reverses the plot and propriety of *Mr. Smith Goes to Washington*, but keeps intact the populist mythos and ethos of the earlier movies. *Bob Roberts* shows how the populist project in American politics could be, per-haps already has been, hijacked by a fascist Mr. Smith and his cynical con-spirators. The 1939 film directed by Frank Capra earned a chilly reception at its premiere in Washington, DC. Still it has become *the* popular template for American movies about professional politics.

The Capra film has plenty of critics among scholars and politicos.[10] They complain that the movie is naïve in tracing America's troubles to the bad characters of its politicians, and it's perverse in equating compromise with corruption. As Hendrik Hertzberg summarizes, "Jefferson Smith (James Stewart) is a Boy Ranger leader in a prairie state who is chosen by the party machine's puppet governor to fill out the tail end of a dead senator's term." Soon "Smith introduces a bill to establish a boys' camp, on land to be bought with a government loan." But he doesn't know that powers behind the scenes plan to sell the land for building a dam at a greater profit. Surprised to be opposed and smelling something rotten, Smith denounces the dam deal. Then he's stunned by a smear campaign from his respected colleague,

Senator Joseph Harrison Paine (Claude Rains), who lies that Smith is the one conniving to make a killing on the land. On the verge of expulsion from the Senate, Smith mounts the filibuster that's made the film famous. He manages 24 hours of pious talk, but apparently to no avail. Unaccountably, though, Paine "suddenly suffers another attack of conscience, is restrained from blowing his brains out in the cloakroom, and rushes to the floor, shouting 'I'm not fit to be a senator! I'm not fit to live! Expel me! Expel me, not him!' Applause, cheers, The End."[11]

The Capra movie is populist in part because it treats professional politicians as intrinsically inclined to corruption. Even more, it suggests that ordinary people include heroes who can go into the secular temples of government and cleanse them simply through the exercise of good, possibly pure intentions. The populist notion is that ordinary people need no craft, compromise, or capacity for complication to improve American politics. The honest among us common folk need only common sense to tell right from wrong. To move others to knowledge of their plain truths, these populist anti-pols require only the eloquence of plain speech and the down-home charisma of the common touch.[12]

Hertzberg is like others with experience in government in protesting Capra's devaluation of political expertise and sophistication. Reviewing *Primary Colors* (1998), which rebuts the conception of American politics in *Mr. Smith Goes to Washington*, Hertzberg insists on the need for compromise and glad-handing explored by novelist Joe Klein and director Mike Nichols in relation to a fictionalized Bill Clinton.[13] By contrast, Hertzberg laments a populist susceptibility of the Capra film to antidemocratic politics.

> Never mind that Senator Paine had served the public interest honorably for thirty years, at the relatively small cost of not directly confronting the machine—less a Faustian bargain than simply a bargain. Never mind that Smith could have a hundred equally good sites for his boys' camp. Never mind that the filibuster is the most undemocratic of political methods. Never mind that Smith has behaved like a thug, punching four out-of-shape reporters in the face after their papers poke gentle fun at him for being a rube. All that counts...is that Smith has "plain, decent, everyday common rightness. And this country could use some of that. So could the whole cockeyed world."
>
> Oh, please. Played strictly for laughs, all this might have amounted to a tolerable, if off-target, lampoon. But it was meant to be taken seriously.[14]

The idea is that some Mr. Smith could wave a wand of common sense, and he soon would know everything a political representative should know. He could wave a wand of common values, and everyone worth including in the community soon would be cooperating for the common good. He could wave a wand of common virtues, and everybody with the least decency soon would be looking up to him as an icon of good government. How innocent. How romantic.

How perverse! Or how humorous. As Hertzberg says, however, *Mr. Smith Goes to Washington* is not (intended as) a satire, whether humorous or biting. It's a populist romance of non-, un-, or anti-politics.[15] Mythically this is the tale not only of *The Candidate* (1972) and *Dave* (1993), but, with twists, of *The Distinguished Gentleman* (1992), *The American President* (1995), *My Fellow Americans* (1996), *Man of the Year* (2006), and more. Some of these films are self-conscious satires, usually more genial than *Bulworth* and *Bob Roberts*, and the reach for humor is their saving grace. All but *The Candidate* and *The American President* play their plots, settings, and characters principally for laughs—at the expense of the present system of official politics. The same goes for *Bulworth* and *Bob Roberts*, except that they display the savagery of attack that has made satire among the most feared devices of politics in the West. *Dave* and *The Distinguished Gentleman* go for a grin with a chuckle; *Bulworth* and *Bob Roberts* want the bark of laughter that goes with the bite of condemnation. When *Bulworth* and *Bob Roberts* loose the cynics for satire, we learn how these *are* among the dogs of war—if by means verbal, visual, musical, and mythical.

The title tells the story of *Mr. Smith Goes to Washington*. Capra's is a republican myth of political redemption for the corrupt city.[16] An unsophisticated savior brings virtue from the countryside to rescue the people and the polity from their own (de)vices. In the Capra film, the hero played by James Stewart goes from an ordinary fellow to a US senator. He has been inspirited with a call to public service, and he resists temptations and smears from the political establishment in Washington to speak the truth. Toward the end, he breaks down; but he triumphs nevertheless by earning the conversion of a hardened official (and generations of sentimental audiences) to his cause.

Satire often works by inversion or reversal. *Bulworth* turns around the Capra plot. Its title figure goes from the US Senate to the gangsta-land of South Central Los Angeles. At the beginning, he breaks down from his own sellouts, telespots, and hypocrisies. Crazy with sleep deprivation and self-loathing, he agrees to keep insurance reform from the floor of the Senate in exchange for a ten-million-dollar insurance policy on his life. It's to benefit his 17-year-old daughter rather than his estranged and snippy wife. Then to add a touch of conspiracy, he arranges for himself to be assassinated at the end of his primary campaign for reelection.

Back in LA, though, the strangest things start to happen. Bulworth crosses paths with a black shaman, the Rastaman, who summons him to song. At a church for African-Americans, Bulworth begins to babble the hard but simple facts that no politician would utter in his right mind—pun intended. He literally levels with his listeners, at once insulting but also ennobling them by trusting them with "the truth." Soon he is appropriating their dances, their songs, their looks, their radical perspectives. As a hip-hop politician, Bulworth begins to rap his way back to popularity by becoming the scourge of politics, news, and entertainment as usual. He becomes the darling of C-SPAN and the toast of Larry King. He wins the heart of his would-be assassin, he converts a hardened drug-dealer into a political crusader, he triumphs in a televised interview, then he gets some sleep—and gets assassinated anyway, by the insurance lobbyist he spurned. Viewers do not learn whether Bulworth survives as a vital spirit—or dies to become another martyred ghost. Evidently his victory is up to them. Do they heed his call, his rap, his song?

Bulworth reverses *Mr. Smith*; yet the Beatty reversals might leave the Capra myth intact, even updated for different times. Science-fiction writer and literary theorist Samuel R. Delany observes that, "In myths, things always turn into their opposites as one version supersedes the next."[17] In one version of the Orpheus myth, he is a great singer; and in the next, he is the lone silent one. So the mythos extends itself. In one version, Mr. Smith goes to Washington to save it, breaks down, but wins anyway. In another edition, his opposite goes from Washington to spread its corruption through extortion, advertising, and assassination. He breaks down and gets saved. But he suffers assassination nonetheless. Flip from one extreme to another, and the larger pattern can stay much the same. Critics who lambaste a naïve populism in *Bulworth* need not look past *Mr. Smith* to find the template.

Has Beatty satirized the Capra myth? Sort of, but not entirely. In a way, he has expanded it from US senators and other officials of government to consultants, lobbies, corporations, entertainers, reporters, along with the politics of race, ethnicity, religion, and culture. "With all its hip-hop and jive, *Bulworth* may seem new-style," observes Peter Reiner, "but actually it's proffering a populism that Frank Capra would have loved. In a movie such as *Meet John Doe* (1941), Capra gave us his archetypal citizen-politician—a blubbery, guileless Gary Cooper who was such a hayseed he couldn't help but talk straight. In *Bulworth*," writes Reiner, "Beatty is harvesting that same old Capracorn, but in place of the hayseed innocent, he gives us the guy who is so much the politician that it deranges him. His only therapy is to spew the 'truth.'"[18] Bulworth's targets are many. Thanks to his reliance on rap, the arrows are sharp and barbed, with at least some of their shafts long and profane. *Mr. Smith* is a nice movie; *Bulworth* is a naughty, at times a nasty, one. Still the populist mythos of *Mr. Smith* remains the backbone of Beatty's film. *The Majestic*, a 2001 Jim Carrey vehicle directed by Frank Darabont, makes many similar moves with regard to popular movies, but without attention to comparable musics.

Bob *Roberts* relates differently to the myth of *Mr. Smith*. This film by Tim Robbins fears the power of Capra populism. It warns that the enterprising, entertaining sons of the military-industrial complex and the national-security state have been seizing the republican myth of the Man on the White Horse. More than that, it shows how their ilk can steal the American myths of Horatio Alger, Mr. Smith, and Miss America for fascist purposes. *Bob Roberts* warns that Wall Street, the "culture industry," and the "infotainment telesector" are using the power of popular music against the people.[19] It seeks to expose this mythic racket. It wants to inoculate viewers against further manipulation through coöptation of their myths and musics. Its strategy is to make the coöptation catchy but amusing and to exaggerate how the manipulation works.

The Robbins movie is a mock documentary of the title character's campaign for a Senate seat from Pennsylvania in 1990. Roberts is a right-wing rebel who left the hippie commune of his parents for military school, got an MBA, made a fortune as a folk singer for the far right and a player on Wall Street, then added philanthropy and politics to his portfolio. Brit Terry Manchester (Brian Murray) and his camera crew travel with the Roberts campaign throughout the concluding days of its general-election contest with the old liberal incumbent. In playing Democrat Brickley Paiste, a 30-year veteran of the US Senate, Gore Vidal gets to drone about national-security conspiracies against public government. He also gets to debate the self-righteous Roberts and fend off lies that allege a sexual relationship with his granddaughter's teenage friend. As in *Bulworth*, viewers see a couple of mock telespots for the focal candidate: one is a content-free celebration of the New Day Dawning with Bob; and the other is a viciously, hilariously sleazy spot that purports to show a drunken senator slumped and sleeping at a desk that displays jejune love doodles with a picture of his teenybopper mistress.

The Roberts campaign combines concerts with other public appearances: on a morning interview show for television, in a photo opportunity at an elementary school, with the doctor at a drug clinic that Roberts finances, at a beauty pageant for a philanthropic foundation that Roberts endows, and for a spoof of *Saturday Live Night* as a travesty of political satire and cutting-edge entertainment that actually shills for corporate profit. The Broken Dove operation funded by Roberts seems to have shifted from running drugs for the CIA in Central America to aiding children and advertising against drugs. The gray eminence behind the Roberts career, not just campaign, is Lukas Hart III, enacted with sinister relish by an Alan Rickman auditioning for Professor Snape in the Harry Potter movies. Tied to the Iran-Contra Affair, but cleared by a sanctimonious Senate, Hart and Broken Dove become implicated in the Savings and Loan scandal of the late eighties and early nineties—but again get absolved by a complicit Congress and a puppy-dog press of white-bread anchors who stay totally out to lunch when it comes to political realities.

Roberts defames the idealism of the sixties while coöpting its political interest in popular music. Resistance to Roberts comes mainly from documentarian Manchester; Kelly Noble (Lynne Thigpen), a black interviewer for a Philadelphia morning show; and counter-journalist Bugs Raplin (Giancarlo Esposito): all are figures from the margins of American politics and society. Writing for *Hard Times*, Raplin dogs the Roberts campaign throughout, seeking to expose its evil connivances. When he finally gets a measure of success with the mainstream press, by linking Broken Dove to S&L skullduggery, he gets framed by Hart and company in a faked assassination that supposedly paralyzes the legs of candidate Roberts and rescues his fading prospects for election. Raplin is freed eventually, after police learn that palsy in his hand would have made shooting a gun impossible. But he is still vilified by rabid fans of Roberts, and one soon assassinates Raplin. Roberts takes office in a wheelchair. His singing career continues too, and the film closes with the documentary camera giving viewers a glimpse of the toe of Roberts' shoe. It taps in time to his latest "protest" ditty, against "Godless Men," as Roberts sings from a wheelchair for an elite audience in Washington.

The myth of *Mr. Smith* is dangerous for America, the Robbins film seeks to show. Like the popular musics of America, the populist myths of America can be coöpted by corporate and military powers behind the scenes of government, campaigns, news, and entertainment. These shadowy forces can commandeer popular forms for politics antithetical to popular democracy. Bulworth's primary opponent characterizes him as "an old liberal whine trying to pour himself into a new conservative bottle."[20] That is a comment on his campaign spots and speeches before the breakdown. The reborn Bulworth, like the satirizing Beatty, is an old liberal whine trying to pour himself into new bottles of hip-hop and rap. Likewise Bob Roberts is working to pour old conservative, or more likely fascist, whine into new populist and "democratic" bottles.

Both films experiment with shifting the elective affinities of political forms and contents, pointing to the neglected significance of aesthetics and cultures for politics.[21] Both put to work a postmodern disposition to juxtapose old and new, familiar and strange, pious and outrageous. What happens if established ideas find different forms? What results if different ideas infuse familiar neighborhoods? The plots of *Bulworth* and *Bob Roberts* satirize election campaigns in the status quo, but they also explore possibilities for cultural politics that depart radically from the present system. What happens if Bob Roberts, rather than Mr. Smith, goes to Washington? What results when Mr. Smith stays in Washington? And what goes down later if he leaves for the hinterland, even Hollywood? Acting as auteurs, Beatty and Robbins become provocateurs. This is why they transpose their politics into words, words into musics, and musics into movies. The purpose of *Bulworth* and *Bob Roberts* is to remake political myths for America.

Politics into Words

Satire works in important part by turning politics into words. Literary satire is not alone in this. Satire as a distinctive form of politics began in the amphitheaters of ancient Greece; and to the present day, theatrical satire depends on the deft delivery of closely worked and clever wording—more than it does on props, costumes, makeup, or even the inspired performance of physical comedy. Cinematic satire follows suit. The editing that paces satirical films can be crucial, but it cannot save political satires where the dialogue does not snap. The images that drive home the lines in political satires can help their words take flight. In fact, the most potent individual fragment from *Bulworth*, the enduring emblem of the film as a whole, is an image that does not even appear in the body of the movie. The poster art and advertising logo for the film show the title character emerging in hop-hop dress as he dances and raps from the distended mouth of a politician in cartoon caricature: presumably Beatty as Bulworth, but drawn to resemble Ronald Reagan. Yet a great logo doth not a great film make, especially when the genre is satire. Horror movies might work through overwhelming images; but the claim of *Bulworth*, *Bob Roberts*, or any other film to significance as political satire rests primarily on the provocative power of its words. The satirical premise is that political criticism depends on articulate speech.

There need be nothing reductive or otherwise disreputable in the disposition of satire to turn politics into words. Nor is satire the only art or practice to do so. The same may be said of law, to take an example especially respectable in the civilization of the West.[22] The Latin root of *law* is *legere*, to read. When politics were taking specific shape in the agora of Greece and the forum of Rome, politics largely were words, mostly uttered by the mouth. The words refined raw behaviors into articulated actions.[23] These politics coalesced as "primary oral practices," and they remain "primarily oral practices" even in our "secondary oral cultures" of electronic media.[24] As a group, American politicians talk and listen more than they write and read. The ancient Greek name for *words uttered by the mouth* is *mythos*.[25] Thus the political power of satire is mainly mythic: unmaking the symbols and remaking the stories that people live together in their governance and everyday lives. Political satire can multiply the mythic power of its words through poetry, melody, and movement, especially in theater and cinema. Even satirical prose, though, must pack a sharp punch. This holds for plays and films as much as stories and novels.

Name symbolism is one manifestation of the satirical urge to turn politics into words. It might not stand out as much as other devices of satire in *Bulworth* and *Bob Roberts*, if only since name symbolism is a prominent practice in the popular mythmaking of films, novels, television, video games, and more. Still the names of the characters and some of their settings are charged with commentary by both films. 'Tis easy to parse the symbolism of names like Jay Billington Bulworth, Constance Bulworth (Christine Baransky), L. D. (Don Cheadle), Nina (Halle Berry), and her little brothers Marcus Garvey (Brian Hooks) and Paul Robeson (Jermaine Williams). The same goes for Bob Roberts, Brickley Paiste, Bugs Raplin, Lukas Hart III, the satirically silent Polly Roberts (Marrilee Dale), the campaign manager Chet MacGregor (Ray Wise), the smiling Dr. Caleb Menck (Tom Atkins), the satirical television show *Cutting Edge Live*, the Roberts campaign superbus called Pride, and such fans as Roger (Jack Black), Calvin (Matthew Faber), and Burt (Matt McGrath). The fatuous anchors and reporters in *Bob Roberts* get such names as Chip Daley (Fred Ward), Carole Cruise (Pamela Reed), Tawna Titan (Susan Sarandon), Rose Pondell (Helen Hunt), Dan Riley (Peter Galagher), Ernesto Galleano (Robert Hegyes), Chuck Marlin (James Spader), and Rock Bork (Fisher Stevens). Or take the feckless staffers—Delores Pettigrew (Rebecca Jenkins), Franklin Dockett (Harry J. Lennix), Clark Anderson (John Ottavino), and Bart Macklerooney (Robert Stanton)—whose names evoke their stereotyped ethnicities, genders, and roles.

Some of the names are satirical puns so broad that they make us groan, but always there are semantic connections to the kinds of characters or settings enacted under the names. If the game were subtext, the present analysis would need to dwell on this verbal level for the satires at hand. But *Bulworth* and *Bob Roberts* emphasize musics rather than subtexts. Western politics stress the words in speeches, in what the ancient Greeks and Romans practiced as oratory and studied as rhetoric. Classical and modern philosophers wanted to separate speech and song, just as they tried to keep rhetorics from becoming poetics.[26] Yet satire always already has been postmodern or postwestern in resisting such divisions. As a popular genre, satire relies so strongly on the susceptibility of politics to display as words that critics often fault it for turning dialogues into monologues and conversations into orations. What such commentators decry as crude literary or dramatic art, however, we do better to appreciate as political and rhetorical genius.

The uncanny quality of speeches accounts for the enduring excellence of *Network* (1976), widely acknowledged as a masterwork of cinematic satire. Edited for audiences used to a slower pace, less reliant on action sequences and special effects than current films, *Network* depends as much on speeches as any play by Shakespeare. Still its ideas and speeches, especially, are so sharp in their conception and dynamic in their delivery that *Network* retains the capacity to engage even teen viewers more than a third of a century after its release.[27] I know, because I still use it on occasion to teach political communication to college students, who are still giving it rave reviews. When we talk about how such a speechy film from another era can enthuse them, students say that it's the brilliance and passion of the speeches by Paddy Chayevsky that give *Network* legs.

Listen to Max Schumacher (William Holden) denounce television or Diana Christensen (Faye Dunaway) defend it. Harken to the declamations by Laureen Hobbs (Marlene Warfield) on communism and Louise Schumacher (Beatrice Straight) on marriage. Hear Frank Hackett (Robert Duvall) and Arthur Jensen (Ned Beatty) tell how the world works as a business. Heed the Oscar-winning monologues of Howard Beale (Peter Finch) on alienation, dehumanization, and dying democracy. From Beale's speeches, especially, we have learned to say with this Mad Prophet of the Airways that "I'm as mad as hell, and I'm not going to take this anymore!" As anyone can see from characters noted in this paragraph, *Network*, too, deploys name symbolism. As viewers readily remember, *Network*, too, uses conceits of conspiracy, assassination, and news as amusement more than information. Yet speeches drive the film's satire. They are what make *Network* a devastating caricature of television politics. Its orations are prose-poems: powerfully composed, subtly rhythmed, brilliantly directed, and wonderfully delivered. They are near music.

In fact, *Network* in general and its speeches in particular turn out to be the main satirical standards for judging *Bulworth*. This holds for commentators who celebrate *Bulworth*'s energy, ambition, and imagination.[28] "Warren Beatty's *Bulworth* is a raucous, profane, bitingly funny rant," wrote Mark Caro when the film débuted. It is "the cinematic equivalent of Howard Beale's 'I'm mad as hell, and I'm not going to take it anymore' speech in *Network*."[29] Barbara Shulgasser argued then that "Echoes of Paddy Chayevsky's *Network* speech about the dominance of multi-national conglomerates are unmistakable." She concluded that, "In many ways this is Beatty's *Network*."[30] And Roger Ebert maintained that "*Bulworth* plays like a cry of frustrated comic rage. It's about an archetypal character who increasingly seems to stand for our national mood: the guy who's fed up and isn't going to take it anymore. Funny," added Ebert, "how in the...years since we heard those words in *Network*, we've kept right on taking it."[31] *Network* looms equally large in the minds of critics who have denigrated *Bulworth*'s naïveté, stereotypes, and execution.[32]

The reviewers have recognized in the film's reliance on rap a transmutation of *Network*-style speeches into chants and lyrics. Telespots have supplanted oratory in the Bulworth campaign, even before the candidate's breakdown at the beginning of the film. The speeches that remain merely echo its advertising themes: "We stand at the doorstep of a new millennium," where welfare, equal opportunity, and affirmative action have gone out of fashion even for "liberals." Returning to California, the candidate truncates his first speech into a sentence, then invites the people in the pews to ask questions. At first, he answers in the prose of plain speech. But by the occasion for the second speech, Bulworth simply dispenses with it and raps outright. Let a little of that first performance suffice: "As long as you can pay, I'm gonna do it all your way. Yes, the money talks; and the people walk."[33] Not high art, especially as rap, but soon even Bulworth's interviewers are drawn into hip-hop rhythms. Overall there are three long "speeches" in *Bulworth*: two in rap by the titular senator and one in prose by Nina, the contract killer who later becomes his lover. Bulworth delivers the first to a fund-raiser with entertainment types, and he improvises the second for an "American Politics Election Special" on television.

Verbally the *Bulworth* raps function more or less like the *Network* speeches: converting politics into words as a way to make fun of our practices and pretensions. No doubt Kenneth Turan has been right to say that the antic character of *Bulworth*'s physical comedy and the niceties of the film's analysis leave its raps with no chance to achieve the anger, eloquence, or insight that has distinguished rappers on the order of Public Enemy, Ice Cube, Dr. Dre, L L Cool J, Lil' Kim, or Eminem.

What gives *Bulworth* its unique character is that all this silliness is periodically punctuated by cogent, carefully thought-out mini-manifestos about such serious issues as the state of African American leadership, why health care costs so much and how those in power have always tried to drive a wedge between the poor of all races. It is surprising to hear commentary like this in any kind of Hollywood picture, let alone a comedy.

But even though Beatty makes sure these sound bites are delivered in a glib, antic manner engineered to be audience-friendly, their presence is too awkward to mix well with the slapstick. The audacity of the concept carries things along for a while, but, as *Bulworth*'s peculiar ending points up, it is far from a seamless weld.[34]

Yet Turan has been right as well to summarize the film's raps as thoughtful "mini-manifestos about...serious issues." Their satirical combination of gravity and glee derives partly from the fact that the rapping is done by a pillar of the white establishment: whether senator (Bulworth) or star (Beatty). It also arises partly from an odd meld of the high politics of sovereign states (and their policies of trade, diplomacy, campaign finance, medical insurance, and banking) with the low politics of everyday lives (sex, school, jobs, drugs, classes, television, and other entertainment).

In the vague sense that folk music stems from ordinary people, sympathizes with them, and sometimes celebrates or empathizes with them, rap music attacks the situations of urban blacks as an underclass. Occasionally it talks up some kinds of response, but mainly it makes angry sense of what's happening. More than other popular music in America, rap carries a chip on its shoulder. Rap is gangsta music because its makers and listeners feel like outlaws within a condition of degeneracy where government has abdicated responsibility but not repression. Its settings favor gangs, pressuring the people trapped there to act like gangsters. Rap captures the jagged, profane speech of people who desperately need to rationalize and repoeticize their lives. As Giambattista Vico understood even better than Thomas Hobbes, the rationality and the poetry depend on each other because they need to create each other.[35] Rap knows that, rap enacts that. This is a matter of the music as a network of pitches and beats, yet it is even more a matter of the words conventional for the genre of rap.

In his breakdown, Bulworth simplifies and appropriates the music; but he remakes the words. How could he not? Bulworth is no black brother from the inner city. No disquisition on black leadership, no liaison of the heart, no visit to the ghetto can change that overnight. Clothes might make the (gentle) man, but they do not inspirit the rapper. Baggy shorts, large sneakers, dark glasses, and a watch cap do not a rapper make. Anger and bitterness Bulworth does have in sudden abundance, and insight of a sort. But it is not an underclass, inner-city insight. Radical accusations and possibilities stream from Bulworth's tongue. Yet his are left-liberal indictments. They spring from sensibilities at home in Hollywood or Washington more than South Central or Detroit. Neither Beatty nor Bulworth has become a Public Enemy. Neither should try. Instead Beatty as Bulworth is pouring white whine into black rap. Contrary to the critics, this is not some political stupidity or artistic travesty. It is an intelligent, intriguing experiment in new political aesthetics: infuse ideological politics of the radical left into musical-mythical forms of the gangsta culture, to see what sparks go where.

Journalist Charles Taylor has spoken for me in allowing that, particularly as speeches, "The political arguments in *Bulworth* may sound depressingly trite—that corporate money has put both political parties in the pocket of big business, destroying any real differences of principle between them and reducing the whole concept of representative democracy to graft."[36] Yet as David Edelstein has observed of the raps, "Beatty's glee in seducing us with language overrides the movie's shaky construction and embarrassing hero worship."[37] Taylor has noted that "their force comes from their context and their source. Beatty's involvement with Democratic politics has gone on far too long now for it to be mere fashion on his part." Rap usually draws persuasive power from the ethos of the rapper as the hipster who's been down there and suffered all that. Thus Beatty's ethos as a rapper, much like Bulworth's, can be the opposite that improves the rule. "Rich celebrities who espouse leftist ideals are almost always targeted as hypocrites, but wouldn't it be easier (and more likely) for them to move to the right? How many (not nearly as rich) people do you know who turned Republican as soon as they got any money?"[38] And the converse holds as well, with Bulworth's lyrics gaining bite from rap's standing both culturally and politically, as well as from its angry tones and engaging rhythms.[39]

The only speech we see Bob Roberts give, in snippets, is from the brief summation at his televised debate with Brickley Paiste. In the current style of campaign politics, Roberts is like Bulworth in conducting many conversations, giving myriad interviews, previewing plenty of ads, and contributing to several debates, but seldom standing still for anything like a classical oration. Where Bulworth lapses instead into rap for leftist diatribes on our political maladies, Roberts relies on songs in several genres for right-wing lyrics against drugs, welfare, affirmative action, women's liberation, the civil-rights movement, and so on. Songs are even more prominent in *Bob Roberts* than in *Bulworth*. Thus both these satires compound their political power through turning speeches into songs.

Words into Musics

The prejudice of our times is that "Speeches are boring."[40] This goes double for speeches in movies. A film advertised as a fine collection of political speeches would fail at the box office. As satires, *Bulworth* and *Bob Roberts* turn politics into words; but as they do, they set the words to music.

Transforming speeches into songs is what carries *Bulworth* and *Bob Roberts*. The two augment the images and dialogues usual for satires with lyrics, melodies, harmonies, rhythms, and orchestrations—rather than orations. That, principally, is how these films persuade. *Bulworth* uses the musical rhythms and cultural resonance of rap to help make its condemnations credible. *Bob Roberts* uses the public familiarity with popular songs from Bob Dylan and various colleagues to help make its mockumentary funny yet chilling.

Satire seems like magic in relying on words for its power.[41] Keeping words powerful is crucial for satire. This is why *Bulworth* and *Bob Roberts* do well to have their title figures break into song. The beat of a song enhances the energy and heightens the rhythm of its words. The tune for a song intensifies the meaning of its words and enriches their voice. In both ways, *Bulworth* and *Bob Roberts* benefit as satires from turning many of their words into musics.

For these reasons, the Rastaman, who summons Bulworth into song, threads through the movie as "a roving street shaman."[42] Shulgasser wrote that "The poet Amiri Baraka plays a street person/Greek chorus who approves of Bulworth's reformation."[43] It is more, though, that the Rastaman is Bulworth's demiurge: almost magically visiting upon him a new power of music. Or perhaps he is Bulworth's muse, calling forth a latent talent for dance and song. As Maitland McDonagh cautioned, "The rhyming is more Dr. Seuss than Dr. Dre," so it is Beatty's enthusiasm and dancing more than his poetry or voice that make the rapping work as well as it does.[44] For an old WASP politician, at any rate, the effect is transformative. And for *Bulworth* as a political satire, the result is—as the Rastaman promises—inspiring.

Bob Roberts is a singer from the start. He might well owe his talent for song to countercultural parents and a permissive upbringing he came to detest. Until he ran away from home to enroll in a military school, Roberts seems to have imbibed the folk rhythms of the 1960s and 1970s that he later puts to work in many of his compositions. Roberts' words are incantations of the charismatic right. They combine capitalist true-belief with a perfectionist cult of high lives and leaders. Is there anything more ludicrously oxymoronic than a "march for self-interest?" The movie's songs were written and composed by David and Tim Robbins. As director, Tim has refused to release a soundtrack album for the film, because he has worried that its parody might be misplaced and some of the songs might be claimed as anthems for the politics that he made *Bob Roberts* to satirize.[45] The worry is neither naïve nor self-congratulatory. More than a few of the film's experiments in melding fascist and capitalist politics to populist styles of song succeed enough to scare populist democrats like Robbins—or cheer his political enemies.

Nazi and fascist politics in the twentieth century showed affinities for the bombastic music of Wagner as well as the sentimental chauvinism of some patriotic hymns and marches.[46] I would hesitate to say that capitalism as an economic ideology has established an enduring affinity for some musics above others. As the enterprising bourgeoisie have diffused into middle classes in cultures such as America, they have developed most of the popular genres current in television, cinema, fiction, and other media accessible to most people, including music. Before *Bob Roberts* and its compositions from the Robbins brothers, we had few songs in a popular vein to celebrate inheritance, profit, self-interest, T-Bonds, corporate takeovers, and such. Music promoting "the American Dream" might be about as close to capitalist music as we usually come. "Charlie on the M.T.A.," as it is nicknamed, does protest an increase in taxes; but American protests in popular music against socialism and bleeding-heart liberalism come seldom to my attention. (Maybe they've flourished in country music while I was not listening? Not really, I'm told.) Popular music in America has included lots of racist and sexist songs, to be sure; but few pursue the fascist principles of leadership, racial purity, and feminine inferiority in the explicit terms of the Roberts lyrics.[47] Nostalgia is prominent in American ditties; but the reactionary ideology of "Times Are Changin' Back" is rare, to say the least. Bulworth's raps are fascinating, satirical mismatches of forms and contents; and the same can be said of Roberts' songs.

If we look in the two films for dynamics of satire other than savage destruction, the question becomes how such experiments in political aesthetics might contribute to inventions that evolve into new politics. Murray Edelman argued that the path of innovation runs *From Art to Politics*.[48] If so, cinematic satires like *Bob Roberts* and *Bulworth* stand to make significant political differences, through creation as well as criticism.[49] How to test such a proposition is elusive; but a good possibility is to study the dissemination of political aesthetics—that is, the political styles—that such films invent or oppose.[50] Hence we could keep an eye on popular movies and an ear on popular musics, for their informal and unofficial politics, even as we pay full-bodied attention to the high and formal politics of state.

Since the movies learned to talk, sustained attention to music has been commonplace for popular films. Political films are no exception. Campaign movies about elections have gravitated toward images of parades and the musics of marching bands, even though these devices have receded in practical prominence. In 1986, *Power* as a conspiracy thriller used a patriotic march ("Stars and Stripes Forever") rather ironically for one of its themes; by 2011, *Ides of March* sounded its hardball realism by avoiding patriotic music altogether. A satire rather than a thriller, *Bulworth* works the conventional playlist, with John Philip Sousa providing "Semper Fidelis" near the beginning and "Stars and Stripes Forever" near the end. Presumably both these marches are meant with a wink and a twinkle in the eye.

As advertisers now show by running issue-advocacy spots throughout the political calendar, not all political campaigns connect with elections. (The long-standing terminology of advertising and military "campaigns" reinforce that.) The broader and more ambitious the campaign, the wider the array of music summoned for its pursuit. As a satire, *Wag the Dog* (1997) encompasses an election campaign, an imaginary military campaign, and more.[51] In consequence, it becomes a virtual tutorial in how the standard musical forms work for politics, especially in the realm of song. It includes an anthem, a ballad, a blues song, a country ditty, a hymn, a march, and more. All are patriotic and sentimental, and all prove intrinsic to the political machinations of the campaign's director (Robert De Niro) and producer (Dustin Hoffman). The film offers them as the work of professional composer Johnny Deam (Willie Nelson), though they stem in fact from several musicians. The campaign presents itself as relying also on a sentimental speech written by its producer for the US president in the movie. But mere speeches can be boring, and the film is too smart to subject us to the full text. It cuts from the oration's beginning to viewer emotions at the end. By contrast, it gives us one session of musical brainstorming or performance after another in the middle of the film. Each of the songs amuses and serves the satire—more of Hollywood, it must be admitted, than of Washington—because they follow so strikingly the culture's elective affinities for forms and contents. They are well-done just to the point of over-done, as with the songs for *South Park* (1999), the Trey Parker and Matt Stone animated satire of movie musicals that springs from their long-running television series (1997–).

Bulworth and *Bob Roberts* share the converse principle of strange matches between words and musics. Both films pour different wine into familiar bottles. The tunes are new enough, yet they are done to be instantly familiar from popular forms of music. *Bulworth*'s raps are simple in their conception and crude in their delivery. They are more reminiscent of early and overtly political efforts by Public Enemy than later brands of rap. Still they seem tame by comparison. The images from Public Enemy are sharper, angrier, and more personal; the language is rougher; the rhymes and rhythms are more inventive.[52]

From the start, nevertheless, rap has been what *Bulworth* needs: a political poetry of the underclass, the under-race. Rap is at times a kind of music that rallies the debased and demoralized to self-respect, self-instruction, self-defense, and self-assertion. (At other times, to be sure, rap inflicts debasement and disrespect, especially for women.) It indicts the oppressors and builds a sense of solidarity among their victims, but it does not settle for lamentation or even protest. It does not merely sing the blues or sling the news. More than that, it agitates, it aggravates, it animates brothers and sisters into action. Rap demands motion, it induces dance, it informs deeds. Often it does, at any rate. Earlier slave narratives demonstrated rationality, gentility, and the capacity for improvement. Thus they reached for common humanity.[53] Rap goes further, engaging folks in forms and rhythms that move them beyond expression and improvement to empowerment. It does this through self-definition and social reconstruction.

Bulworth appropriates rap for self-indictment by the upper-class, the ultra-race, even the über-sex. Beatty uses rap to turn the rant of the accuser on himself. Bulworth's raps embrace a contempt for lobbies, governments, and corporations, without denying the capacity of politics to do better. His raps endorse a condemnation of current money, media, and medicine, without wishing them away. Beatty is "playing out a hallowed, white-liberal fantasy of being as black as any soul brother."[54] To savage the system while saving the polity, *Bulworth* needs the alarm, the anger, and the articulation of rap. As Taylor has contended, "political satire without savagery is finally a comfortable old mutt."[55] Satire can serve a system rather than destroy it. "Why," asks Gary Trudeau of *Doonesbury* fame, "is satire such an effective form of social control? Because at its rotten little core, it's unfair. It's rude and uncivil. It lacks balance and proportion, and it obeys none of the normal rules of engagement. Satire picks a one-sided fight, and the more its intended target reacts, the more its practitioner gains the advantage." Consequently satire is a "savage, unregulated sport."[56] It can ridicule, lambaste, and delegitimate a system too.

Part of the cost in Beatty's borrowing from rap seems to be a descent into stereotypes. With its musics come hip-hop styles of dance, costume, discourse, and conduct. The language alone teems with the figures attacked by *Bulworth*. "When Bulworth asks Nina where all the black leaders have gone, her answer is as intelligent and plausible as a year's worth of op-ed columns," opined Ebert. "But when the movie presents black culture as automatically more authentic and truthful than white, that's a leftover knee jerk; the use of blacks as repositories of truth and virtue is a worn-out convention in white liberal breast-beating."[57] These presumably are the stereotypes that the movie tries to disarm, dispute, disrupt, destroy. Yet the repertoire of devices for satire depends so much on twisting clichés, contesting conventions, confronting through caricatures, and assaulting with stereotypes that (whether they know it or not) people who want satire to avoid all simplification and prejudice actually want no satire at all.

People who dislike *Bulworth* often pounce on its use of ghetto stereotypes. Peter Reiner has complained, "Beatty isn't that far from the mind-set of '70s blaxploitation movies like *Superfly*, which often had its pimps and pushers performing double duty as truth-tellers and victims of 'the system.'" In fact, "At one point, Beatty actually shows us a South-Central movie marquee announcing *Superfly*." Yet "those movies were at least aware of their own hypocrisy," Reiner has declared, whereas "Beatty is almost touchingly naïve. Make ice cream, not Uzis."[58] In much the same vein, Owen Gleiberman has lamented that:

Instead of taking its joke further and further, as *Network* did, *Bulworth* ends up shamelessly embracing the very white liberal sanctimony it had already shown to be an irrelevant con job. The film becomes a rambling high-concept comedy, a burlesque of the pure image of Warren Beatty as aging homeboy. But that image alone won't cut it. The movie ends up saying: Here, at last, is a way out of our mess—if those nasty politicians would just acknowledge inner-city African-Americans and "their" culture. By now, that statement is an insult to blacks, to whites, to anyone, in fact, who has watched the first part of *Bulworth* and understood that symbolic compassion of this sort isn't the solution, it's part of the problem.[59]

Yet satire typically uses stereotypes, trying to turn them against one another and themselves. This can make satire a dicey game. It is what causes Mark Twain to be called a racist for writing *Huckleberry Finn*.[60] The test is whether the savagery and lunacy of a satire manage to undo or at least redo the stereotypes it invokes—more than reinforce them. If *Bulworth* seems to you "thin, repetitive, and intoxicated with its own outrageousness," then the types have stayed cardboard cutouts, developing little of the depth needed for mythic archetypes or political inventions.[61] Ebert countered that "It's better when Bulworth abandons political correctness and says what he thinks, however reckless."[62] Yet even successful satire can seem at best a mixed performance.

McDonagh has noted that "Bulworth's scathing, vitriol-laced riffs on race relations, incestuous media, corporate monopolies, the distribution of wealth and—of course—Hollywood are as incendiary as they are profane." As she has conceded, the question can be, "How valid is an agenda appropriated from disenfranchised African Americans by a privileged white man?" And as she has observed, Beatty "stages a preemptive strike against accusations of propaganda by seeding the film with nagging questions about Bulworth's conversion on the road to Washington. Has he seen the light or simply succumbed to middle-age jungle fever, embodied in the beautiful, whip-smart Nina, whom he spots at a campaign stop?"[63] The difficulty with a defense based on ambiguity, nuance, or even realism is that satire invites, actually insists, on accusations of propaganda. Irony pursues ambiguity; satire takes sides. In this is the idealism of satire. Thus satire usually makes a stand and proclaims it to the world.[64] It typically lives to declare an idea and take on all comers. Some think that a golden rule of satire is "no sacred cows," but they mistake satire for farce.[65] The bite of satire is fierce, not because its maws open wide for everything, but because its jaws are strong, and its teeth are as long and sharp as needles.

Satire takes sides, and it proclaims categorical truths, but it still leaves ambiguity in its wake. Its idealism is ironic. In making the target into a fool, the figure that the ancient Greeks called the Eiron, satire does ironize the target; but satire also ironizes itself. In turn, this does proliferate possible meanings and truths, as this chapter's ending section explains. That is not because good satire eschews one-sided complaints; it is because it can cut so deeply in any of its directions as to unsettle social conventions in many dimensions. Bulworth's attack on politics as usual skewers the culture industry, energy companies, health care, banking, fast food, cosmetics, immigration policy, the drug war, and a whole lot more. The conspiracies behind Bob Roberts have similar breadth. Cinematic satire at feature length can hardly do less.

The ambiguity and nuance in Bulworth spring mainly from its challenges to the cultural and political aesthetics of these American times. Do you think that hip-hop is a style for home boys in the Ghetto, not white guys in the Senate? See Bulworth rap. Do you know that gospel is a sound for southern or urban blacks? Hear Cheryl (Michele Morgan) and Tanya (Ariyan Johnson) bring it to a California church for suburban whites. In Shulgasser's words, the "two black girls first seen singing gospel in a neighborhood church shame the uptight singers in a WASPy white church by wailing the hell out of a hymn at the top of their beautiful voices." Do you fear that black women have no voices? "They tell the truth with their singing even more thrillingly than Bulworth does from the podium."[66] Putting black gospel into white churches is the same sort of aesthetic, cultural, political juxtaposition as putting young black rap into the mouth of an old white politician, fitting that pol for hip-hop dance and dress, or letting him scratch records after hours in LA. It is much the same as having L. D., a black drug dealer played by Don Cheadle, defend his use of kids to run crack by talking empowerment like a weird amalgamation of Huey Newton and Jack Kemp.[67]

There is a similar moment in Bob Roberts. The title character sings in an urban church with a black choir that "Times Are Changin' Back." The old white priest who introduces them delivers the credentials of Bob Roberts in tones and rhythms straight from black gospel in the south. Moved by the music, his prim and proper white parishioners fairly dance in the aisles. The arsenal of satire for both films is full of conflations, juxtapositions, inversions, reversals, oxymorons, outrages, bedfellows altogether weirder and sometimes worse than strange. Some would turn away from the ensuing sounds as painful or the resulting sights as silly. "Like Newt Gingrich singing 'My Yiddishe Mama' or Hulk Hogan doing needlepoint, the sight of Warren Beatty rapping is not on the top of most people's must-see list," Turan has written.[68] Yes, Tim Robbins is a better singer than Beatty for folk or rap. But straining the talents of the lead actors in such awkward directions is less a theatrical shortcoming than a satirical strategy for both films. To experiment with rewiring our standard relations between aesthetics and politics is to satirize our realities and extend our possibilities.

Bob Roberts does this mainly by putting right-wing reaction against political ideals from the 1960s into musical templates from that era. Just as he has in popular music since the sixties, Bob Dylan looms large in this gambit. The titles of the three albums supposedly released by Bob Roberts are telling: *The Freewheelin' Bob Roberts*, *Times Are Changin' Back*, and *Bob on Bob*. For the most part, the sounds echo early Dylan, acoustic rather than electrical; yet the lyrics drive in antithetical directions. "Complain, Complain, Complain" attacks people who are homeless or unemployed. "What Did the Teacher Tell You" is an assault on political correctness and bans on prayer in public schools as well as a paean to inherited wealth. "Don't Vote" is a Roberts song for voter self-suppression that also would fit political campaigns for 2012 and probably beyond. Along other tracks, Roberts uses a country sound for "Drugs Stink," whereas "Beautiful Girl" celebrates women as sexual objects with a simple, soporific tune that suits the beauty pageant hosted by Roberts. "Wall Street Rap" reaches beyond *Bulworth* to dramatize sardonically the empty, perverse excitement in finance. "Retake America" is an anthem for right-wing populists. Anticipating apocalypse from "Godless men," "This World Turns" resembles "The Sounds of Silence" by Paul Simon, but with starkly different politics. Roberts uses other forms too.

The music of Bob Roberts also has other inspirations—which can be to say, other targets. The music videos included in the film evoke Michael Jackson and Robert Palmer as much as Bob Dylan. They even tap rap for urban rhythms and George Romero's *Night of the Living Dead* (1968) for zombie images. The Roberts look is an elegant blend of Hollywood, Wall Street, and "yuppie"—as his fervent denouncers have it. For a touch of perfectionism, there is Bob's nearly Nazi salute to fans. Bob doesn't exactly dance, but he does sashay through production numbers, as in the pageant to select Miss Broken Dove from the annual cast of Philadelphia beauties.

For adornment, Bob's staff on the Pride provides a politically correct blend of color and gender, along with an economically crucial mix of languages. Bob's wife is a prim blonde, seen but not heard. For harmony, Bob plays guitar and harmonica; and he sings with Clarissa Flan (Kelly Willis), Miss Broken Dove from a year not long gone by. Stereotypes are rife in *Bob Roberts*, which aims them against the hypocrisies of Congress, the corruption of the national-security state, the greed of corporations, the emptiness of mass media, the persistence of racism, and other targets familiar from populist and leftist satire. Its most distinctive move, though, is to show how popular forms of aesthetics and charisma are being hijacked for capitalist and militarist strains of perfectionist politics. And as with *Bulworth*, the emphasis in *Bob Roberts* falls mainly on the politics of popular music.

Musics into Movies

An even more recent satire takes much the same turn. *O Brother, Where Art Thou?* (2000) by the Coen brothers rollicks through an Odyssey plot and an epic structure to satirize racism and modernization in Mississippi. Along the way, it plays at making the "old-timey music" of the gospel south into a force for populist re-form. By night, Homer Stokes (Wayne Duvall) is a Wizard of the Ku Klux Klan. By day, Stokes is campaigning for governor as the champion of The Little Man (Ed Gale), who promises to sweep out the political corruption of the incumbent, Menelaeus, better known as Pappy, O'Daniel (Charles Durning). O'Daniel is not about to cede the mantle of re-form to a hijacker. Soon both pols have pickers and singers out entertainin' folks with an indiscriminate combination of hobo, mountain, blues, bluegrass, gospel, and otherwise "country" songs. This extends the experiments in recombinant aesthetics for politics that have been ventured by *Bob Roberts* and *Bulworth*. It crossbreeds tunes and rhythms to rework everyday lives.

"Mass-communicatin'" by radio, the two populist politicians inadvertently promote public appreciation for musical inspiration and professional talent, regardless of race or prison record. The "old-timey music" that results is a popular reconstruction more than a mere recuperation. (The same could be said of the Grammy-winning soundtrack for the film itself.) It responds to the changing ears of listeners being educated by newly diverse sounds. The old-timey music is authentic enough in its own right, but not by a Western standard of true origins. Thus it turns out that Odysseus can go home again, but not exactly as the man he was before—and not entirely to the people or places he left a long time ago. This also holds for the Coen equivalent, Ulysses Everett Megill, played by George Clooney. Likewise the old-timey music mixes cultures and politics along with races and genders and classes. These form a postmodern mélange that helps free listeners from the outdated conventions that prevent modern progress. It pours old wines well-aged together with promising vintage from new grapes into a vast array of bottles and vats, cups and casks. The satirical sting stays intense, but the invention can reach beyond savaging individuals and institutions toward re(con)figuring them.[69]

O Brother, Where Art Thou? shares with *Bulworth* a general kind of focal character. Both Jay Billington Bulworth and Ulysses Everett Megill are fools. Bob Roberts is not, although the Robbins movie has an acute concern for the fools who are his actual and potential fans, including us as viewers. 'Tis not that Bulworth and Megill do foolish things from time to time: all humans do, even Bob Roberts. Instead Bulworth and Megill are fools in the archetypal, mythic sense. Both play off the Eiron, the stock character for satire in ancient Greece, whose idealistic or otherwise confused head stays so foggy in the clouds that his practical feet forever stumble on the rocky road of life. That is how Greek comedians conceived Socrates, and Cervantes used the mold for parts of Don Quixote. The fool is the character who tilts at windmills and mistakes many another figure that comes his way. Typically his intentions are good and his ideas are clever, sometimes too clever by half, but his judgments are off—way, way off. (Let me reserve more on such fools and their windmill-tilting to the fourth chapter on Tom Selleck's neo-noir figure of Jesse Stone in a series of made-for-television movies set in Paradise, Massachusetts.)

But why fools? Why would films interested in political aesthetics, especially of speech and song, feature fools as their leading figures? In going from musics into movies, how do fools contribute to the strategy of political invention through juxtaposition and patchwork? Think of the court jester. In the West, jesters are official fools for medieval and early modern politics.[70] By stereotype, the dress of jesters is motley: literally a patchwork of odd colors, patterns, and fabrics. This is evident in the strangely constructed cap that comes with the caricaturistic bells. The conduct of jesters is motley too. One minute these fools are tumbling over tables, the next they are bursting like Bulworth into rude song, soon they are juggling whatever comes to hand, then they are conducting disquisitions with the nobility, now they are making clever rhymes to ridicule some of the same people, later they are sporting with the children, but occasionally they are counseling kings. They satirize everybody at court, so nobody gets too glorious to serve the realm; yet sometimes their humor gets out of hand and heads roll, some of them royal. Fools of this sort live the experimental aesthetics for politics projected by musical moves in *Bob Roberts*, *Bulworth*, and *O Brother, Where Art Thou?* Motley are the political aesthetics and strategies of all three films.

To break down existing conventions and experiment with new ones, these foolish films match forms and contents in ways aesthetically and politically incorrect. The tradition of folly that generates jesters is one that spans both "natural fools" without the wit to handle ordinary affairs and "artificial fools" with wit to burn.[71] Neither kind can help but unsettle social conventions, for fools transgress these relentlessly, sometimes maliciously.[72] Yet Bulworth and Megill are both fortunate fools. Despite their profound folly and maybe even because of it, the two take mostly happy turns and stay mainly oblivious to painful costs of their foolishness. (At least that holds for each fool until the ending of his film.) The recent template from Hollywood is the title character in *Forrest Gump* (1994). Anything but fortunate are the fools in *Bob Roberts*. The fans of Bob have their day, during the film, but its implication is that they are headed for terrible consequences. The prophecy is not of a rude awakening, since the movie winks that Bob's fans know about his scams and take sick pleasure from them. Rather it is of an apocalyptic, dystopian "reckoning" of the kind sought by the title character in *Wyatt Earp* (1994) or by Bane in *The Dark Knight Rises* (2012). *Bob Roberts* gives prominent roles, some of the satirically richest in the film, to the singer-candidate's fans. All the while, though, *Bob Roberts* is warning us viewers that we easily could find ourselves cast as the political equivalents of those fans: played for fools by cynical charismatics.

Bulworth and Megill differ in subtypes of folly. Ulysses Megill is an aesthete, a dandy, a fop.[73] He is only one of four mighty foolish misfits who manage, fortunately but inadvertently, as the Soggy Bottom Boys to remake southern (maybe also Western?) politics. They pick up the tempo to turn that old-timey music from bluesy complacency with gospel salvation to modern re-formation of the political and economic kinds. None of the four intends anything like these consequences. Their aims, in the time-honored anti-tradition of dandies, are to make a fast buck, live high off the hog, and especially stay cool on the cutting edge. This puts aesthetes crosswise with social conventions, almost by definition; and it often takes them literally outside the law—as with escaped convicts Ulysses, Pete (John Turturro), and Delmar (Tim Blake Nelson) in the Coen film. As the film shows, though, dandies often turn their worlds upside down. Their arts are their lives, and their experiments conflate high and low, left and right, inside and outside to make a motley mess of social orders. Such fools fit perfectly into the hi-jinks of the Coen film.

By contrast, Bulworth is a holy fool. Like Howard Beale in *Network*, Bulworth seems to have lost his mind but found his soul. Moreover his soul is now instructing his tongue. When ordinary rationality as well as personal or social control break down, the holy fool is beset by a divine madness. It imbues him with special understanding and inspired speech. He is the high man cast down into mental and social darkness—but also the low man raised up into heavenly light. "I have seen the light!" proclaims Howard Beale. When indoctrinated later by Arthur Jensen, Beale adds, "I have seen the Face of God!" Jensen's calm reply is fit for a fool: "You just might have...Mr. Beale." Bulworth's sources of inspiration, Nina and the Rastaman, are black and under-class, not white captains of business after the fashion of Jensen in *Network*. Yet they, too, inform the gospel of their holy fool.

These are key functions of the Rastaman and Nina as muses for Bulworth. They help compound Bulworth's breakdown and make it productive—as a holy fool. Edward Guthman has argued that the Rastaman's injunctions to sing and be a spirit "may be the closest Beatty comes to a pure statement here: Take control of your life, he seems to say; don't let the system play you for a fool."[74] As Turan has explained, "The heart of this willingness to play the fool is the new Bulworth's determination to speak as much as possible in amusing rap-type rhymes, something that seriously disconcerts the senator's all-business staff, played by Oliver Platt, Jack Warden and Joshua Malina."[75] Speaking in truthful tongues can make holy fools potent advocates. Even commentators who do not like *Bulworth* as a whole have found its initial moments of revelation to be powerful.

> Campaigning before a group of African-Americans in a South Central L.A. church, Bulworth looks down at the speech he's supposed to read, but he can't bring himself to get the words out. Instead, he begins to speak the truth. The ugly truth. Before long, Bulworth isn't just speaking the truth—he's rapping it. Like Howard Beale in *Network*, he's become a crackpot sage, driven to preach the realities of corruption in the voice of the dispossessed.[76]

Even from the start, "Beatty is already nudging us to accept the senator's ravings as a higher truth. Even his name is metaphoric: Bulworth—his bull has worth. The sick joke at the heart of the movie is that, in politics, it takes a loony to level with us. Bulworth alone is unfettered enough to tell it like it is."[77] Yet it is only when Bulworth's words find music to become raps that his rants acquire the incantatory power to improve politics.

Beale helps turn his network upside down, and his ratings are highest when his ravings are greatest. Bulworth helps turn his campaign, his party, his country, his culture on its ear. Traditional fools include the faux popes and kings-for-a-day of the medieval Festival of Fools. That whole practice of folly inverted whole societies for wild periods of indulgence, license, and frenzy. Many commentators see in them safety valves for systems of oppression, just as satire can function. Yet their main dynamics are more creative. They turn societies upside down and shake them around—to open them up for radical innovations.[78] Europe still has such festivals. Their festive fools dance in the streets, as Bulworth dances through the second half of his film. In this full-bodied mode, satire operates as a counter-chorus, not only singing but also dancing against social custom and conventional wisdom. The hip-hop and rap adopted by Bulworth bring the underside of American society to the top, at least for a couple of wild and crazy days.

Raps are closely akin to rants and chants: the words of holy fools. With Bulworth, raps invite others into the declamations. As poetry slams imply, raps can become contests; and that is how their participants increase. The delirium of the holy fool can be contagious, spreading in rapid waves throughout a community. Rapping on television, Bulworth re-forms L. D. and his 'hood, including Nina's extended household. Body and soul, Bulworth seems to be filled with uncanny energy. Enthusiasm makes both Beale and Bulworth charismatic. Infused with divine spirit, *theos*, they grace the lives of the others who hear and see them. They are present for those others, and they move them. We know these kinds of politics from diverse movements of late.

Bulworth and Beale do all this with graceful, charismatic criticism of their targets, with rap and rant that ridicule and accuse. By contrast, *Bob Roberts* "displays" its targets.[79] *Bob Roberts* presents itself as a documentary. It shows the Roberts campaign through a mocking lens, hence the name "mockumentary" for such a cinematic satire. When *Bulworth* offers C-SPAN coverage and commentary for the title character, this is to authenticate and amuse; when *Bob Roberts* puts documentarian Terry Manchester on the screen or turns to Nodding Nigel, the cameraman, it is to frame and enact. Like *Bob Roberts*, *Bulworth* attends to media coverage as an intrinsic part of campaign politics. Both show various differences that television in particular can make. Yet the C-SPAN cameras are not the Bulworth cameras, and we see all kinds of things that C-SPAN cannot see or show. If Nodding Nigel does not go there, neither do we, keeping the satire sharp in its insistence on a particular perspective borrowed from the documentary conception of truth.

A Coda on Political Truth

This is where we need to be especially careful with *Bulworth* and *Bob Roberts*. Satirical truth is political truth: not simple or singular, not absolute or even assured. No satirical truth-teller like Bulworth or Beale, no matter how "holy," turns out to have divine truth. No satirical target like Bob Roberts or Bulworth's Congress, no matter how vile, turns out to be utterly false and unredeemable. Political truth is mythical truth: figural, poetical, symbolical.[80] It can found polities—and epistemologies—precisely because it is plural, debatable, evocative, inventional.[81] We must not take satirical certainties literally, even though the cinema sometimes induces us to do so. If we forget that satirical truths are figural, multiple, ambiguous, and provocative, rather than proven, we invite them to make fools of us. Holy fools do not give transcendental truths.

The conceit of *Bulworth* is that its title figure has become a truth-teller. Maybe Bulworth has lost the will or ability to lie. As Turan has described it, "Bulworth is suddenly stricken, like Jim Carrey in *Liar, Liar* (1997) with the compulsion to tell the truth."[82] Bulworth "loses his senses," Edelstein has said, "and begins to babble the truth on the stump."[83] "Liberation via nervous breakdown is an unpredictable thing," McDonagh has acknowledged, "but there's something to the notion that there's nothing like a little disaster to sort things out."[84] By this account, of course, Bulworth repeats the madness of Howard Beale: "The movie *Network* had a premise similar to *Bulworth*," N'Gai Croal has observed: "A veteran news anchor becomes a national sensation when he loses his mind and starts speaking the truth—but it had a truly incisive take on politics and race, and it smartly skewered our longing for a populist leader to guide us out of the wilderness."[85] Maybe Bulworth instead has made a conscious, strategic decision. Shulgasser has held that Bulworth "chucks his mealy-mouthed campaign speech and starts uttering the jarring truth in public."[86] Likewise Maslin has maintained that "Bulworth goes bonkers enough to take desperate measures. He does something that works here almost as galvanizingly as it did in *Network*: he speaks the unspeakable truth."[87] Either way, though, "This is Beatty's premise: Imagine a politician who drops his phony, elect-me facade and decides to spill the blunt, unvarnished truth about race, class and economics."[88]

Satire counters Truth. Even its holiest of fools contextualize and deconstruct the foolish Truth of a target—before they create other possibilities. Ebert was right to raise a red flag about *Bulworth*'s encouragement to "encode" the Rastaman's "incantations" as "universal truths."[89] Often we do well to treat satire as a challenge to conventions rather than a contest of Truths. Then we can recognize that "The movie is about what happens when Bulworth stops mouthing pre-fab catch phrases and starts being brutally honest with everyone around him."[90] Honesty is not necessarily *Truth-Telling*. At most, honesty and satire provide what David Ansen has left in lowercase and pluralized as Bulworth's truths: "Instead of emitting the usual high-minded gas, out of his mouth issue rude, uncensored truths about politics, race, the media and money." As Ansen has indicated, this is "A dizzying mixture of the sophisticated and the naïve, the deft and the clumsy." Satirical truths can be—in fact, satirical truths typically are—one-sided, simple-minded, nasty, and inconsistent without losing their mythical and political merit as truths. "*Bulworth* is overstuffed, excessive, erratic—and essential," Ansen has concluded, because "No other Hollywood movie is raising these issues, or puncturing so gleefully the conservative pieties of our day."[91]

No matter how hard satires insist on privileged visions, especially as they try to tear down opposing people, structures, or systems, satires mostly make room for more truths than before. Almost always they ironize in order to satirize. Taylor has been unhappy that "Beatty hasn't decided if we're supposed to find Bulworth grotesque or sympathetic, if his truth-telling is a symptom of his breakdown or of mental health."[92] But this kind of ambiguity, multiplying the possibilities, can be good satire as well as good drama.

The complaint I'd endorse against *Bulworth* is that it idolizes straight talk in much the same way as *Mr. Smith Goes to Washington*. Reiner has made the case in terms that miss some of the virtues of *Bulworth* as a cinematic satire, but his criticism is fair as far as it goes:

> The movie overvalues Bulworth's straight talk. Hasn't Beatty been listening to American political dialogue in the past decade? This fanfare-for-the-common-man/down-with-big-business rap is indistinguishable from the patter that passes for populism these days from the right, left, and center. Even Ross Perot and Steve Forbes get away with it. When Bulworth tells us that "the rich are getting richer" and the corporations lock out free speech, he may be preaching from the heart but he's hardly breaking new ground. Bulworth is supposed to be about the power of truth in politics, but it's so tone-deaf to the way the game is played that it becomes something it never intended: A movie about a con artist who finds a new con.[93]

"Spewing his flood of truth in the form of white boy rap," Bulworth might not be saying much that is new, let alone insightful.[94] Still the delivery is an important part of the meaning, and the delivery of *Bulworth*—the film even more than the character—is provocative.[95] The same goes for *Bob Roberts* and *O Brother, Where Art Thou?*

What is most provocative in these films is the motley, foolish, unconventional matching of aesthetical forms with political contents. As we've been seeing, the relations of idealism and realism are similarly peculiar, complicated, even motley in these satirical movies. In all three, moreover, the musics are where the main experiments transpire in strange matches of form and content. *Bulworth, Bob Roberts,* and *O Brother, Where Art Thou?* put their motley musics into action by performing them as political provocations. The products are possibilities for politics different from the populist vision of Mr. Smith going to Washington, and the ensuing chapters explore several such alternatives: realist, idealist, and otherwise.

CHAPTER 3

Realism as a Political Style: Noir Insights

(Featuring *L. A. Confidential*, *The Prestige*, and *The Illusionist*)

The standard objections are that pluralism gives too little weight to the power of ideas and of social and economic forces, and that it leaves no room for morality. (Pluralism's equivalent in foreign relations is realism, which strikes people who don't like it as having the same flaws.)[1]

—Nicholas Lemann

Obama was learning that one of the greatest skills a politician can possess is candor about the dirty work it takes to get and stay elected...if there was any maxim from community organizing that Obama lived by, it was the Realpolitik commandment of Saul Alinsky...to operate in "the world as it is and not as we would like it to be."...Like many politicians, Obama is paradoxical. He is by nature an incrementalist, yet he has laid out an ambitious first-term agenda... He campaigns on reforming a broken political process, yet he has always played politics by the rules as they exist, not as he would like them to exist. He runs as an outsider, but he has succeeded by mastering the inside game.[2]

—Ryan Lizza

ealism is an abiding aspect of politics. In aspiration and criticism, practice and theory, deed and word, politics return insistently to facing hard facts, making tough choices, then doing whatever needs to be done—in the conviction that true responsibility requires no less and that the ends will justify the means. Some people take realism to be the whole of politics, some the soul of politics, some their bane or debasement, and some just one perspective among others. But few would (or think they could) banish realism altogether from politics. Rather most see realism as present in the origins, prominent in the destinations, and persistent in the machinations of Western—even world—civilization. And the same goes for its principal contrary, idealism.

This is how debates between realists and idealists form a defining problematic of Western philosophy. Thus Sophists parry Platonists and Aristotelians. Machiavellians attack Utopians. Marxians as Materialists oppose Hegelians as Idealists. Pragmatists deconstruct Rationalists. Empiricists debunk Theorists. Realists impugn Moralists. And so on. Political science often distinguishes between the local and global or the national and international versions of realism, contrasting pluralism (and company) with Realpolitik (or the like)—as Nicholas Lemann does above. Yet as Lemann implies, there are strong reasons to recognize how much these variants share, meriting the same label in overall contrast to similarly numerous inflections of idealism.

The consecutive issues of the *New Yorker* quoted at the beginning of this chapter mention many of realism's characteristic tropes: skill, especially at doing dirty work; a peculiar kind of candor; practicality; and rationality in facing "the world as it is and not as we would like it to be." Realism is ambitious politically as well as personally, yet it is mostly incrementalist when pursuing change. It takes politics to need reform, often because corruptions mask themselves in pretty words, debilitating myths, manipulative illusions, or empty dreams. Accordingly realists take themselves to be plain-speakers who talk hard truths in the tough terms required to spur effective action. Seeing through the frauds that mystify others, realists escape the cynicism of using their fallen knowledge for personal advantage. Instead realists debunk the myths that bewitch others, and they appreciate politics as contests among similarly enlightened leaders separated by different interests. Typically they play politics as hardball. This means pushing inventively and vigorously against the rules that define not only fair and honorable deeds but politics of any kind. Realists argue their hardball to be justified by the rampant mistakes and corruptions of others. Yet realists also take their hardball to be enabled in part by their own pervasive manipulations and self-deceptions of other people.

Realism regards its name as grim but admirable. 'Tis politics for hard bodies and minds, tough enough to confront unsettling truths in troubled times. That's how romances of realism tell its stories: as the muscular and imaginative politics needed by everyday lives as much as imperiled republics. To sample recent editions of these romances in the all-too-imitable style of realist fables pioneered by Niccolò Machiavelli's *Prince*, consult *Hardball* or *Life's a Campaign*, the same handbook for realist action written twice by Christopher Matthews.[3] The ethos is evident in rough synonyms for *realism*: not only *hardball* but *authenticity, down-to-earthness, genuineness, literality* unto *literalism, materialism, matter-of-factness, plainspokenness, practicality, pragmatism, rationality, secularism,* and *worldliness.* Likewise the neighbors in outlook for realism are said to be cynicism, pessimism, and skepticism. We should take care not to conflate any of these three with realism, yet we also should resist overdoing distinctions among supposedly contrasting sorts of realism. In terms of style, realism coheres strongly as a network of tropes and dispositions.

Much of the distinction-making arises from attempting to render realism (or idealism) as a code, creed, philosophy, ideology, or some otherwise "substantive" doctrine. There are good reasons, at times, to do so. Yet the irony is that this literally *ideal-izes* political realism. As the word *ideo-logy* suggests, this strives to reconstruct realism as a modern, formal logic of-ideas: a singular, deductively consistent list of propositions that human realists supposedly endorse in (prior, abstract) principle and (subsequently, perhaps merely) apply in practice. Then analysts individuate different kinds of realism into contrasting lists of tenets; and they name each apart, whether or not the names surface often—or in the same senses—within our political practices.[4]

Still the kinship among subspecies of realism deserves attention too, because it can be helpful in practicing and apprehending our politics. Especially this holds for inventing and interpreting our political myths: the symbolically charged stories we coordinate our lives by.[5] As sketched in the introduction, one good way to do this is to treat realism as a complex of political styles. And as suggested then, this means regarding realism as a loose form of political action.[6] This encourages us to analyze recurrent figures of realism for their family resemblances rather than their propositional logics, and it reminds us to identify instances of realism by their prominent uses of these tropes rather than strict sets of necessary or sufficient conditions.

As before, let's seek these conventions of realism at popular more than elite levels. This can lead us into popular culture. It is largely of and for, if not always by, ordinary people in their everyday lives. Concentration on popular culture can steer us to popular media and, in electronic times, to electronic media especially. Media are mythic through and through; and in America for the last century, the electronic medium preeminent in myth-making has been movies. Their myths help us make sense of our situations, structure our routines, and inform our actions. Media interact incessantly; even so, movies have been particularly potent in electronic cultures to date. As the British theater critic Kenneth Tynan reflected:

> The most powerful influence on the arts in the West is—the cinema. Novels, plays *and films* are filled with references to, quotations from, parodies of—old movies. They dominate the cultural subconscious because we absorb them in our formative years (as we don't absorb books, for instance); and we see them again on TV when we grow up. The first two generations predominately nourished on movies are now of an age when they rule the media: and it's already frightening to see how deeply—in their behavior as well as their work—the cinema has imprinted itself on them. Nobody took into account the tremendous impact that would be made by the fact that films are *permanent* and *easily accessible from child-hood onward*. As the sheer number of films piles up, their influence will increase, until we have a civilization entirely molded by cinematic values and behavior patterns.[7]

The vaunted attunement of realism to reality might suggest that cinema and mythmaking are among the last places to seek political dynamics of realism. As novelist Marge Piercy observes, however, "myth forms reality and we act out of what we think we are."[8] Even as they announce a project to dispel myths as though they were mere falsehoods, realists appreciate their political importance, especially on the levels of everyday lives. So we do well to seek realism in movies.

The popular genres of cinema most often regarded as realist in style are documentary and neo noir.[9] Documentary has not been a prominent mode of cinematic mythmaking since the era of the newsreel. These two (somewhat) realist genres of cinema intersect in documentary noir, yet that has been no more in vogue of late than other kinds of documentary.[10] The onset of digital moviemaking might be changing this, by enabling rapid and inexpensive production of documentary movies from a much greater range of people. Nonetheless a concern for current mythmaking would lead us instead to neo noir. As a cinematic initiative from the United States in the 1940s and 1950s, classic noir has enjoyed off and on prominence since. Gradually noir became conventionalized into a popular genre known as neo noir, which has moved into a fourth straight decade of boom times.

All noir is known among movie commentators importantly for the realism of its aesthetics—which is to say, its mythic, visual, and aural styles. In noir, these are everyday styles of political action for some of the stock, focal characters. They are also styles of political mythmaking for the moviemakers. Nobody thinks that noir is only realist in style. Its look and sound are widely agreed to be expressivist, too, and noir myth often is existentialist even more than it is realist. These complications can be advantages, however, because they can keep us from temptations simply to equate noir style with realist style. Popular forms of our political culture taken by convention to be more exclusively realist in style surely would include news and documentary. Like noir, though, those forms actually participate in political styles beyond realism; even as popular senses of news and documentary as strictly realist can make their other political dynamics harder to recognize, analyze, and take into separate account.

Associated with the expressionism that helped inspire its aesthetics, neo noir is pervasively existentialist in its politics.[11] Yet the cinematic realism also persistent in neo noir often implicates political realism as a style. Let's return, accordingly, to what it might mean to take politics as style. A good step is to sketch at least a few figures of realism as a style. I say "a few" because the present ambition is not a full inventory of realist tropes but just enough stock characters, deeds, settings, sounds, and looks to start analyzing examples that can teach us more. Next we do well to acknowledge the existentialist and expressivist aspects of noir, to provide a sense of the noir surroundings for political realism. Then we can put these figures to work in contrasting the political realism of *The Prestige* as neo noir with the political idealism of *The Illusionist* as neo noir. These are two of the only three neo-noir films I know to feature stage magic, and they were released in consecutive months of 2006.[12] Both are excellent exercises in political mythmaking within neo noir as a film genre highly important in America's popular movies of the past several decades. Yet their politics are contraries in some respects, and their styles follow suit. Together these two movies enable us to appreciate some features of realism as a political style.

The Pledge: We See Politics as Style

Are you watching closely? Every magic trick consists of three parts or acts. The first part is called the pledge. The magician shows you something ordinary: a deck of cards, a bird, or a man. He shows you this object; perhaps he asks you to inspect it, to see that it is indeed real—you know, not out of the normal. Of course, it probably isn't. The second act is called the turn. The magician takes the ordinary something and makes it into something extraordinary. Now you're looking for the secret, but you won't find it, because of course you're not really looking. You don't really want to know. You want to be fooled. But you wouldn't clap yet, because making something disappear isn't enough: you have to bring it back. That's why every magic trick has a third act: the hardest part, the part we call the prestige.

Ingenieur John Cutter as *The Prestige* starts

A favorite theorist of politics, Hannah Arendt, once argued that Western civilization could have done politics as public action far better had the ancient Greeks added to their ideas of doing good and telling truth a further sense of "doing beauty."[13] At the time, Arendt was working on a trilogy about thinking, willing, and judging as *The Life of the Mind*.[14] She linked doing beauty with thinking, but we would do better to appreciate political judging and acting as doing beauty-in-style. This pun can be complicated, since the republican-rhetorical tradition where we could locate Arendt tends to construe doing beauty *as* style.[15] No less relevant, too, is the American version of virtuosity as doing almost anything "with style."

To educate a sense of style is to cultivate "taste" in experience and "touch" in action. It avoids fixing an exclusive, determinate set of standards for distinguishing good from bad, right from wrong, apt from not. Yet to analyze taste in philosophical terms is notoriously difficult, and to analyze touch has barely been tried at all.[16] As Arendt was beginning to intuit, this is why aesthetics—as practices and studies of beauty or, in a larger compass, experience—turn out to be highly relevant to prudential judgment. Studies of political style can become substantive when we attend to aesthetics in action.[17] This is a major reason that aesthetic forms—such as popular genres of films and other current devices of mythmaking—deserve sustained scrutiny as enactments and accounts of our politics.

When political theories pay better attention to political action, a signal result can be more stress on political style. "In brief," writes Robert Hariman, "a political style is *a coherent repertoire of rhetorical conventions depending on aesthetic reactions for political effect*."[18] Therefore figures that comprise a political style can "account for the role of sensibility, taste, manners, charisma, charm, or similarly compositional or performative qualities in a particular political culture."[19] Kim Stanley Robinson, who writes savvy political theory in the popular genre of science fiction, writes that "Beauty is the promise of happiness. And the only happiness is action."[20] Sustained and iterated action is performance; performance is style; style is doing beauty: that's the proposal.[21]

At issue here are two forms of political action, thus two complexes of political style, that routinely connect in the United States since the onset of the Second World War. Realism is a prominent style of domestic and international politics in this period. The theory as well as the practice of American politics are rife with pluralism, Realpolitik, pragmatism, hardball, and other inflections of realism. In fact, political science reinvented itself throughout the twentieth century as a family of realist takes on politics, especially politics in America.[22] From 1940–1941 onward, noir became for the popular cinema centered in Hollywood a persistent and successful form for realist concerns and sensibilities that arise in the politics of everyday life. As noir reaches beyond the politics of celebrity into most aspects of American existence, it coalesces into a popular genre of neo-noir films.[23] The project here is to treat realism and noir as styles of political action that connect in mythmaking.

The present interest is in political action as doing-beauty-in-style. Then why focus on the political style of realism in popular culture? Especially why focus on popular movies and their genre of neo-noir films? Among our premier venues for ordinary people to participate in making our political myths as our political realities, popular media are superb places to see and do political styles. So we do well to study the political myths in popular genres—without accepting the prejudicial suppositions that they are popular falsehoods, romantic mistakes, or other species of political error to be overcome by academic analysis. The need is to approach film, television, and other popular media in electronic times as cultural practices and political realities with varying dynamics in terms of truth and power.

Hence popular genres in mass media are good places to theorize about postmodern and postwestern politics. These genres are modes of practical action, because they remake the political myths we live every day. The theories implied or articulated in popular genres can improve academic accounts. The popular counts can be more vivid in evoking political events, origins, and prospects. Especially they can express politics in our everyday situations. I've been learning this by moving among contrasting genres such as epic, satire, thriller, horror, news, and romance. This lets me parse their politics through myriad comparisons among their conventional characters, settings, and occurrences. The purpose is to engage us where we live, foregrounding our own experiences of the unofficial but pervasive politics of daily existence, where we participate in person and completely.

Here we focus on neo-noir movies for their affinities to the politics of realism, particularly at levels of style. But we cannot analyze neo noirs, fantasies, westerns, or films in any other popular forms without gaining a decent sense of how several of these genres operate politically. We need to compare their families of conventions: the stock figures that we learn to associate with each genre. We appreciate these as political styles when we respect them as vernacular forms of action, and a way to do this is to analyze the political styles that emerge from specific works in a genre. An important part of this analysis is learning from subgenres, especially where they share territories or boundaries with subgenres in other genres. Political insights can spring from seeing how the horse opera as a subgenre of westerns overlaps with the space opera as a subgenre of science fiction. Political lessons emerge likewise from noting how super-noir movies blend conventions of the superhero saga with figures from neo-noir realism. This strategy looms large in comparing *The Prestige* to *The Illusionist*.

The genres must be popular rather than academically defined. Popular genres, like popular styles, form apart from any scholars who might analyze them. The conventions of neo-noir and realism are genuinely popular, not just theoretical. Like realism, noir has been increasingly popular as a form of political mythmaking in the United States from the Cold War onward.[24] Neo noir is not just a collection of films, videos, and ads that analysts list in promoting arguments about their shared features. Instead we attend as closely as we can to how neo noirs get configured by their writers, directors, producers, actors, cinematographers, and—as myths—by their popular audiences. The argument here is that analyzing neo noirs can help us explore political dynamics of realism as a family of styles in our everyday lives.

The Turn: We Recognize Realism as Style

Magician Borden to Magician Angier on Magician Su hobbling to a cab: This is the trick. This is the performance: right here. This is why no one can detect his method: total devotion to his art, real self-sacrifice. You know? It's the only way to escape all this . . .

Angier to Julia, his assistant and wife, on Su above: He's been pretending to be a cripple for years! . . . Any time he's in public, any time he goes out. It's unthinkable! Borden saw it at once. But I couldn't fathom it: living your whole life pretending to be someone else.

Julia to Angier: You *are* pretending to be someone else.

As *The Prestige* turns

To many a realist, it is surprising, paradoxical, even perverse to treat realism as style—particularly in politics. The pledge of political realism is to face actualities without distraction or distortion. It is to see through styles, myths, words, hopes, utopias, illusions, ideas, pieties, pretenses, and other manipulations to the bare facts and interests beneath. Realism takes itself, in other words, to be antistyle—even *the* antistyle. When realism turns out to be (presentable primarily as a) style, Americans sense something uncanny occurring. Is the demonstration one of stage magic, a rhetorician's feat of misdirection and sleight of hand, as realists might insist? Is it a theorist's way of taming danger and doing good, as idealists might imagine? Or is it, as realists might dread, an exercise of dark but real arts by enemies who unravel our realities to unhinge our rationalities? In other words, is it some realists outdoing others? Instead it is, I suggest, a more realistic and politically intelligent sense of realism in politics. (But maybe that just *is* some realisms trumping others?)

The first trick is that to recognize realism as a political style is to disappear realism as most have regarded it politically. To turn true realism into tropes is to make it vanish from the usual view. With a wave of the wand, does realism as substance become style...? Where did the real realism go? With a snap of the cloth, realism as rationality is now art...? What happened to the hardheaded, hard-hearted, hardfisted, hard-charging realism that was just there? With a twist of the wrist, realism as deeds and consequences becomes words and gestures...? How is the true realism to return? As John Cutter (Michael Caine) says in *The Prestige*, realism remains; but we don't exactly see it, because we don't actually look—because we don't really want to see. As Cutter intimates, we dread the unknown but suspected implications of what we might see. And as Cutter concludes, we "want to be fooled." Fools for firm and settled realities are we, even as we tell ourselves that realism faces the hard facts that people with less courage or calculation contrive to miss. As a political style, realism of every kind—even epistemic—is something that we modern Westerners would rather not see.

Analyzing Machiavelli's texts, Robert Hariman offers an early treatment of realism as a political style. Hariman shows how Machiavelli's writing "crafts an aesthetically unified world of sheer power and constant calculation."[25] Even as Machiavelli mobilized words to perform his politics, though, he denied their importance, their legitimacy, their power in action. "The realist style radically separates power and textuality," says Hariman, "constructing the political realm as a state of nature and the political actor as someone either rationally calculating vectors of interest and power or foolishly believing in such verbal illusions as laws or ethical ideals. Since this style operates as the common sense of modern political theory, its deconstruction removes a major obstacle to developing alternative conceptions of politics, particularly accounts—such as this one—that highlight artistry."[26] In masking the roles and powers of the words, Machiavelli concealed his reliance on them, making his rhetoric—his style in action—all the more powerful as political realism. Time and again, his words declare a no-spin zone of hard truth, plain speech, and pure rationality. Learn to look past words to deeds, the realist says, and past appearances to interests—for deeds and interests do not lie. Fortune can frustrate even the clearest vision and the coldest calculation, so success is not assured. But that is what makes success especially sweet, and success can be cultivated through political arts of realism.

Hariman focuses on rebutting realist arguments against style and realist claims to escape it. His main argument is *that* realism is a political style, so he gives some attention to *how*, but it remains introductory. "The gist of [Machiavelli's] innovation is that he repudiated the genre's [the princely mirror's] most basic assumption—its belief that politics is circumscribed by words. Thus, an interesting sign of the break is his omission of the one element of the genre that most signified the metaphysic of textuality: the frequent citation of prior writers."[27] From this crucial turn arise the figures that Hariman takes to endure in realism as a political style.[28]

> reality rather than textuality,
> > where reality is materiality;
> strategy rather than prudence,
> > where strategy is self-control of temperament and
> > sovereign control of historical memory;
> experience rather than reading,
> > where experience includes observation;
> originality rather than tradition or common sense,
> > where originality is the source of authority;
> action as self-assertion,
> > where self-assertion is audacity or boldness and
> > ambition for survival and glory is honorable;
> politics as war,
> > where war involves force, fraud, and fortuna; and
> calculation of interests,
> > where a sovereign self abstracts from the world and
> > the ends justify the means for survival and glory.

To this roster, Sheldon Wolin has added another important figure: economy of violence, where bold force and fraud can nip escalation in the bud to minimize the violence that people suffer to some extent inevitably in a turbulent world.[29] That trope seems particularly important to the international realists, such as Hans Morgenthau and Henry Kissinger, who promote updated versions of Realpolitik.[30] These figures do not exhaust realism as a style of politics, but they serve well for a start.

Yet notice how limp and logological the items can seem in such a list. Thanks as much to Machiavelli as to Hariman, it's mainly a scholar's summary. It offers abstruse canons, concepts, definitions, and propositions for what (Hariman correctly maintains) should instead—as a "style of conduct"—be "performances."[31] After rebutting the realist pretense to escape style, Hariman turns in his next chapter to the courtly style; and there he repeatedly tells stories in order to evoke performances—just as Machiavelli relates anecdotes for his realism. Since the goal here is to augment Hariman's account of realist style, particularly for analyzing political realism in popular films, let us reach for realist figures more overtly suited to stories, dramas, and movies. These realist tropes could resemble an inventory of standard figures for a political genre of films: standard characters, deeds, settings, sights, sounds, and themes. And that's exactly the point: realism *is* a popular form of politics in America. This means that realism operates in important ways as a mode of action, which is to say, a style of performance. It also means that popular forms such as westerns and noirs, which plainly are styles of performance, work in significant ways as modes of action too. One of these action projects of popular cinema is what I'm calling mythmaking: shaping the meanings that we take from—and give to—our shared lives.[32]

Again the aspiration is simply to get started, with claims in this section to be given initial evidence by the analysis of specific films. Something to notice right away about realism, something resonant with noir, is that its mythic repertoire of characters is strongly gendered. Realist accounts of politics mostly have males for their movers and shakers. Their characteristic celebration of hardball with hard truths, hard choices, and hard deeds makes the realist ethos macho. Machiavelli is an easy example. He portrayed the realist prince as a male who must go boldly where moralists, idealists, utopians, and Christians hesitate to tread. The prince "must learn how not to be good."[33] He should prefer being feared to being loved. He should master force and fraud. He should do whatever it takes to stay in power and stabilize the principality. Violence will be needed at times, so the realist should not flinch from the effectiveness of early use, both to maximize prospects of success and to minimize amounts of violence required. In our real world, fallen and difficult, this is to show the realist's sense of political responsibility. The idealist hope and pursuit of nonviolence, by contrast, are really apt to multiply our need for force as well as fraud to maintain decent order.

Satire relies on exaggerating genre conventions, so notice how *The Colbert Report* (2005–) and *The Daily Show with Jon Stewart* (1996–) spoof the masculinist realism of American news and punditry. As a pretend pundit, Colbert uses his Lord Byron looks to enact egomaniacal narcissism and sexism. As fake reporters of fake news, Rob Corddry, then Rob Riggle, and eventually Jason Jones have played supermacho men in the field. *The Daily Show* contrasts them with John Oliver as the mild-mannered and vaguely effeminate Brit or John Hodgman as the Resident Expert, who both seem more often at home in the studio. The caricatured man's-man roles are rough, tough, gritty, and profane, but otherwise blunt and plainspoken. They mock any measures short of force and fraud as sissified in their civilization—and insufficient in the severity of their effects.

The masculine prince should beware the ineliminable, disordering dynamics of fortuna, aka Lady Luck. She foils the best-laid plans; and though she ensues from unpredictable interactions of ambitious males, she stays a female principle that can unman even the best of realists. Hence she should be wooed and subdued as an audacious man might court but take a woman who is far from entirely willing.[34] In the dramatis personae for political realism, the other females are mostly idealists or deceivers. The idealists might be good; but they usually are weak or undone early in the story, which nearly never turns on them. The deceivers typically are charming but destructive, at least to the realist and likely to the regime. In the colorful language of neo noir, they are simply—without any need for translation or qualification—spider women. The audacious realists should drive the action, but spider women—like fortuna—can turn events in directions that nonetheless disadvantage or defeat the men of realist virtues. For the realist actor, a female in either mode is seldom the enemy but often the nemesis.

Realists develop their skills as bulldozers and debunkers in the school of hard knocks. Rather than the mentors prized by republicans and martial artists from the Mysterious East, the Western realists at most have models that they admire and imitate from afar. Put macho realists and their ambitious models in the same room, and butts get kicked or heads soon roll. Realists also learn from tellers of hard truths. What they learn is to distrust words and manners, which mislead even when they are not meant to. They also learn to tackle troubles early and head-on. As a realist character, the debunker is literally of (a) bunker mentality, under siege by enemies seen and unseen as well as fortunes unforeseeable. The realist does not want to get his hopes up: any realistic assessment of almost any situation sees hopes as recipes for disappointment.[35] The realist works in the world as it is, not as he might want it to be. To practice this maxim, the realist armors himself against feeling too much in one way or another, because sentiment just interferes with calm, cool, accurate calculations of his interests and the means to realize them. The realist injunction, as Matthews says, is "Don't Get Mad; Don't Get Even; Get Ahead."[36]

Princes have advisors rather than mentors. Machiavelli detailed how realists must take advantage of skilled advisors, but keep them at arm's length or more. Never trust them much, he instructed, and always assess their advice in terms of their own interests—which are bound to dominate their recommendations. Never ever let an advisor come to the fore, save to take a fall for the realist who needs to punish a failure or a perpetrator, even when the person fingered is transparently a scapegoat. With the idealist, the scapegoat brings to a revealing total of two the count of characters shared by realism and Christianity; and these might only be two faces of the same figure for the realists, who seem relentless in scapegoating idealists above all.

There is a fourth female character for realism, at least of late. This is the professionalized or otherwise masculinized woman. She strives and even succeeds as a realist by cultivating in herself the masculine virtues of the realist prince. Unlike the prince, the realist female often has a mentor, who often is a male rather than a female. The mythos of realism implies that female and male realists could share a room without butting heads, but the further implication is that the female is apt to remain deferential and inferior—as a realist—to the male. Possible cases in point are the femme focale and title character (Keira Knightley) in *Domino* (2005), Madeline White (Jodie Foster) as the system fixer in *Inside Man* (2006), and Karen Crowder (Tilda Swinton) as a system minion in *Michael Clayton* (2007). By contrast, a bold and tough Clarice Starling (Jodie Foster) in *The Silence of the Lambs* (1991) is undoubtedly an idealist; yet that non-noir horror film reinforces most of the points here about realism as a political style by showing it as mostly evil, especially in its sexism. Audacity and toughness alone doth not a realist make.

We do well to notice that, mythically, the Machiavellian or Realist Prince is not the only kind of prince by political style. The Dark Prince is the perfectionist nightmare, exemplified by Dracula as a vampire in the Byronic mode.[37] William Shakespeare's Hamlet is the Sweet Prince, please remember; and this makes him a republican by political style, even though he is a prince and Friedrich Nietzsche analyzed him as a Dionysian man more akin to Dracula.[38] *The Little Prince* by Antoine de Saint-Exupéry is conservative in political style, more or less in the mode of Edmund Burke.[39] The game of comparison could continue through the Frog Prince passed along by the Brothers Grimm, Will Smith's television character on *The Fresh Prince of Bel-Air* (1990–1996), *The Princess and the Pea* by Hans Christian Andersen, *A Little Princess* by Frances Hodgson Burnett (the Artist Formerly Known as) Prince, J. K. Rowling's *Half-Blood Prince*, Diana as the People's Princess, Jesus as the Prince of Peace, Satan as the Prince of Darkness, the Joker as the Clown Prince of Crime, and so on.[40]

Another important character for political realism is the people, the public, the crowd, the mass, the nation: in short, the tertiary targets for realist manipulations and audiences for realist performances. The realist's primary target and observer is himself, whom he manipulates and monitors incessantly. The realist's secondary targets and witnesses are the other competitors in the arena, players on the stage, or the like. Some are realists, some are idealists, and some are otherwise by style. The same goes for the background people who line the arena or turn toward the stage, and they are significant (if individually intermittent and weak) actors in realist dramas. (Republicans differ from realists in part by insisting that all other participants, no matter how momentarily distant or inattentive, can and should enter at times into public action.) It is as the people, the nation, or the like that these third-level participants in realist politics gain power as a kind of collective character. This sideline character is crucial as the diffuse arbiter of realist reputation. As Thomas Hobbes joined Machiavelli in reminding us, reputation *is* reality and power in realist politics. 'Tis a maxim fundamental for the hardball celebrated by Christopher Matthews too.[41] Realism emphasizes paradoxically that what the people "know" about politics, whether materially true or not, matters immensely in making realities for realist politicians.

Yet what the people don't know can have decisive effects as well. This leaves backroom operators—such as advisors, pleaders, specialists, and sometimes even their bosses—second in realist importance only to the politicians more or less "in public." Realist stories take us behind the scenes to view more of what is "really" happening than can be seen by usual audiences. There we see that backroom operators often work as conspirators whose roles and contributions never (should) come onto the stage and into the light. Denied the satisfaction of associating themselves with public successes, these operators must be moved and supported in other ways to serve the people and especially their favorite politicians. Often the operators glory quietly in pulling the strings of publics and politicians. This can make them all the more dangerous as cynics. To me, the police elders in *Training Day* (2001) epitomize not only backroom bosses and counselors but the nearly cynical operatives offstage in other capacities too. They delight in their own tiny "publics" of the few other realists "in the know," who appreciate their genius while taking their counsel and fronting for them in the larger arenas of police and political endeavor.

We find these characters of realism in settings where the times are troubled, the stakes are high, and the tactics are hardball. The realist stress on strategy and tactics turns into a craft of political moves, gambits, and tricks of the trade. Advisors to realist politicians, like the politicians, see themselves as continually recalling apt devices from earlier situations in order to invent variations of these tried-and-true moves that might fit the specifics of new challenges.

Outlooks are cloudy for realists, who face fortuna as well as knowable troubles. Hence realist settings look worn and gritty, dark and grainy. Once recognized, troubles can come into strong and disturbing focus, as objects with obdurate solidity but sometimes unnaturally sharp edges. Often the scenes are shadowy, with realist landscapes bleak and cityscapes occasionally in grayscale. Colors typically come bleached, washed out, or otherwise distorted.

The sounds of realism arrive in layers. Ambient noises initially establish attunement to the real situation. This sometimes happens with one distinctive tone, voice, or effect added at a time until the individual sounds merge into a mood—more or less as a melody, a harmony, and an overarching arrangement. This holds especially for realism's third-level participants, largely spectators, since what they sound or hear establishes a sense of expectation for events to come.

Then whispers or their functional equivalents might come into notice, as though drifting from backstage or slipping under closed doors. These might say quietly what the über-realists who operate behind the scenes are advising and why, or trying to arrange and how, even hearing and doing as they go. Eventually we hear a focal actor or two emerge onstage. They might narrate the backstory in hard-bitten voices, or they might announce the times in portentous tones reminiscent of a newsreel. At other times, their deliveries might sound more matter-of-fact or ingratiating.

Generally their words or other sounds guide participants on levels three and four, with the fourth and outermost "ring" for us as analysts who begin by observing some third-level audiences seemingly more within the realist dramas. What we hear steers us and others into the ongoing action, directing observations and structuring experiences. And at last, the realist contests among several deeds or voices commence, often with thriller music that is potboiling: troubled but energizing, at once agitated and a little forlorn, yet steeled to action and evoking changes to come. In recent decades, at any rate, this is how I've been experiencing realist dramas and movies as well as realist episodes of "real-world" politics in person or on television.

As a mythos, political realism amounts to inventions informed by stock stories that meld the genre's conventional doers, deeds, situations, sights, and sounds. As a philosophy, realism typically resists the idea of a mythic inventory of standard tales. It holds, in effect, that there are more than eight million stories in the naked city. It takes these to be susceptible to anticipation or summary only at the level of realist method, whether scientific or philosophical, where doers calculate arrays of interests for each incipiently unique

situation. Yet if this echoes the stance of act utilitarians who doubt the existence or the efficacy of any rules beyond the one injunction to account for
particular pains and pleasures, it also admits of comparison to the approach
of rule utilitarians who rely in practice on rules and institutions rationalized
by in-general, in-principle accounts.[42] In other words, realists work from a
repertoire of stylized, schematized narratives that trace specific plots, each
evoked by a rule for action that maximizes prospects for success.

Would-be counselors from Machiavelli to Matthews popularize realism in guidebooks, accordingly, and these articulate realist rules through
anecdotes that make the rules into punch lines for their respective stories.
These resemble republican-rhetorical handbooks in the service of prudence; and the two distinguishable kinds can overlap, as they do in works
by Machiavelli and Matthews.[43] As Hariman observes, however, the realist
turn from republican prudence to interest calculation makes for distinct
sets of tales and rules (technically, myths and epimyths).[44] From Hobbes
to Kissinger and Morgenthau, moreover, realists often produce scientistic
texts that downplay intermediate maxims and stories of action, meant for
individual realists in particular settings, in favor of demonstrating chronic
truths about human nature and national interest in world-historical conditions.[45] Still the Machiavelli-Matthews form evokes many of the specific
plots that comprise a repertoire for political realism. The present project
is not to rehearse a large number but merely to remind us of a familiar few
from recent political news.

In domestic settings, Pluralism as a drama of crosscutting interests is
a realist myth—evoked among many others by Arthur Bentley, David
Truman, Robert Dahl, and (noted here at the start) Nicholas Lemann.[46]
Hardball is a second standard plot for national politics, telling the needs
for it and the disasters in departing from it.[47] Realpolitik as a stock realist
story of grand strategy conducted on- and offstage is a familiar form for
international politics.[48] Working the intersections of national and international affairs are realist accounts of State Origins, complete with conditions
of nature and sovereign enforcers from Hobbes and Locke to *Hero* (2002).[49]
Also at the intersections of national and international politics are realist dramas of Dirty Hands, such as *24* (2001–2010) on television or *Zero Dark
Thirty* (2012) on film, sharing the recent (but unrealistic?) bent for torturing
terrorists to save cities.[50]

If there is an Ur myth for realism, it might be the Realist Awakening.
And if the label recalls America's "awakenings" as periods of mass religious
conversions, the resonance can be defended. Both brands of awakenings
share a sense of eyes opening or scales falling away, so that people can
see clearly for the first time (at least in a long time) the basic realities of

their human conditions. By contrast with Paul on the Road to Damascus, though, a realist awakens not all at once and beatifically but in painful steps of compromising his former ideals in order to confront urgent challenges and act effectively enough to survive. As with Paul, nevertheless, the awakening might simultaneously—paradoxically—blind the realist step-by-step to relevant complexities and compunctions. He might have prized these as an idealist, but he learns as a realist to disregard them as distractions and distortions that hide the real troubles and opportunities.

Some awakening realists don blinders that keep them focused on what really matters; others just remove their eyeglasses. *L. A. Confidential* (1997) taps genres of hardboiled detection and neo noir for a tale of Realist Awakening. This is one of three story lines interwoven well by a nicely complicated novel then superbly dramatized by the ensuing movie.[51] Each skein turns on problematics of realism and idealism faced by a leading character. Ed Exley (Guy Pearce) is the one who undergoes a Realist Awakening; and he might be the movie's single most central figure, even though he is not the most sympathetic of the three leads. Together the three must overcome big antagonisms and sinister obstacles to ally into a team. Only two survive, realistically enough. The sympathetic lead, Bud White (Russell Crowe), ends exiled and grievously injured but with the spider woman redeemed; while Exley as the new realist ends momentarily wounded—but with another promotion already in hand and well on his way to running the police department.

Exley's version of the Realist Awakening involves resisting but eventually meeting three tests for hardball policing. These come at Exley from his police superior, Captain Dudley Smith (James Cromwell), in the film's first scene at the Hollywood Station. It introduces both these men:

> *Smith*: I saw the test results on the lieutenant's exam: first out of twenty-three. What'll it be then? Patrol Division? Internal Affairs? What?
>
> *Exley*: I was thinking Detective Bureau.
>
> *Smith*: Edmund, you're a political animal: you have the eye for human weakness but not the stomach.
>
> *Exley*: You're wrong, sir.
>
> *Smith*: Would you be willing to plant corroborative evidence on a suspect you knew to be guilty in order to insure an indictment?
>
> *Exley*: Dudley, we've been over this.
>
> *Smith*: Yes or no, Edmund.
>
> *Exley*: No.
>
> *Smith*: Would be willing to beat a confession out of a suspect you knew to be guilty?

Exley: No.

Smith: Would you be willing to shoot a hardened criminal in the back in order to offset the chance that some lawyer...?

Exley: No.

Smith: Then for the love of God, don't be a Detective! Stick to assignments where you don't have to make those kinds of choices.

Exley: Dudley, I know you mean well; but I don't need to do it the way you did or my father.

Smith: At least get rid of the glasses. I can't think of a single man in the Bureau who wears them.

In ensuing events, Exley repeatedly and specifically turns away from each of Smith's acts of hardball realism. In the short term, each moral, idealistic counter-course seems to impose heavy costs on Exley and others. But in the middle and longer terms surveyed by the drama, Exley actually turns out to be prospering; and his realist capacity to protect citizens from crime seems to be increasing. Nonetheless the corruptions coming to his attention swell rapidly; and as Exley flails to keep his head above them, he manages moments of cool reflection for changing course, step-by-step. First he plants evidence to clinch the indictment of a man he knows to be guilty. Next he browbeats, then he literally beats confessions from suspects he takes to be guilty. Finally he shoots a hardened criminal in the back to keep that man from lax justice. Thus Exley awakens to realism, with each of Smith's three tests posed as cases where good ends justify bad means. By the way, the hardened criminal is Smith.

Along the way, the police chief (John Mahon) joins Captain Smith in telling Exley to lose his eyeglasses; and the film uses Exley's glasses to evoke four aspects of political realism. First, they suggest the masculinism of hardball realism: look macho, not like a sissy. Second, they symbolize the acute sensitivity of hardball realism to public relations and appearances: look heroic, strong, and self-sufficient, like a clear-eyed visionary who sees far without aid. Third, they mark the moral myopia of realism: only when Exley doesn't even try to see distant details in the lives of others but instead handles the big things close at hand does he advance. And fourth, the pocketed eyeglasses suggest that realism blurs vision at a distance, into the future, thus diffusing and softening a realist's detailed sense of the bad consequences to come from bad deeds done with only crude objects in the foreground coming vaguely into focus. With glasses gone, Exley can only see well what's close at hand. This makes precision shots impossible; to shoot effectively at a distance, Exley must use a shotgun, blasting big holes in—or only near—his targets. Thus the eyeglass motif implies that the advertised acuity in realist style is largely a lie. The main gains in effectiveness come from magnified firepower rather than precise targeting.

On the whole, therefore, the novel and film ironize realism. (Relatively few Hollywood products directly endorse it.) The third lead, who dies mid-movie, is Jack Vincennes (Kevin Spacey). He is the only lead who begins the film as a full-fledged realist: always calculating the angles. The irony is that he is the one who fails to survive, implying that realism is not adequate to its own bottom-line tests of survival and success. White begins as a moralist avenger who punishes bad men, especially for abusing women, so he breaks plenty of eggs but makes no omelets. That's why he needs to learn the rational and relational aspects of realism; and they help him survive, but barely and far from L. A. policing. The rest of the police mistake Exley for an exclusively self-interested realist, with little sense of police solidarity or personal honor; they miss that his honor and solidarity reach beyond police to the larger community that they are to serve. A step-by-step descent from his moral high horse, down to a realist republicanism, lets him retain his personal honor and enhance his community service. Another irony is that learning realism lets Exley be the one lead who succeeds, not just survives, yet he does it by limiting his realism.

The Prestige—We Return Neo Noir as Realism

Losing still tears him up. This is his greatest asset and his greatest albatross all at once. Bob [Knight, longtime coach of Indiana University men's basketball team] thinks he can beat the game. Nobody can beat the game. If you could, there would be no game. But Bob keeps trying to beat it anyway and when he doesn't he thinks of it as failure, *his* failure, and it tears him apart.[52]

Al McGuire

One way to analyze political realism in everyday life is to articulate its mythos; and as we have just seen, this can amount to specifying realism as a popular genre of politics. When we do this, we see realism operating more emphatically as myth than style, more insistently as style than strategy, and more effectively as strategy than ideology. As the invocation of *L. A. Confidential* suggests, a complementary way to analyze the popular politics of realism is to find them in performances of the (somewhat) realist genre of neo noir. A bonus for us is that this can help spotlight the stylistic aspects of political realism, especially because neo noir is so highly and self-consciously stylized.

A focus on style lets us appreciate political realism in (and as) the everyday aesthetics of looks and sounds. These looks and sounds are not merely instants or accidents of visibility and audibility, whatever their sources or significance. Instead they are carefully composed and persistent complexes of visual and aural meaning: the gothic look of a cathedral by comparison with the streamlined look of a bullet train; the lush sound of a symphony orchestra by contrast with the grunge sound of a garage band. In political terms, this approach to style is principally republican-rhetorical. Then the stylistic components of deeds are gestures (of performance) by contrast with the strategic components of deeds as moves (in competitions). Since realism as a political style makes strategy one of its most prominent tropes, or gestures, there's no need to fear that the resulting takes on realism will lack attention to strategy. But there's a need to keep in mind that, for political realism as a style of conduct in everyday life, strategy is more a gesture than a move. Yes, politics can be complicated; and realist politics are never exceptions, even when they claim a simple adherence to reality or necessity, as they sometimes do. But none of this is news, let alone a distinctive fault—or insight—of rhetorics, aesthetics, or any other aspects of the present analysis.

Commentators continue to debate whether the early classics of noir, during the two decades that bracket 1950, comprise a "series," a "cycle," or a "genre" in the special senses most useful for theorizing cinema. But there is no doubt that the neo noir of the last two or three decades constitutes a popular and considerably self-conscious genre.[53] Although a small start, the independent account just ventured of realism as a political mythos can help us learn further about realist style in popular politics by contributing to an analysis of the political aesthetics of neo noir as a popular genre of cinema. For the trick is to coax realism and neo noir into teaching us about each other without slipping into a virtual identification of the two. An additional assist comes from tapping prior accounts of neo-noir politics that begin as existentialist. This enables us to sidestep any vicious circularity that could come from relying on an initially realist take on neo noir.

In a sentence, the existentialist politics of neo noir involve awakening to resistance of corrupt systems. This is consistent with existentialism in philosophical terms, but it relates more specifically to the conduct of our everyday lives. In addition, it recognizes and explains more of the conventions that characterize neo noir through family resemblance and generic recurrence. At most, even recent books on neo noir acknowledge 20 or 30 notable conventions, and that is probably because they work with abstrusely philosophical takes on existentialism. Again let a single sentence suffice: "This philosophy [of existentialism] emphasizes contingency and chance, a world where there are no values or moral absolutes, and which is devoid of meanings except those that are self-created by the alienated and confused 'non-heroic hero.'"[54] The more philosophical the sense of existentialism, the less concrete and practical the implications. When we articulate the politics of awakening to resistance of corrupt systems, we get twice as many prominent complexes of conventions: 40 going on 60. Explaining the bulk of them can wait for the next chapter, but we can get acquainted with enough to follow their political logic—and learn more about realism—for now by considering such neo-noir topes in *The Prestige*.

Neo Noir as Realism: The Prestige

Christopher Nolan's film between *Batman Begins* (2005) and *The Dark Knight* (2008) is neo noir, like those two blockbusters.[55] Each movie in the Dark Knight trilogy by Nolan is super noir, a hybrid of superhero and neo-noir films, and *The Prestige* intersects that subgenre somewhat as well.[56] Distinguished by archetypal plots, neo noir as a set of political exercises in existentialism has seven of these subgenres. If the Ur Myth for political realism is the Realist Awakening, the originary drama for neo noir is Shakespeare's *Hamlet*.

1. The Hamlet Drama displays how the noir protagonist awakens to a system so rotten that the protagonist cannot figure out what to do. Neo noirs often make a change in Shakespeare's model for the protagonist, then they let the difference produce happier turns than Shakespeare's premise can promise.[57]

2. The Faust Myth traces how a human overreaches in seeking fame, fortune, charisma, or other power that the protagonist cannot gain without doing evil and cannot handle without messing up. Even Goethe finds salvation for Faust in the end, so it's not surprising when neo noir eventually lets a Faust figure off the hook that classic noir usually twists home in the end.[58]

3. The Quixote Quest examines how a solitary champion of justice comes to tilt nobly but foolishly at windmills. Classic noir finds catastrophe in the folly, but neo noir sometimes plays the foolishness for fun or saving grace.[59]

4. The Chinatown Tale considers how a pervasive yet inscrutable system of corruption can overwhelm a more or less well-meaning protagonist long before this lead character even figures out what is happening. Again neo noir is more likely than classic noir to find the humor in such a situation: *The Big Lebowski* (1998) by the Coen brothers is a case in point.[60]

5. The No-Exit Narrative shows how the protagonist learns the hard way that there is no path out of a system seen almost from the start to be

corrupt. In neo noir, this plot sometimes turns sunny at the last moment; but a sudden escape at the end still mires the film's overall ethos in gloom and doom.[61]

6. The Payback Plot explores how the protagonist is undone by a campaign of cold-blooded vengeance. Neo noir occasionally lets the lead triumph instead, as the audience revels in pleasures of vicarious revenge. *Payback* (1999) with Mel Gibson exaggerates the pains and pleasures into parody.[62]

7. The Superhero Saga invents superhuman powers to symbolize how the surprising resources of emerging movements can help a protagonist resist, escape, or even overthrow an incipiently totalitarian system of social control. This kind of tale appears in American comics with the Batman at the same time that noir films are taking shape, but it does not truly claim the silver screen until Tim Burton films *Batman* (1989) as neo noir.[63]

The Prestige is a chaotic, fractal film of enormous complexity in plot. This fits the often endless machinations of political realism. Depending on how we count, the film provides between two and four focal characters, and they produce several interacting dramas. Their overall mythos is arguably Faustian, and that might be a surprise. For the Faust Myth is an idealist (not a realist) drama. It demonstrates why we should not make the realist mistake of embracing evil means to allegedly good ends. The devil is in the details of any such contract or strategy; and we humans never manage to see or think through all the crucial details, even when they stay in plain view. Yet this mythic matrix makes the film's stylistic attention to political realism all the more engaging, and it makes the movie's critical attention to awful consequences of realism as a political style all the more telling.

If you have not already seen *The Prestige*, I hope you soon will; and I don't want to spoil it for you. There is no way to analyze its complexities without providing information that the film long conceals from first-time viewers. To be sure, these details typically lurk in plain sight; but the filmmaker distracts us from them, exercising the illusionist's stagecraft throughout the movie. *The Prestige* is an excellent film; and it might engage you even more in further viewings, as you understand it better and can look for how its tricks of attention and perspective operate. But do not miss the chance to experience its manipulations in the absence of backstage knowledge. So please consider your reading done for the moment unless you've viewed *The Prestige* before. And in any event, you need to have seen *The Prestige* in order to assess the plausibility of the following approach, let alone any insights that it might offer into the film. Similar considerations hold for *The Illusionist*, to be discussed in the comparison that concludes this chapter. Therefore if you are yet to watch either movie but might in the near future, this is the place for you to call a temporary halt in your reading.

Back again? *The Prestige* pits two British illusionists, two stage magicians, against each other in what turns tragically into a competition to the death. Almost magically, both these figures are doubled in the movie. Rupert Angier (Hugh Jackman) has not wanted to be recognized as Lord Caldlow, at least initially to spare his family an unwanted association with the unsavory world of theater. Alfred Borden (Christian Bale) has a deep secret that he will do whatever it takes to keep: he is sharing life interchangeably and in every respect with his identical twin, Bernard Borden. They trade everyday performances between Borden as magician and Fallon as the ingenieur (engineer) who assists with the technological work offstage. This is the basis of their greatest feat of stage magic. In "The Transported Man," Borden disappears into a doorway that can be seen to lead nowhere, whereupon he instantly exits a distant door visibly unconnected to the first. It is Alfred entering door one, and Bernard exiting door two, or vice versa. In a rivalry that springs from Borden's early role in the death of Angier's beloved wife and stage assistant, Julia (Piper Perabo), Angier becomes determined to outdo Borden by improving on this trick. But how does Borden do it? Angier does not know. So he steals Borden's diary of magic. It misleads Angier to commission Nikola Tesla (David Bowie) in America to build better equipment that does the trick differently. Then Angier outshines Borden on the stage, and further tragedies ensue.

Borden is the better magician by far, in technical terms, but Angier is the better stage performer. Besides that, Angier is rich (as the British Lord Caldlow). And the vengeful desire to outdo Borden eventually makes Angier as fanatically dedicated to magical success as Borden has always been—or more. But even though the doubling of Borden is an inference plain to the least reflection, and it's said by several characters to be the only way that the Transported Man could be done, Angier does not learn until the end—when it's too late—that "Borden" has been twin brothers. And even though the film shows us early the brutal realism of stage magic, by killing birds to make them vanish, then using "their brothers" to bring them back for the prestige, few first-time viewers figure out the Borden trick much—if any—earlier than the desperately corrupted Angier.

Many tropes of neo noir surface insistently in *The Prestige*. It even includes the long plot loop from classic noir. Thus it begins with the trial and incarceration of a noir protagonist. Next it leaps back to move carefully through developing relationships among the focal men and women. Then it rejoins the bracketing tale with the protagonist in prison, where he is condemned to die and coerced to do a desperate deal for his daughter's future. Yet the movie also jumps back and forth among many other moments. This makes for an especially striking example of the more complicated time lines in many neo-noir films. To stay decently concise, the present treatment skips many neo-noir tropes in *The Prestige* in order to focus on several crucial to the film's fusion of existentialist and realist politics.

If there is a single required character for neo noir, it is the noir protagonist. This is the lone champion of justice. Typically he is a tough little guy with a residual code of honor that he is too honorable to admit. Often he carries another's cause into troubles that this hardened but caring character barely senses in advance, unfortunately compounds along the way, and seldom subdues in the end. Yet every once in a while, a noir protagonist attains some telling triumph. In classic noir, this is partial and momentary; in neo noir, it might be complete and lasting (but still less often than not).

The indisputable candidate for noir protagonist of *The Prestige* is Borden. Immersed in the craft and ambition of stage magic, which entails relentless competition, he awakens late to its systematic corruption. Too late? Well, that depends on whether we are talking about Alfred or Bernard. Framing is a major figure in noir, both in pictures and in plots; and at the level of plot, Angier frames Alfred for murder. (The film parades visual frames one after another to suggest how stage magic relies on frames to construct—and manipulate—viewer perspectives.) Alfred goes to the gallows, leaving his story a Faust Myth of selling his soul to the devil without fully comprehending the price that he must—and does—eventually pay. Unknown at this time by Angier, Bernard escapes the frame. This leaves him free to avenge his brother by killing Angier; and this also lets him get back Jess (Samantha Mahurin), the Borden child, who had been (legally) taken by Angier. Bernard's story is the one reminiscent of a Superhero Saga: as though he has the superpower to survive the execution of Borden arranged by Angier, Bernard emerges to live a full and avenged life of his own. He is reunited with Jess, no longer twinned to Alfred, and able to collaborate at last with Angier's ingenieur—John Cutter—in making further magic off and on the stage. In the end, Bernard is Borden free and whole.

Yet Bernard has suffered grievously for the realist project shared with his brother. He has lost half his own life in sacrifice to his career. He has lost his beloved wife, Sarah (Rebecca Hall), to suicide induced by her derangement from dealing in ignorance and confusion with one husband who loved her but, on alternate days, a different incarnation of the same husband who did not. He has lost two fingers through the realist duplication of painful consequences from a Borden trick sabotaged in public by a vengeful Angier. As part of the Borden rivalry with Angier, Bernard has dirtied his hands by returning the trick, laming Angier permanently in gait and morality. The humiliation goads Angier toward exceeding the great Borden trick and framing Borden unto death. And so Bernard has lost his brother, too, with whom he shared more life and love than even twins can readily imagine. Bernard's hands are filthy, his realism detailed and discredited. Yet a virtual superpower, a virtual feat of magic, lets him off the immediate hook: not entirely a surprise in neo noir.

Even more than Borden, Angier functions as a hard-boiled detective, another character recurrent in neo noir. Like classic noirs, the newer versions usually include a private eye, a policeman, a journalist, or another kind of investigator who intervenes in some corrupt system while its crimes are ongoing. Typically the detective and the noir protagonist are one, but far from always. In *The Prestige*, both magicians repeatedly investigate the competition to see how their tricks work. But brief observation is usually enough for Borden to figure out the tricks of others. It is Angier whose investigations extend into hardball and the depravity beyond.

Angier joins Borden in doing voice-over narration of events in the film, and this often is a device associated with noir protagonists. The film's complications and reversals arise even here, with Angier's voice-over including words from the Borden diary as well as Angier's own responses to what he is reading. Is Angier/Caldlow another set of noir protagonists? The case could be made, with only a slight shift in sympathy and thus perspective. Then this pair would change places, pretty much, with Borden-Fallon. Were this the movie's emphasis, then its noir protagonist would come to an unqualifiedly bad end. This is because Angier dies for his many mortal sins: not only against Borden-Fallon but also against himself—time and time and time again, as we see unmistakably toward the film's conclusion.

With bad ends to this point outnumbering good ends three to one, it's no surprise that the overall tone of the film is grim. In a mode conventional for neo noir, as well as classic noir, the pervasive ethos of the movie is the bleak, dark outlook of fate and doom that gives the genre its name from the French for *black* or *bleak*. What corrupt system dooms most of its protagonists? In *The Prestige*, there are at least two good answers to this question. One is (stage) magic or, more generally, triumph in public performance. Just as good an answer is political realism. Even in their everyday-life rivalry, doing whatever it takes to prevail lures the protagonists into vicious cycles of invention and revenge. Realist styles in competition run away with three or four of the film's candidates for noir protagonists. Yet a further inference available from the film is that the two ways to identify the corrupt system themselves turn out to be one and the same. Just as Angier and Caldlow are one, and just as Borden and Fallon are identical twins, triumphal performance in public competitions is exactly what political realism pursues. They share the pervasive corruption of systematically irresistible inducements to do whatever it takes to succeed.

Two other characters have voice-overs also. The one whose voice-overs begin and end the film—in the fashion standard for noir—is Cutter, the main ingenieur. Cutter is important but not exactly central to the film. Still this does not disqualify him for consideration as a neo-noir protagonist. Classic noir almost always centers on the protagonist; neo noir usually does, but some instances move the protagonist somewhat to the side. Likewise the philosophies of existentialism focus intensely on the humans adrift in a world where they must make their own meanings, whereas the politics of existentialism focus as much or more on the systems that encompass and corrupt the protagonists. Thus some neo-noir films give more attention to the system bosses, minions, and fixers than to the system sleepers who awaken to resist their systems. Cutter has thought he understood the full commitment required to excel at stage magic, to which he has devoted his whole career and possibly his life. But he only learns through entanglement in the tragedies of the younger magicians how ruthless and disastrous the realist pursuit of success in a strongly competitive enterprise of public performance *can* become—and all too readily, almost inevitably, *does* become. Has Cutter, as a system sleeper then later a minion who serves the system's corruptions without quite knowing it, awakened to resistance before the film's conclusion?

Cutter makes common cause with Bernard to kill Angier, avenge Alfred, get Jess back, and make better stage magic with the other two survivors. Cutter is unmistakably a mentor and a wise old man, but neither of those archetypes is a noir identity. (Mentors are standard in super noir and epic.) As ingenieur, Cutter is too routine a supporting figure for him to act as a system fixer, summoned from afar to save the system in its times of greatest peril. Cutter does not lurk so far on the margins of the system as to be a virtual outsider. The noir fixer has great powers, or he would not succeed repeatedly as an emergency man, cleaner, or last resort. Distance from the system boss as the symbolic center of power is a crucial source of autonomy for the fixer. This is a further source of the fixer's power within the system, but also of his power over it, and potentially over the system boss as well. In neo noir, the fixer can exceed even a resistant protagonist as a danger to the system boss or even to the system itself. If turned against the boss or the system, a fixer can harm or undo either. In the end, Cutter works with Bernard to undo Angier/Caldlow. Yet Bernard's astonishing survival—or emergence—is the decisive contribution, and Cutter's role in Angier's demise fits better with Cutter as an awakening sleeper. Accordingly we do well to respect Cutter's credentials as a noir protagonist—and actually as the one who might be offered to us viewers for identification. Is Cutter *our* double in the film, where otherwise we might remain merely the audience for the magic of stage and film?

However we answer that question, let's notice that Cutter's is the existentialist myth of neo noir: awakening to resistance of corrupt systems. Does this mean that *The Prestige* is not, as promised, highly realist? No, for Cutter is still close to a sideshow in comparison to Angier and Borden. Especially for Angier but also for the two Bordens, *The Prestige* is exactly a realist myth of awakening to hard realities and harder responses. These realists are the men at the center of the movie. The genius of the film is to interact their mostly Faustian stories with the largely idealist tale of liberation eventually shared by Bernard and Cutter. But when all this is said, it makes decent sense only if we resist the idea that Cutter might be a fixer.

As it happens, another figure is a much clearer candidate for system fixer. Nikola Tesla stays on the geographical margins of the story. He works on a mountain outside Colorado Springs, while the rest of the film occurs in London, then he leaves in haste for places unknown. At this point, we hear Tesla relate in voice-over his departing letter to Angier. But we have learned that voice-overs are like other genre conventions: none is a sufficient or necessary condition—in this case, for being a noir protagonist. For genre conventions work instead in looser modes of family resemblance, mythic recurrence, and particular importance. Misdirected by the supposedly stolen diary, Angier has asked Tesla to repeat what he has (not really) done for Borden: build a machine that can teleport people. With the letter, Tesla leaves the result for Angier: a machine that can reproduce people—in their adult and clothed entirety—but only at some distance from the original. Angier learns how to work this contraption, and soon uses it to fool audiences into seeing his teleportation from stage to balcony in the barest of instants. So Tesla is the powerful fixer, called into the picture to save the system—or at least its boss, the privileged Lord Caldlow—from the peril of losing to Borden in their realist contest to be acclaimed as the world master of stage magic.

This means, of course, that Angier/Caldlow is better appreciated as a system boss than as a noir protagonist. He is the symbolic embodiment of political realism-in-style-in-action. He is the symbolic center of the magical thinking—covertly cultivated by realist expectations—that "doing whatever it takes" will yield whatever the practitioner wants. He equally symbolizes the magical thinking of realists that intensely desired victories will justify conclusively the evil machinations intended to achieve them. In neo noir, the system boss is seldom a dictator or puppeteer whose minions are the means of controlling everybody in the system. In existentialist systems, the ordinary people and other functions work effectively to maintain the system without much recognizing that this is what they are doing. This is how they don't always recognize when their system is corrupt, when they are perpetuating its corruption, or even when there is a system and they are part of it in the first place. Instead the system boss is a striking figure that recurs in smaller or weaker ways throughout the system to model the styles that secure its persistence. Such repeating figures also show the coherence of a social system in the absence of any direct puppeteering. Angier has minions, from his magician's assistants to his manservant, and they sometimes include an unwitting Cutter as the magician's ingenieur. As minions, they do help make his acts effective; but these do not control every part of the system in some linear sense. Most others in the corrupt system of stage magic as (paradoxically) realist politics coordinate their acts with his out of their immersion in the same, mutually reinforcing, projects rather than any specific responses to his directives. They mostly live in the same style, and that is how their acts coordinate—not because they share a common dictator at some literal center of the system.

In neo noir, the system boss often turns a woman into system bait to lure an awakening resister to his doom. Most of the deadly females in classic noir are spider women who act more or less on their own to weave webs of deceit, entrapment, and doom for noir protagonists. Yet many of the femmes fatales in neo noir are less personally culpable. A little like the loved ones taken hostage by super villains to manipulate superheroes, these neo-noir women are used by the system boss to manipulate resisting protagonists. Sometimes the women do not even know that they are serving as bait; and sometimes it is their simple, "sleeping" participation in the system rather than any specific manipulation by a boss, a(nother) minion, or a fixer that makes these women deadly to awakening protagonists.

The Prestige gives us several variants. Angier's love for Julia McCullough positions him for a fall into a realist campaign of competition (to get ahead) as well as a largely republican campaign of revenge (to get even) when he recognizes that negligence by Borden might have contributed to her early death. Without any intention on her part, she becomes a kind of bait that lures the rich, willful, and talented Angier into a realist-magical system where he quickly becomes the central symbol of its machinations.

Bernard's love for Sarah lures Borden into marriage and a family life largely incompatible with the realist style taking hold of the twin brothers. In response to her entrapment in the crazy coldness of realism as a system, Sarah kills herself. This is a neo-noir wake-up call for Bernard and even Alfred. It alerts them to the systematicity and perversity of their realism.

Every dirty trick before that point could have and should have awakened all the magicians to their corruption by the systematic practice of realism as a political style; but none of those nasty stunts has sufficed, and it is Sarah's sacrifice that at least starts to awaken the Borden brothers. The ruthlessness of realist competition and the escalation of republican vengeance are not easily recognized or resisted. By the time of Sarah's suicide, both these dynamics had gone so far—even for the Bordens, let alone for Angier/Caldlow—that the noir trope of a fated doom hangs over just about everybody featured by the film. Bernard survives, along with Cutter and Jess, but without Alfred, Sarah, or even Olivia Wenscombe (Scarlett Johansson), whom Alfred has come to love. The residual guilt for Sarah's death, guilt that realism promises to crowd out in favor of interest calculation, seems to push both brothers further into their vicious competition with Angier. So they goad Angier to even more extreme measures, including the tricky fame for him that proves deadly to Alfred.

As system boss, Angier tries to use Olivia as system bait to undo Borden. But the ruse backfires when she comes to love Alfred. For this contributes to Sarah's suicide. Yet it also leads to Alfred's use of Olivia and the Borden diary as bait meant to mislead Angier into seeking Tesla in Colorado. That backfires, too, when the Tesla machine enables Angier to become "The New Teleported Man" and frame Alfred for murder. Even this backfires. These measures induce each desperately realist copy of Angier to murder his prior self repeatedly—so that the ruse of teleportation cannot be exposed as the arguably more astonishing reproduction—before Bernard finally murders the last version of Angier. We might say that all these murders are justified, at least by Mosaic standards, because every one of Angier's earlier incarnations has murdered its predecessor too. Just before the film's coda, we see most of these Angier bodies floating in their watery coffins. Before Bernard burns down the theater building, each body floats in the locked tank into which that realist has plunged to drown, beneath the stage, even as its copy materialized at the back of the far balcony.

And there, argues *The Prestige*, is the awful truth about political realism as a style that practices its figures systematically, relentlessly, ruthlessly. The truth is that the political realist must murder himself, over and over again, almost with every passing moment. It is the realist's style to put aside all attachments to previous times and people—including himself—in order to calculate advantages for the present and interests for the future. This is to deny completely to the realist any hold on continuing who the realist has been or what he has done. Neither move is easily accomplished in full, but the realist style insists at least on emphatic gestures in both directions: the realist is to sever himself utterly from who he's been and even who he is now in favor of who he's to become. *The Prestige* literalizes this figural truth about extremities of realist style in the politics of everyday life. William Shakespeare observed that the coward dies a thousand deaths, yet *The Prestige* shows that the realist outdoes even this by intentionally inflicting the deaths on himself. Teeming with realist tropes, *The Prestige* turns out in the end to provide an idealist lesson about troubles with realist politics.

Neo Noir as Idealism: The Illusionist

The idealism of *The Illusionist* is, by contrast, evident from the start. The music is a bit of classically inflected potboiling by Philip Glass, so the opening credit sequence relies instead on sepia images of Victorian scenes in soft focus to suggest that something of a romance is on the way. And a romance, genred additionally as neo noir, is exactly what we get. In the manner of popular conventions, "everybody knows" that there is an elective affinity of idealist politics for romance. So this is not a film where doom overhangs just about every event. Instead the mood is one of mystery and wonder. *The Illusionist* does use the same long plot loop from classic noir that appears in *The Prestige*, with the focal figure shown from the start to suffer deep trouble much later in the movie. But the romantic look of *The Illusionist* gives viewers confidence that the male lead can prevail. *The Illusionist* also uses other temporal tricks, but these do not leap around a lot as in *The Prestige*, and we recognize right off that *The Illusionist* is not a fractal film about times too turbulent for protagonists to survive. Even so, fate appears in this film as a noir trope—not in the film's atmospherics or plot so much as in its dialogue and narration, where a persistent theme of the talk is the tragedy possible in class destinies inescapable from birth.

Again, though, the strongest candidate for noir protagonist is not entirely central to the action. The title character is Eisenheim the Illusionist (Edward Norton). This is his stage name, so that there is some doubling in his development. But as a genuine magician, or at least as his own brilliant ingenieur as well as a dazzling performer, Eisenheim can call upon the functional equivalent of superpowers. This is seldom promising as an indicator that a character should be taken as a noir protagonist, since superpowers diminish a figure's vulnerability to domination by a corrupt system. In the end, Eisenheim acts to liberate not only the love of his life but the entire political system of Prussia from corruption by its Crown Prince Leopold (Rufus Sewell), an incipient totalitarian. Eisenheim uses stage magic to disgrace and delegitimate Leopold, who kills himself rather than submit to public humiliation or, worse, discipline by his father's agents. As in *The Prestige*, there is a noir frame for murder. This time, however, the murder is not real.

It is instead a real-world illusion staged by Eisenheim and his confederates to free his love and to discredit Leopold. Thus Eisenheim is a Liberator, and the neo-noir plot is a Superhero Saga.

The charismatic Eisenheim is intriguing, but the neo-noir protagonist holds his own in this film. Chief Inspector Walter Uhl (Paul Giamatti) drives lots of action in *The Illusionist*. He is a minion of Leopold, who bosses the corrupt system. Uhl has been corrupted in his service to Leopold without quite seeing how much the monarchy is slipping not merely into tyranny but even toward totalitarianism. Yet Uhl is being asked to function more and more as the head of a proto-Gestapo. Eisenheim suspects nonetheless that Uhl is not completely corrupt, and he uses magical craft to manipulate Uhl into parting company with Leopold in a series of crucial steps that leave Leopold dead and Uhl out of the minion business. Most of the "tricks" that Eisenheim pulls on Uhl in particular are tricks of right-direction rather than misdirection: they point Uhl toward evidence (true or fake) of the (urgently true) corruption of Leopold and Viennese politics. Just as Uhl is Leopold's minion, Uhl has police at his call; and these also function as system minions. They include Jurka (Jake Wood) and Willigut (Tom Fisher).

Uhl provides the noir narration in voice-over. Each trick pulled on him by Eisenheim, even the stage magics, works as a wake-up call for Uhl. Eisenheim also calls Uhl repeatedly on his misstatements, which Eisenheim implies Uhl could not actually believe upon the least further reflection; and these exchanges seem comparable to "calling somebody's bluff" at, say, poker. For example, Eisenheim provides an early test of Leopold's worthiness to lead by calling on him to lift his sword from the floor, where Eisenheim seems to have stood the sword impossibly on its point. Carefully phrased patter compares the scene to King Arthur's call to demonstrate his right to rule by pulling Excalibur from the stone where Merlin had impossibly inserted it. This spurs the courtiers present for an evening's entertainment to think about Leopold's right to rule when, in coming years, his father has died. Uhl is prominent among the courtiers who hear—and see—Eisenheim's implication. But at this point, Uhl is not yet thinking hard about Leopold, so Uhl spots Eisenheim as political trouble. As chief inspector, Uhl is a detective; and his slide at the urging of Leopold into police-state tactics to deal with Eisenheim marks Uhl as a plenty hardboiled detective.

Sophie von Täschen (Jessica Biel) is Eisenheim's love from childhood onward. She has become Leopold's fiancée, although more for reasons of state than her own heart. She is the film's femme fatale, even its spider woman, because Leopold and Uhl try to use her to manipulate and doom Eisenheim. But she also qualifies because she conspires with Eisenheim to fake her murder at the hands of Leopold. This baits Leopold into revealing his stripes further, and it baits Uhl into recognizing Leopold's political derangement. In alliance with Eisenheim, Sophie literally deceives and becomes deadly to Leopold. In fact, we might even infer that it takes something of a superhero to use the system's gambits in this way against the system's boss.

A Coda on Idealism as a Political Style

Every magic trick consists of three parts or acts. The first part is called the pledge. The magician shows you something ordinary. The second act is called the turn. The magician takes the ordinary something and makes it into something extraordinary. But you wouldn't clap yet, because making something disappear isn't enough: you have to bring it back. Now you're looking for the secret, but you won't find it, because of course you're not really looking. You don't really want to work it out. You want to be fooled.

Ingenieur Cutter as *The Prestige* ends

Here in *The Illusionist* is unadulterated idealism for politics. The film's visual style and its tale of liberation for a whole polity from seemingly inescapable corruption are unusual for a neo-noir movie. In a way, we might say that the idealist conclusion of *The Prestige* is hard-earned by the movie's pervasive realism. But we also might say that the final lesson of *The Prestige* comes only at its end, as a possibly transformative gesture. Still we should not say in contrast that *The Illusionist* is idealist through and through. For it's not. The realist style of neo noir is evident throughout the film, even as it keeps getting trumped by an idealist style familiar from elsewhere but nicely suited—detail by detail—to this film. Both movies show how neo-noir realism is vivid and instructive. Nevertheless *The Prestige* also shows how neo-noir realism can sometimes serve the kind of residual idealism evident in the cautionary tales of classic and neo noir. And *The Illusionist* shows how neo-noir realism can sometimes be trumped by the sort of triumphal idealism apparent in romances where love conquers all. As promised from the start, these two movies might be argued to end somewhat dismally for their protagonists, or they might not; but at least, both films hint at how we viewers might do better.

And we might begin to do better by respecting idealist politics for their distinctive modes of practicality. As political styles, realism *and* idealism can become crafts; and that's what starts to happen when we develop a political style into a popular genre of information or entertainment. Thanks to Machiavelli, Matthews, and seemingly a million imitators in how-to-succeed manuals, we've long known that realist politics can become an intricate and productive craft. But realist genres such as noir, news, and documentary have been contributing mightily to our cultural sense of realist craft over the last century and more. It's arguable that a similar take on idealist politics as a craft has been available since Plato, although this is not how he's usually read.[64] But it's clear that *The Illusionist* as a demonstration of idealist craft shows how other genres such as romance, epic, and even satire can refine respect for ideals into practical talents for politics.

The film shows how ideals should be recognized and practiced as beneficent, productive illusions. It rebuts the realist insistence from Machiavelli onward that idealists and utopians must be exploitative poseurs or disastrously naïve. Like real realists, the film implies that ideal idealists know themselves to be illusionists. It also suggests that excellent idealists practice their politics self-consciously as a style, even a craft. With Eisenheim, moreover, they proclaim their craft as well as perform it. This differs crucially from realists. Consummate realists know themselves to be manipulators of appearances and people, but contrive to hide this from others in order to make it most effective. Realists want us to see them instead as cool calculators of real, hard, material interests. Is that their distraction, their misdirection, for us in the audience?

As avowed illusionists, idealists privilege textuality rather than reality. This reverses the realist priority identified by Hariman in Machiavelli's writing. For idealists such as Eisenheim in *The Illusionist* and Spock (Zachary Quinto) in *Star Trek Into Darkness* (2013), textuality is taken as "ideality," by contrast with the realists' materiality. Ideality features the idealized standards and arrangements that we can recognize as the rules, ideals, principles, and interpretations that we have written—or otherwise formalized and enculturated—as a community. Idealists defend their priority of textuality as making room for a fuller range of better informed reflections on what has happened and how, what to do and why, even who to be where and when. The idealist conviction is that there can be ethical and practical advantage in sidelining the realist pretense of no pretense. Bill O'Reilly might insist that his Fox program (1996–) is a "no-spin zone," but only fools take this literally, while the rest of us (realists and idealists included) take this way of branding O'Reilly's sort of spin as a figure to enjoy or to annoy—just like the Fox claim to be "fair and balanced." So in its sustained studies of spin, figurality, and other aspects of textuality, the postmodern academy has generated a smart and extensive repertoire of idealist moves and implications. Theorists of literature and other kinds of communication have been articulating our devices of textuality. Likewise our writers, filmmakers, and other artists also have been helping (even more than our politicians?) to refine our crafts of political idealism and mythmaking.[65]

It's not that Eisenheim the idealist declines to bend or even break our rules and our other realities; it's that Eisenheim the illusionist respects them, their makers, and himself enough to advertise that this is his craft. It's not that Spock the Vulcan is incapable of lies by legalism or omission to protect his people and his mission of peace from the machinations of a warmonger; it's that Spock the idealist loves people and truths enough to treat them as ends more than means. This does not keep Spock the illusionist from misdirecting potential adversaries by reminding them that Vulcans cannot lie. Nor does it keep Eisenheim the lover of Sophie from framing Leopold for her fake murder, in part to save her for life with Eisenheim. The lesson is not that idealists are sincere and selfless angels, while realists are duplicitous and scheming devils. Nor is the point that idealism disregards realities, any more than realism disregards rules. Both politics, on occasion, pursue the construction and contestation of our rules and realities. They just do it in in contrasting ways: idealism plays it up, whereas realism plays it down. Still the different styles can produce specific, significant differences in what we do.

As we've already started to see, contrasts between idealism and realism can be expressed by overt idealist reversals of the first four realist figures that Hariman elicits from Machiavelli. Notwithstanding the reputation of idealists for radicalism unto absolutism, a reputation promoted more by realists than idealists, we do better to say that idealism practices prudence rather than strategy. "Where strategy is self-control of temperament and sovereign control of historical memory," as Hariman says, prudence is self-discipline in decision and second-nature cultivation of political judgment.[66] This leaves idealists seeming imaginative and intuitive more than cognitive and calculative in the manner of realists. Reborn as an idealist, the title character (Warren Beatty) in *Bulworth* (1998) hip-hops beyond his Senate liberalism and realism into politics that disconcert his earlier friends *and* foes. What he's doing cannot compute for them; it must seem crazy and unpredictable. Both Eisenheim and Spock surprise even the realists, foes or friends, who have studied them most closely. Yet as the two explain, neither has stopped acting rationally and predictably. It's just that idealist rationalities can differ from realist rationalities—as prudence departs from strategy.

Realists favor experience (including observation) over reading, because they know not to trust the accounts of others and want to see directly for themselves. Idealists favor reading over experience—not because they are fools for authority, as Machiavelli intimated when promoting (realist) originality over (idealist) tradition or common sense, but because idealists take reading to include interpretation. In other words, idealists recognize that experiences are not so much given as made or taken—by interpretation.

Idealists are often constructivists, holding that observation just is interpretation.[67] And idealists are often perspectivists, seeking diverse interpretations, even as idealists see political advantages in tradition and common sense.[68] These projects are where epistemics of idealism and realism merge into politics of idealism and realism. Or better, they help show how epistemology is political.

For good reason, Hariman treats realism as *the* antistyle, with his analysis of Machiavelli focusing on refutation of the realist attack on style and the realist claim to avoid style. There could be other candidates for the premier style-against-style, including a more rationalistic take on the bureaucratism that Hariman lambastes as low mysticism, in the manner of Franz Kafka.[69] Nonetheless realist style in Machiavelli is an especially apt target for Hariman, and he leads with an analysis of it in order to defend political styles in general. This paves the way for readers to respect the other three styles that Hariman proceeds to examine. As a result, the move here to evoke idealism by reversing the first four priorities of realism that Hariman finds in Machiavelli might imply idealism to be *the* epitome of political style, treating it as the political style of styles. Hariman might leave that role by default to republican style. He links courtly style centrally to unsavory politics past and present, whereas his main worry about republican style is merely that it's too demanding to become more than "an insiders' game."[70] Among the twentieth century's premier opponents of realist politics was its principal proponent of republican politics, Hannah Arendt.[71] This fits with Hariman's own inclination to favor republican style, and it's telling that critics persistently fault Arendt's politics for undue idealism and elitism—as an insiders' game.[72]

Idealists typically regard action as performance, which is standard for republicans such as Arendt. In contrast to Machiavelli's realist celebration of action as self-assertion, the idealist emphasis on performance takes action to be embodiment in motion, in gesture. As we've already noticed, Hariman and other theorists of style see performance as the gist of style, and vice versa. Idealism admires performance when serving reflective commitments to goodness and justice. Both our movies about stage magic present action as performance, of course, but so do the most effective protagonists in *L. A. Confidential.* Exley and Vincinnes repeatedly prove productive because they pay acute, largely theatrical attention to the staging of what they do. Other police make fun of them for their self-conscious attention to aspects of performance. When these two get into the deepest trouble is when their deeds are the most impulsive and least pondered for audience impact. Like Captain James T. Kirk (Chris Pine) in *Star Trek Into Darkness*, White is (initially) the LAPD realist whose action is sheer self-assertion. And like

Spock with Kirk, Exley and Vincinnes work with White on idealist arts and perspectives of performance in order to help save White from himself.

White joins Captain Smith and his other thugs as LAPD realists who practice politics as war—in a Machiavellian vein replete with force, fraud, and fortuna, but especially force. Like Angier and Leopold, White's tactics—but even more his eruptions—of violence are what make him formidable yet also seem ready to doom him in the end. The initial idealists such as Exley, Cutter, and Eisenheim—and even the eventual idealists such as Vincinnes—practice politics as invention rather than war. Their invention involves inspiration and persuasion rather than force and coercion. It relies on (overt) illusion rather than (covert) fraud. And it pursues improvisation rather than (suffering frustration in the end by) fortuna. Unsurprisingly invention is central to the republican-rhetorical tradition of political thought and action.

Calculation of interests and economy of violence are key tropes of political realism; and they loom large in the justifications offered by Admiral Marcus, Captain Kirk, and Captain Smith for preemptive strikes in *Star Trek Into Darkness* and *L. A. Confidential*, respectively. For realists, interests are material resources for survival and glory; and realists measure these resources in units of pleasure and pain, or credit and debit, to decide which acts are most advantageous or least disastrous. By contrast, idealists invoke the specifically republican notion of inter-est as what is among or between us, connecting us into communities.[73] So idealists promote construction of interests, where people help make publics for sharing resources and stories of who we might be. This is exactly what Exley, Vincinnes, and White manage among themselves as well as what they eventually hope for Los Angeles in *L. A. Confidential*. It also is what Spock, Kirk, and the rest of the crew achieve for the Starship Enterprise at the end of their *Star Trek Into Darkness*, just before they embark on an unprecedented five-year mission to contact distant civilizations. Thus idealists seek expansion of communication, where this leaves individuals and people different in their interests and views yet increases their mutual understanding and advantage.[74] Of course, realists soon literalize this figure in retorting that it's naïve to assume more communication means more sympathy, prosperity, or peace. And the antagonism continues.

At the conclusion of *The Illusionist*, Eisenheim has a boy deliver to Uhl, presumably no longer the chief inspector, a manual. It tells how to perform the Orange Tree trick that Uhl first admired from Eisenheim. As the hand-off happens, Eisenheim in disguise brushes past Uhl on the street in order to pick his pocket. Eisenheim retrieves the "magical" locket that he had long ago made for Sophie and that they had used to frame Leopold for her murder. In part by attending to Eisenheim, Uhl has slowly been learning the craft of illusionism—as the style of idealism. So it only takes Uhl a moment to realize that the locket is gone, but already Eisenheim has escaped, and Uhl recognizes that he would not want to catch the illusionist anyway. This climaxes the film's antagonistic—but productive—communications between Eisenheim and Uhl. It is a final wake-up call from Eisenheim, alerting Uhl to his beneficent manipulation by the illusionist and others to keep Leopold from terrorizing their realm. It also suggests that the idealists' subtle interventions into Viennese politics—and Uhl's life—have come to an end, for now, and a good end in each case. Uhl, too, has become at Eisenheim's instigation a free and moral man.

CHAPTER 4

Noir in Paradise: Testing and Twisting Realist Politics

(Featuring the *Jesse Stone* Series)

par•a•dise (paŕ-uh-dīs) n.

1. A place of ideal beauty or loveliness.
2. A state of delight.
3. Paradise, Massachusetts (town, FIPS 55520)
   Location: 42°40677' N, 70°81223' W
   Population (4587): 25408 (7633 housing units)
   Area: 17.3 sq. mi. (land), 41.8 sq. mi. (water)
   Zipcode(s): 02587

   —Opening legend for *Stone Cold*

Bearing heavy baggage, Jesse Stone drives cross-country to Paradise, Massachusetts. To Paradise, Stone brings drunkenness that cost him a job with the LAPD, obsession with the wife he has lost to careers and affairs and divorce, grief for his old dog soon to die, resistance to facing his failings and feelings, plus disregard of rules in the way of justice. "Jesse" is from the Hebrew for "wealth." Is this name an ironic reference to Stone's baggage; or does it note his talents for survival, detection, and justice? Jesse is played by Tom Selleck, an actor known for tough but sympathetic cops, cowboys, and detectives in dramatic series and movies made for television. As a result, he has even become a corporate representative of CBS Television. Like Charlton Heston before him, Selleck also has become known as a spokesman and board member for the National Rifle Association. They have been similar as heroic, macho figures, although Heston's career was centered in cinema whereas Selleck's has focused on television.

It's surprising that Jesse Stone's sad, old SUV manages the trip; and it's amazing that a job as Paradise Chief of Police awaits a man as damaged as Jesse. A competent predecessor has left for no clear reason, and the Town Council has inexplicably hired Stone instead. He is to lead only three officers, none especially experienced. But the town is small, and its policing is less about major crimes than reassuring appearances for seasonal tourists and commuters to Boston. Paradise is a beautiful place, the police "force" is smart and respectful, then Stone lucks into an affordable old house on the seashore. Stone is a clever and rugged guy, with a wry tongue. He has learned the craft but also the politics of policing in the big leagues of Los Angeles. He works with great skill and will to make a new life for himself in a town where its name is mostly its condition. What a wonderful turn of events! What could go wrong?

Answers to this question tell us about the political mythmaking implicit in American television as well as movies. In turn, that can clarify contributions of television and cinema analysis to theories of politics. The logics that link communication media and technologies to dramatic forms and political implications are loose, elective, and historical rather than deductive or deterministic.[1] So the politics are more cultural, conventional, and stylistic than creedal and ideological.[2] Moving their title figure from a notorious city to an idyllic town, the Stone series of television movies puts a noir protagonist of realist politics into an earthly paradise supposedly better suited to epic heroism and idealism—but supposedly lacking in neither. As Stone and Paradise learn otherwise, we learn about an affinity of American television for epic politics. We also learn about their tension with the political realism and existentialism of neo noir as a popular genre.

Argument

American television has mostly been episodic and serial in structure, while American cinema has not, and this has political implications. Even on "the small screen" of television, episodic politics are principally epic politics; and serial politics are primarily idealist politics. Both epic and idealist politics favor mythic archetypes over settings that develop historically and characters who develop psychologically. In aesthetical and political as well as historical and psychological terms, therefore, the "realism" on American television has largely been limited to news and documentaries. Or at least that has held until the advent of so-called "reality television" and a few of the far-better-funded series on such cable channels as AMC, FX, HBO, Showtime, and TNT. Even then, the cinematic form most renowned for "realism" in the time of television has seldom surfaced on TV, save for the replays of noir and neo-noir films shot first for theatrical release on "the big screen." Series made for TV feature hosts of hard-boiled and other detective shows, but few articulate the aesthetics or the politics of noir.

The scarcity of noir on American television is a cultural and political curiosity. It is especially provocative since the initial cluster of classic noir and the later genre of neo noir are principally inventions of American cinema, although with crucial help from European talent. In the time of television, many of its American programs have issued from the same people, places, and studios as many American movies. We know these sources of television and movies loosely, collectively, and colloquially as "Hollywood." The main argument here is that one of the likely reasons for the surprising scarcity of Hollywood noir on Hollywood TV is a resistance to that popular genre's realism and existentialism that lurks in the episodic and serial structure of American television.

A signal exception is the noir series of made-for-CBS movies based loosely on the Jesse Stone novels by Robert B. Parker. I argue that this series is an exception that proves the rule. So far there have been eight movies about Stone in Paradise, at nearly 90 minutes each. They help us see what happens when affinities of Hollywood TV for epic and idealist politics interact with noir's increasingly generic politics of realism and existentialism. They do this by adapting Parker's thought experiment of moving a fired veteran of the LAPD cross-continent to lead a tiny police force in Paradise—as an imaginary, small-town exurb of Boston.

Generic noir explores the politics of awakening morally ambiguous "protagonists" to resistance of corrupt systems that encompass them.[3] The Paradise series relocates noir tropes from the prototypically postmodern civilization of a big but decentered city to the archetypal and televisual contrary in a community still consonant with picket fences.[4] Paradise is a fabric of epic tropes, and each film in the series functions as a TV episode in the story of Stone as a noir figure transplanted to Paradise. What results are television experiments in epic noir, and these inflect in telling ways the existentialist and realist politics generic for neo noir.

Neo noir often melds with other popular genres in specific movies to produce fantasy noir, gangster noir, horror noir, sci-fi noir, super noir, and so on. Yet epic noir is rare. Some three hundred neo-noir films (in English) have been released since 1980; but aside from the eight Paradise movies made for television, only 1–2 percent of neo-noir films are epics as well. In the Paradise series, epic ingredients help shift noir from its early urbanism and constructivism into moments of environmentalism and naturalism. Many epic elements in the Stone shows help move noir from insistent realism toward resurgent idealism. And epic tropes in Paradise turn noir from a nearly Nietzschean misogyny toward a kind of feminism. As noir's lone knight of justice, the hard-boiled protagonist is arguably all along a crucial, if isolated, figure of idealism in a genre otherwise inclined toward political realism; so to find idealist politics in neo noir need not be a major surprise. Even for neo noir, however, feminist politics appear prominently in only 12–15 percent of films in the last three decades. The environmentalism and naturalism of epic-noir politics in Stone's Paradise are similarly remarkable. Accordingly the project here is to advance an analysis of epic-noir politics in the Paradise programs—to show how analyses of television can contribute to theories of politics.

Noir

Neo noir as a popular genre prospers in many media from the 1980s onward. It stems from classic noir as a film cluster in the 1940s and 1950s, which traces in turn to gangster films and tales of hard-boiled detection in the 1920s, 1930s, and 1940s.[5] Politics of hard-boiled detection start with vaguely Marxist exposés of big-city corruption.[6] In general, they tell of tough little guys who fight for justice that must remain minimal and momentary. Gangster movies put their macho men of honor even more inescapably into the midst of crime.[7] Then noir movies use spider women and other femmes fatales to trap their male "protagonists" within fateful trajectories.[8] These men are too aware of their complicity and too ironic in their talk to count as mythical *or* historical "heroes."[9] Still they drive the action by resisting valiantly the noir systems of corruption that they cannot defeat fully.[10] Neonoir movies conventionalize and existentialize many of the recurrent figures and impulses of classic noir, while in the end letting roughly half of their realistically doomed protagonists off the final hooks that these films grimly foreshadow.[11]

Classic noir is a cluster of 140 or more American movies released between 1941 and 1958. As a group, they were neither produced by filmmakers nor viewed by Americans at the time as exercises in a popular form like horror, gangster, or western films. Owing to World War II, early noirs were seldom seen soon abroad. Only after the war did French critics who were catching up on American films recognize so many similarities among these movies that they named them collectively as "noir," meaning "black" as in "bleak," for their shared looks and outlooks. Critics began analyzing devices crucial for these films, even as the critics noted that American filmmaking was turning away from featuring those devices. Sometimes the critical literature reads as though there were nearly no noir-like movies released in the United States for the next two decades, but that was far from true. Gradually the older movies, the further films, and the critical comments interacted with makers and viewers of Hollywood films to feed the construction of "neo noir." For more than three decades, the new noir has operated as a popular genre like fantasy, romance, science fiction, or war movies. For rosters of classic-noir films, noirs in the interim, then neo-noir movies, see the ending appendices.

The argument here is about the politics of neo noir as a popular genre available since 1980 or so for cinema, television, and other media. As a critical cluster rather than a popular genre of films, classic noir is much more miscellaneous and much less conventional than neo noir. This matters because the politics of popular genres are in the uses of their conventions. It also matters because the conventions—hence the politics—of popular genres are made and shared widely in our culture, rather than staying the special preserve of a few commentators.

Of films released in English in the United States between 1980 and 2012, I've analyzed some three hundred where neo-noir conventions predominate. No doubt, I've missed at least a few that I'd count if I were to view them tomorrow. No doubt, I've included at least a few that other viewers would not credit as neo noir, even according to my take on the conventions. And no doubt, I've excluded several handfuls of films widely—but mistakenly, I'd argue—claimed for current noir by various commentators. (Many classifications by recent critics seem to stem from thinking about noir only in terms of the diffuse atmospherics that sufficed for canons of classic noir as constructed by earlier critics looking back on personal favorites.) The presence and prominence of conventions must be judgment calls based on careful articulation of the genre's conventions: its stock characters, scenes, and settings, along with its shared looks, sounds, and strategies. My project for neo noir as a genre is not a few case studies or even a sample but a decently complete census: one good enough to permit inferences from rough portions or percentages.

Because noir begins in cinema, an eye on neo-noir films is more than helpful in making sense of neo-noir politics on television. Because I can't pretend to the same coverage of TV, a focus on the Stone movies is similarly useful. Like many television programs, each Stone film is an episode in a chronologically arranged series. The production values never exceed high-end television, and the overall length is about the same as many a cable-series season. The star and several of the other main actors have been television fixtures: not only Tom Selleck as Jesse Stone, but Viola Davis as Officer

Molly Crane; Kathy Baker as Officer Rose Gammon; Kohl Sudduth as Officer Suitcase Simpson; Stephen McHattie as Captain Healy, Homicide Commander for the State Police; William Devane as Dr. Dix, Jesse's psychiatrist; and Saul Rubinek as Town Councilor Hasty Hathaway. On the other hand, construction of each episode as a made-for-TV movie can make some of the comparisons with cinematic noir more exact—and some of the political lessons more confident—than they otherwise might be.[12]

That said, I need to add that the Stone movies could turn out to be a startling portion of episodic noir on television, or at least American television. So far, only a few other American series strike me as predominantly neo noir: ABC's *Twin Peaks* (1990–1991), *Terminator: The Sarah Connor Chronicles* (2008–2009) on Fox, and AMC's *The Killing* (2011–). It's easy to suppose I've missed some—even many—others.[13] Yet the television classics of moral ambiguity, hard-boiled detection, police procedure, systematic corruption, or foreboding ethos that occasionally get named are surely not noir by genre: not AMC's *Breaking Bad* (2008–2013) or *Dexter* (2006–) on Showtime, not HBO's *The Wire* (2002–2008) or *NYPD Blue* (1993–2005) on ABC, not even *Miami Vice* (1984–1990) on NBC.[14] Even *Twin Peaks*, from noir meister David Lynch, might be more horror than neo noir—making that series similar to such Fox sci-fi programs with intermittent noir touches as *Millennium* (1996–1999) and *The X-Files* (1993–2002). Of course, *The Sarah Connor Chronicles* themselves sprang from three cinematic exemplars of sci-fi noir; and *The Killing* on AMC is an American remake of Denmark's *Forbrydelsen* (*The Crime*, 2007–). Not so incidentally, the Denmark series stands with movies made from the Stieg Larsson *Millennium Trilogy* as epitomes of "Nordic noir," which infuses police procedurals, detective tales, and similar thrillers with moral ambiguity and brooding tones possibly meant to compensate for omitting many other conventions of neo noir.[15]

There is no doubt, though, that Robert B. Parker wrote hard-boiled detection; and before he died early in 2010, Parker wrote nine such novels about Jesse Stone in Paradise.[16] Parker is even better known for his hard-boiled detection novels about Spenser and Hawk, inspiring the television series *Spenser: For Hire* (1985–1988), with Robert Urich in the title role. Urich later made four Lifetime movies as Spenser, and Joe Montagna made three movies in that role for A&E. But these mostly go to show that hard-boiled detection need not be done as noir on film, and seldom is on television. Even in movies, dramas of hard-boiled detection get genred mainly as thrillers. This is all the more likely for the 40 Spenser novels because they are seldom subtextual or otherwise subtle about Parker's politics of race, sex, family, culture, violence, psychiatry, or even food. The Stone novels are higher-concept, perhaps pushing their uses of literary conventions to do more of the political work. A hard-boiled detective moves from the Big City, Sin City home of cinematic noir to a small-town paradise opposite in coast and culture. The novels explore what happens to him and to paradise. Through the eight Stone movies, we also can explore what happens to noir as it interacts with television.

All these movies use *Jesse Stone* as their titles, so we do well to name them by subtitles. The first four rework Parker novels: *Stone Cold* (2005), *Night Passage* (2006), *Death in Paradise* (2006), and *Sea Change* (2007). The next four are products of Selleck and Michael Brandman: *Thin Ice* (2009), *No Remorse* (2010), *Innocents Lost* (2011), and *Benefit of the Doubt* (2012). *Sea Change* gained Selleck an Emmy nomination for acting. At this writing, it's unclear whether there will be more Stone movies.[17] But it *is* clear how the first eight are neo noir, individually and collectively, and that's a good place to begin political analysis of the Stone shows. So let me use a network of neo-noir conventions refined in contrasting hundreds of recent neo-noir films to hundreds of somewhat similar movies genred overall by thriller, gangster, horror, or other conventions instead. Most of these neo-noir conventions are consensual among cinema commentators; the ones I add get a little more explanation (thus justification) along the way.

Neo-Noir Conventions of Character

Popular genres cohere as networks of conventions, meaning that the presence of none of its familiar figures is a necessary or sufficient condition for including a work in a particular genre.[18] Still if neo noir were to have a *sine qua non*, it would be a **protagonist** too complicit in corruption to be heroic in spurring the action. As his name suggests, Stone was imagined by Parker to be about as hard-boiled in character and hardball in deed as they come.[19] (The CBS movies make him more accommodating, but not much.) Yes, neo-noir protagonists are often hard-boiled, but far from always. Moreover hard-boiled, hardball—that is, politically realist—protagonists are a dime a dozen in thriller, gangster, horror, and war movies that are not in any pervasive way neo-noir. The telling trait is that Stone is an ambiguous mix of vices and virtues: exactly the kind of male who drives the action in most neo-noir films. This makes Stone similar to such noir protagonists as private detective Jake Gittes (Jack Nicholson) in *Chinatown* (1974) and *The Two Jakes* (1990), police detective David Mills (Brad Pitt) in *Se7en* (1995), and bodyguard Creasy (Denzel Washington) in *Man on Fire* (2004).

From the start, Stone is implicated in related sets of **corrupt systems** that he tries to police. Early or eventually, all too many of their corruptions are evident (to us) in him. Yet he's not initially aware of many of these systems, their corruptions, or his complicities. The eight films (episodes) show him awakening (more fully) to (resistance of) these troubles, his involvements, and their systematicity. The social systems criticized by neo noir are often the sorts analyzed by Hannah Arendt, Peter Berger, Michel Foucault, Erving Goffman, Maurice Merleau-Ponty, Jean-Paul Sartre, and other theorists attuned to existentialism.[20] Among the systems especially prominent in neo-noir films so far are bureaucracy, capitalism, celebrity culture, social class, colonialism, consumer society, criminal justice, drug war, family, gangs, national security, patriarchy, and suburbia. The travails of a protagonist map the operation of a film's focal system and specify its principal corruption(s). In *L. A. Confidential* (1997) and *Mulholland Dr.* (2001), protagonists are beset by celebrity cultures corrupted by addiction and exploitation; in *Femme Fatale* (2002), celebrity culture corrupts the protagonist through crime and treachery; in *Where the Truth Lies* (2005), celebrity culture corrupts with polymorphous perversity; in *Domino* (2005), celebrity culture undoes the protagonist with boredom from the ready-made life also excoriated by existentialists.[21] *Traffic* (2000) and *Savages* (2012) show the drug war riddled with crime, addiction, racism, and treachery. *Swordfish* (2001), *Syriana* (2005), and *Déjà Vu* (2006) explore the systematic interdependence of terrorism and the war on terrorism.

Consonant with the existentialist fascination with extremes of human experience, the corrupt systems in neo-noir films are sometimes less institutional, perhaps more philosophical, psychological, even epic. *Insomnia* (2002) and *Seven Pounds* (2008) explore guilt as a system (not just a condition) of corruption. *Payback* (1999) and *The House of Sand and Fog* (2003) dramatize vengeance as a system (not just an act) of corruption. *21 Grams* (2003), *The Next Three Days* (2010), and *Source Code* (2011) treat troubles arguably systemic for life. *Edward Scissorhands* (1990) and *The Human Stain* (2003) trace corruptions possibly systematic in humanity, even though *Edward Scissorhands* is also interested in suburbia as a corrupt system. And so on. Corrupt systems appear in many non-noir movies, and they are staples of conspiracy thrillers as well as dystopias.[22] Still they are the most specifically political figures of neo noir as a popular genre, where they are too important to existentialist and realist politics to slight.

To display the systematicity of corruption in particular institutions, policies, traditions, conditions, experiences, philosophies, and other targets of political interest, neo noirs embody their systems in **bosses** who epitomize each system's sinister operation. John Huston's Noah Cross is the boss of *Chinatown*'s corrupt system of water politics. Typically neo noirs evoke further aspects of their systems in the **minions** who assist the bosses, the **fixers** summoned by bosses from the margins to handle unusual threats, the **sleepers** who take part unaware, the **baits** deployed by the systems to lure potential resisters from hiding, and the **gambits** used by the systems to defeat those resisters. These are existentialist tropes for analyzing noir systems.

As neo noir, each Stone movie shows how the protagonist shares in a system and its corruption, then comes to recognize and resist it. The systems and their corruptions differ in each movie. In the eight Stone shows to date, six different systems surface. When *Sea Change* and *Innocents Lost* assail systems featured by earlier Stone movies, each reprise provides a different take on its system's characteristic operation and corruptions. Depending on our analytical perspectives, the six systems suffer more than ten different corruptions. These systems and corruptions get symbolized by eight bosses, with several reappearing as the series proceeds (table 4.1).

One of the many ways in which the Stone movies work together as a television series is that all but the first personify their systems with a mob leader. By the second film, this becomes a more or less continuing character: mobster Gino Fish (William Sadler). He is prominent in five of the seven episodes where "his" mob is a metonym for (aspects of) the corrupt system that Stone soon comes to detect and contest—but stays slow to diagnose and disrupt directly.

Three of the eight Stone shows provide more than one system boss. In each, the non-mob bosses evoke other operations and enact other corruptions of the shared system. Family patriarchs Hank Bishop (Edward Edwards) and Jerry Snyder (John Diehl) respectively enact the sexism and domestic abuse that add to the violent authoritarianism of mobster Leo Finn (Steven Flynn) as corruptions endemic to the patriarchy resisted by Stone during *Death in Paradise*. The human affection featured in *Thin Ice* suffers the systemic self-interest of greed enacted by Fish. But its other boss—of self-interest—is Paradise Councilman Carter Hansen (Jeremy Akerman). Hansen pursues favoritism for his son-in-law and pushes the police to maximize revenue from a speed trap rather than investigate a cold case of kidnapping from clear across the country. The susceptibility of the justice system to corruption by organized crime focuses *Benefit of the Doubt*, the eighth film. But even before that, the seventh Stone movie engages the less sensational corruption of justice and rehabilitation by systemic self-interest. In *Innocents Lost*, corruption from crime is aggravated by corruption from favoritism, greed, and inattention that allows victims to fall through the cracks. Again the Paradise Council pushes dubious priorities, and the mob victimizes people for monetary gain. Moreover Dr. Parkinson (Mark Blum), as director of the Tranquility Clinic, lets his facility neglect rehab clients, making them prey to addiction, debasement, and crime.

Table 4.1 Corrupt systems in Paradise

Stone movies	Social systems	System corruptions	System bosses
Stone Cold	Socioeconomic class	Boredom and power	Andy Lincoln, retired inventor
Night Passage	Community	Crime and politics	Gino Fish, mobster
Death in Paradise	Patriarchy	Authoritarianism, sexism, and domestic violence	Leo Finn, mobster; Hank Bishop, father; and Jerry Snyder, husband
Sea Change	Socioeconomic class	Exploitation	Gino Fish, mobster
Thin Ice	Love, family, and friendship	Self-interest (as favoritism, greed, and inattention)	Gino Fish, mobster; and Carter Hansen, councilman
No Remorse	Everyday life	Sociopathy	Gino Fish, mobster
Innocents Lost	System of justice and rehabilitation	Self-interest (as favoritism, greed, and inattention)	Dr. Parkinson, clinic director; Gino Fish, mobster; and Carter Hansen, councilman
Benefit of the Doubt	System of justice	Organized crime	Hasty Hathaway, mob boss

Actually there turns out, by the end of the eighth movie, to have been something of a boss of bosses all along. This figure has been systematically behind most of the corruptions of Paradise that Chief Stone has come to recognize and resist from the first movie onward. At long last, Stone learns that Hasty Hathaway is the (top) boss of the regional mob that encompasses Boston and Paradise. Like the purloined letter, Hasty has been hiding in plain sight as the Paradise car dealer who even led the Town Council in hiring Stone. This revelation helps explain Stone's recruitment from firing, disgrace, and alcoholism in LA to replace a respected, healthy chief in Paradise: Hasty wanted someone too beset by other troubles to notice fully what was happening beneath his nose. Until the eighth episode, the Paradise movies have Stone suspicious of Hathaway as at least a little larcenous; but mainly they treat him as comic relief.

The nickname implies that Hasty takes advantage of people giving him all too quick a glance to see him for who and what he really is. In other words, his concealment depends on his getting, even cultivating, little respect. His given name of Hastings might reinforce this, at a colloquial glance; yet its etymology from Old English reveals him as a "son of the severe, violent one." What a way to evoke the series preoccupation with patriarchy as authoritarian and abusive of women! Furthermore the family name of Hathaway links him through Old English and Welsh—not only to heaths and paths—but also to strife, contention, and war. At a longer look, "Hastings Hathaway" appears a potent mythic label for the boss of organized crime, both in the big city of Boston and in the small town of Paradise. With the whole series also working as a single neo-noir series, the boss of Paradise as a corrupt system is a bastion of its social establishment, its business network, and its government. Diss him, if you will, as a car seller, a cuckold, a bit of a buffoon; but he secretly superintends the regional crime syndicate.

In this late perspective, Finn and Fish join the many other minions of Hasty's system. Hasty has meant for Stone to be one of them, protecting Hasty's hometown or base, but he has wanted Stone to stay unaware of helping Hasty's criminal organization. This has made Stone a system sleeper, in various ways, throughout the series. That holds also for others in the system of justice: Stone's officers, local lawyer Abby Taylor (Polly Shannon), the medical examiner recruited by Stone, and even some members of the Boston Police and the Massachusetts State Police. Likewise Jake Gittes does not comprehend until the very end of *Chinatown* how he has been advancing the systematically sinister interests of Noah Cross and company. As the truly hard-boiled detective in Paradise, by contrast, Stone is among the first to awaken to Hasty's overarching system of corruption and resist it. This doesn't eradicate Stone's sins or troubles, including his inadvertent services to Hathaway and the crime syndicate; thus this doesn't exactly make him a hero. But it does make him the protagonist of this neo-noir series.

Four of the individual movies develop additional sleepers, perhaps to underscore how easily people can become complicit in corrupt systems. *Death in Paradise* features the writer Norman Shaw (Gary Basaraba) as a celebrity and a sexual predator. Yet that movie displays how organized crime has been taking advantage of Shaw's celebrity and predation to serve its further interests, while having him stay oblivious to its operation until he becomes one of its murder victims. Similarly college student Lewis Lipinsky (Mike Erwin) serves as a clerk at the rehab mill that Dr. Parkinson directs as the Tranquility Clinic in *Innocents Lost*. Deciding to ignore Parkinson's orders and answer questions from Stone, Lipinsky starts to recognize what he's been abetting; and he seems ready to take Stone's concluding advice that Lipinsky seek work elsewhere to go on putting himself through school. And in the last two programs, Thelma Gleffey (Gloria Reuben) keeps the books at Hasty's car dealership without seeming to notice that Hasty is a criminal, let alone the crime boss. (She also becomes Stone's trusted friend and sexual partner, leading us viewers to trust that she's not in league with Hasty.)

Sleepers are part of the system; and they share in its corruption—even if they are good in many ways, even if they later resist and escape the system, or even if they become liberated and redeemed. Lipinsky might escape, and Stone at least resists, but Shaw doesn't awaken in time to avoid murder by the larger system, and Taylor dies unaware of her unfortunate role in it. The very corruptions of neo-noir systems are what engage some participants, who then become bosses and minions. Such systems lure unknowing participants with distinctive baits, then entangle them continually through gambits that can come to characterize each system. In each movie about Stone, he is either the focal participant drawn into the film's system, or he is a representative participant who is apt to feel at least a little tug from the system's main attraction to many of its participants. A roster of Paradise baits, gambits, and minions can be telling (table 4.2).

These neo-noir systems—complete with their characteristic corruptions, baits, gambits, bosses, and minions—clarify the dynamics of Paradise. In a kind of weak irony, these turn out not to be all that paradisiacal. They privilege not only the usual culprits of crime, class, money, and other machinations of power but especially the abusive, patriarchal exercise of power by men over women. Each Stone movie interweaves investigations of two or three focal crimes that parallel each other enough to detail the corrupt system at issue. Of the eight movies, only *No Remorse* and *Benefit of the Doubt* have no focal crime against women; while four of the Stone movies attend entirely to crimes against women. (*No Remorse* focuses instead on

Table 4.2 System resources in Paradise

Stone movies	System baits	System gambits	System minions
	Women (Abby Taylor)	Sex and friendship	Jesse Stone, police chief
Stone Cold	Women (Candy Pennington)	Sex through rape	Bo Marino, football star Kevin Freeney, football player Troy Drake, Bo-Kevin friend
Night Passage	Employment	New start in paradise Payoff and retirement Payoff and power	Jesse Stone, police chief Lou Carson, former chief Joe Genest, mobster
Death in Paradise	Power over women	Patriarchal authority	Jesse Stone, police chief Lovey Norris, mobster
Sea Change	Money	Bribery and blackmail	Jesse Stone, police chief Alan Garner, mobster Terry Genest, mobster Hasty Hathaway, criminal
Thin Ice	Affection and advantage	Impersonal rules to conceal personal gain	Jesse Stone, police chief Alan Garner, mobster William Butler, police officer

continued

Table 4.2 Continued

Stone movies	System baits	System gambits	System minions
No Remorse	Normality (as an absence of differentiating patterns)	Apparent randomness to conceal patterns	Jesse Stone, police chief Alan Garner, mobster John Kelly, mobster
Innocents Lost	Minimizing troubles	Easy "solutions"	Jesse Stone, "retired" chief William Butler, police chief College administrator Public defender Mrs. Van Aldan, divorcé Amanda, Fish assistant
Benefit of the Doubt	Employment and personal fulfillment	Working in plain sight	Jesse Stone, rehired chief Gino Fish, mobster Amanda, Fish assistant Henry Uppman, Fish lawyer

homosexual jealousy in a male triangle of sex and advantage, while *Benefit of the Doubt* concentrates on its revelation of an encompassing system and boss.) Such attention to "women's issues" by the Stone series is uncommon in neo noir, and it strikes me as an elective effect of setting Stone's policing in "paradise." Other peculiarities of the Stone series converge on such an inference.

Neo-noir films typically target their protagonists for (further) entanglement in their corrupt systems. Neo noirs conventionally engage their usual male protagonists through the beauty, wealth, or wiles of women. The intensified involvement often dooms the protagonist, so noir theory treats such a focal female as a **"femme fatale."** Since there are deadly women in many other kinds of films, it is helpful to notice that a specific subtype predominates in neo noirs, where **"spider women"** weave webs of deceit to entrap male protagonists before they figure out how deeply embedded in the system they are becoming. As a potentially deadly attractor through sex and deception, a spider woman epitomizes a defensive strategy of bait and switch by the corrupt system that would dupe a male sleeper and subdue a male resister. Seldom is the spider woman also the system boss; instead she is used by the system just like its other functionaries. Yet her power over the male protagonist is typically great. Accordingly her prominence in a neo-noir film is often second only to the male protagonist, whom she more or less seduces into (further) service to the system's corruption. Evelyn Cross Mulwray (Faye Dunaway) is *Chinatown*'s spider woman; Irene (Carey Mulligan) is *Drive*'s (2011).

For the Stone series as a whole, as for each of its movies, the femme fatale who lures and spurs Jesse further into trouble is Jenn (Gillian Anderson), his former wife. Whether she is a spider woman is debatable, in part because there are several peculiarities that suit Jenn to playing Eve for Jesse in the epical conditions of Paradise. In the novels, Jenn stays in LA for a few volumes but then moves to Boston; in the movies, she stays on the west coast, arguably making Jesse's break with her greater and his new start even cleaner. In both, though, Jesse still talks a lot with Jenn by telephone. He serves her as friend, confessor, refuge, and protector. This keeps him all too tethered to her and his love for her. She does seem to love him in her own, limited way; and she might not be deceptive in the manner of a spider woman, because her excessive self-involvement and her tactics for exploiting Jesse are clear to both of them in her calls. Still she entangles him in emotional webs of titanic strength. Moreover their strands parallel many of the patriarchal plotlines that trouble ties of males and females throughout Paradise, let alone Boston. At times, Jenn seems for Jesse a kind of strange attractor, a black hole in his life: a sucking absence more prominent and consequential than even his friends in Paradise. She "appears" in each episode only as a telephone conversant, a disembodied voice, save for *Benefit of the Doubt*, when she just gets mentioned in a therapy session for Stone. The gradual, overall decline in Jenn's calls seems a carefully calculated measure of how well Jesse himself is doing.

Every episode has at least one woman who attracts Stone sexually, even romantically, but none supplants Jenn as Jesse's love. In *Stone Cold* and *Night Passage*, this is Abby Taylor, who is murdered before these first two movies end. Sybil Martin (Sean Young) in *Sea Change* and Amanda (Christine Tizzard) in *Benefit of the Doubt* are **"good-bad girls"** familiar from neo noir, and they intrigue Stone, but he doesn't sleep with them. Also in *Sea Change*, Leeann Lewis (Rebecca Pidgeon) bids briefly to eclipse Jenn as the femme fatale and spider woman for Jesse; yet her moment soon passes. During *Thin Ice*, *No Remorse*, and *Innocents Lost*, Stone seems to sleep with Sidney Greenstreet (Leslie Hope) of Internal Affairs for the Boston Police; but as her great noir name hints, theirs is sexual play more than anything deeper. Almost as parody, Stone's longest sustained attraction is to Sister Mary John (Kerri Smith), developed in *Death in Paradise*, *Thin Ice*, *No Remorse*, and *Innocents Lost*. Such unusual limits on Jesse's links to every noir candidate for a femme fatale who might doom him to defeat by the system seem televisual and paradisiacal twists on neo-noir conventions shaped over hundreds of films.

In the Stone movies, therefore, Jesse is the central sleeper lured into each system with telling baits, gambits, and women that differ from one show and system to the next. Only by *Benefit of the Doubt*, the last movie to date, does the overarching system boss for Paradise have reason to worry that such resources might be insufficient to defeat Stone's determined (if not always well-directed) resistance. When mistakes or resistance seem to imperil continuation of a system, a neo-noir fixer gets summoned from the margins by its boss. Recourse to a fixer is an unusual, even desperate move, since fixers are costly—not only to the system's coffers but also to the boss's (reputation for) power and thus to the system's vital sense of invulnerability. Only in the eighth movie, as Stone shows an unhealthy interest in Hathaway, does Hasty as system boss assign an assassin to track and ambush Jesse. But this is a small-town paradise, so Stone spots the outsider right away. His jokey name of Arthur "Art" Gallery (Robert Caradine) signals that his looking will trump his shooting, with neither entirely effective. Still his bullets do help Hasty and his ill-gotten gains escape Stone—at least for the moment.

The Stone series also includes many of the other, arguably lesser characters routine for neo noir. Since the setting is Paradise, the two **"damaged males"** are residents nearly as new as Stone: writer Norman Shaw and Mr. Thompson

(Robert Racki), the military veteran who is expert with improvised explosive devices and starts *Benefit of the Doubt* by assassinating William Butler (Jeff Geddis) as well as Anthony D'Angelo (Vito Rezza) of the Paradise Police. Also like Shaw, Thompson is soon murdered by the organized criminals who have just used him. And since the setting is Paradise, the **"deranged males"** are rich outsiders merely visiting for the season. Harrison Pendleton (Nigel Bennett) abuses young Cathleen Holton (Mika Boorem) in *Sea Change*, and Andy Lincoln (Reg Rogers) helps his wife murder in *Stone Cold*. Brianna Lincoln (Jane Adams) is the only deadly female in the series, whereas there are 12 **"deadly males,"** not including Stone: an ordinary proportion for neo noir. But the series has 12 male victims and 16 **"female victims,"** reversing a conventional ratio to suit the paradisiacal sensitivity to violence against women. The contrasting neo-noir figure of a **"helpmate homemaker"** gets a humorous and reinforcing twist when the Stone series fills that role unmistakably with a male dog: Boomer (uncredited) in *Night Passage* and Reggie (Joe the dog) in the other seven shows.

Neo-Noir Conventions of Action

Scholars of neo noir have given much less direct attention to its conventions of action, yet these can be especially important for its politics. The most discussed convention of noir structure is the **long plot loop** often claimed to characterize classic noir. Many a neo noir, too, begins with the protagonist in deep trouble. Without resolving that situation, the film soon cuts abruptly backward in time, often marking the new beginning with a screen legend to say "four hours ago," "three days before," "two years earlier," or the like. Then most of the movie returns the protagonist step-by-step to the opening scene of peril, enabling viewers to see how his action in a corrupt system has brought him to the point of somewhat deserved damage, disgrace, or death. Resuming the pivotal scene, now seen as chickens come home to roost, the film completes the protagonist's devastation as signaled from the start. Or, nearly half the time in neo noirs, the film lets the protagonist somewhat surprisingly off the hook so long prepared for him. *Crash* (2005) and *Broken City* (2013) have their protagonists pay the piper, while *Fight Club* (1999) and *Reindeer Games* (2000) spare their leads for something new.

This classic loop is the platform for explaining several other actions conventional for neo noirs, even when these films lack such a long loop or any at all in the plot. In part, this is because neo noirs often seek functional equivalents of the classic loop, with several flashbacks, dreams, fantasies, time jumps, or even alternate realities. But it is also because the related tropes of action for neo noirs can substitute at times for such departures from linear plots. All three moves are evident in the Stone series. *Stone Cold* is the first movie; then the series jumps back to *Night Passage*, letting this second movie—based on the first Stone novel—function a lot like a long loop from classic noir. For *Night Passage* shows how Stone crosses the country to start his career anew as Paradise Chief of Police, even though the initial movie has him already on the job. Then the third movie, *Death in Paradise*, proceeds from the end of *Stone Cold* to show Jesse inextricably up to his neck in crime plus other troubles in Paradise. And these continue through the eighth movie's late revelation—and escape—of Hasty Hathaway as system boss.

The individual movies each use sizable helpings of other devices that generate effects similar to a long loop in the plot or shorter but more frequent flashbacks. Moreover the sixth and seventh movies feature recurrent flashbacks too. *No Remorse* shows us viewers many a noir "flashback" in dream or imagination, some in classic black-and-white, as Jesse consults for the State Police in reconstructing parking-structure murders in Boston. These brief scenes follow Stone's principle of overcoming obstacles to inference or even evidence by "going back to the beginning." Over and over, he reimagines opening scenes of three seemingly random crimes in the same locale to get a sense of how they connect otherwise. Then *Innocents Lost* provides several flashbacks to Stone's earlier encounters with suicide Cindy Van Aldan, as guilty memories overshadow diverse activities in his present to "replay" their interactions.

Not only in themselves but also in their coherence with many other neo-noir tropes in the series, these devices contribute to a generic sense of doom impending throughout for this protagonist and his town. The retrospective structure of a long loop in the plot means that, from the start, we've seen the protagonist in such terrible trouble that it's hard to see how he could escape unscathed when the film finally returns in the end to his opening scene of peril. The glory of many a neo noir is a **voice-over narration** that introduces or comments on its key events in retrospect. With the emblematic protagonist a hard-boiled detective, the emblematic voice-over for neo noir is **wry**. With a paradigmatic mood of fated doom, the voice-over for neo noir is often **world-weary** too. But many neo noirs lack any voice-over narration, and others assign it to characters bound to sound different from the paradigm.

The Stone movies have no voice-over narration, but their voice and dialogue for Jesse are often wry and sometimes world-weary. Many Stone scenes feature the **snappy repartee** sometimes notorious in neo noir. Parker's novels draw praise for snappy, snarky dialogue: more like theatrical banter than the idiomatic rhythms of speech prized by George Higgins and Elmore

Leonard.[23] Plenty of Parker's verbal formulas and catchphrases find their ways into the Stone movies, even when they have left behind Parker's plots. Due to Parker as well as Selleck, Stone's is a distinctive voice readily recognizable as a neo-noir detective's. As a neo-noir protagonist, Stone often cracks wise—but is otherwise laconic, sometimes leading others to respond in kind. In *Benefit of the Doubt*, this ramps up, with Stone a font of wry, terse remarks that spur especially his psychiatrist, Dr. Dix, to follow suit.

By Jeff Beal, the scores for the Stone movies are **bluesy, brooding, and potboiling music** in ways standard for neo-noir cinema. They make palpable an atmosphere of **fateful fortune**. (The main theme is a beautiful, driving, haunting piece of neo-noir music: one of the best I've heard.) Other figures of fateful fortune in the Stone movies increase as the series proceeds. The early, playful talk of "coply intuition" grows more serious, strange, and bleak as it shifts from Stone to his protégé, Suitcase Simpson. When Jesse is out as Paradise Police Chief in *Innocents Lost*, he wards off the fear that he's finished forever with pursuit of justice as a police officer by muttering repeatedly that "fate won't do that to me." Then in *Benefit of the Doubt*— which is full of ironic gibes about guesses, hunches, and such—Stone also talks twice and darkly about fate. Neo-noir films often rely on dialogue to complement voice-over narratives, musics, and plots to foreshadow trouble or outright doom for their protagonists.

Sometimes in a neo-noir film, its corrupt system comes into an emblematic crisis that its protagonist provokes or experiences. Borrowing from Shakespeare's *Hamlet* as the Ur plot for generic noir, we can think of such tumult as marking **"time out of joint."**[24] Some of the resulting neo-noir scenes show a **holiday unhinged**: Christmas disrupted by domestic abuse then police rioting early in *L. A. Confidential*, Independence Day ironized toward the end of *Hannibal* (2000), a Festival of Fools run rampant to climax *In Bruges* (2008), or Thanksgiving hijacked for the showdown of *Deadfall* (2012). Each of the last four Stone movies unhinges its times in ways less blatant than targeting holidays, but clear enough all the same. Even so, the main dynamic of time out of joint for the Stone series turns on the protagonist seeking a fresh start in Paradise, where he finds instead an intensified personal responsibility for crimes that beset others, especially women. Like many of its namesakes, Paradise imagines itself as a holy-day sustained enough for its escape from ordinary, troubled time to become a place. It is true that policing Paradise, like working with his psychiatrist, helps Stone face his troubles. Yet he can neither end nor tame them, and Paradise is for Stone a holiday place unhinged.

Some baits and gambits of corrupt systems appear as specific people in neo noirs; but more often, they take shape in scenes. By far the most frequent and prominent gambit in neo noirs is **framing**: as a device of plot, it implicates characters (often the protagonists) for deeds—usually crimes—they did not commit. The Stone movies include at least 14 explicit or implicit acts of framing, and only the first movie has none. Aside from these acts of framing, tied to the corrupt systems specific to each movie, the plot that emerges overall for the series implies Hathaway to be a master of positioning others to take the fall for him. Stone stops or solves many crimes that have been orchestrated behind the scenes by Hasty, but Jesse does not adequately detect Hasty's role in most of them until the eighth film is heading for home.

A related neo-noir convention oddly neglected by commentators, although observed far more often than not by moviemakers, is the **wake-up call**. The protagonist is typically a sleeper at the chronological (rather than narratival) beginning of events in a neo-noir movie. In other words, he is unaware of the focal system, its corruptions, or at least his own part in them. Then something occurs that could, should, and (eventually) does start to alert him to what's happening systematically and how it involves him. Asleep in bed in *The Limit* (2003), May Markham (Lauren Bacall) is awakened by a gunshot, followed by the neighbor's knock on her door; and she soon finds herself caught in gangster machinations. Thus noirs neo as well as classic noirs often literalize the figure of the sleeper, and they do the same for the trope of the wake-up call. Ringing at night in *The Maltese Falcon* (1941), a bedside phone informs Sam Spade (Humphrey Bogart), just roused from sleep, that his partner has been murdered. This starts awakening Spade to the film's sinister plot. It's not easy to alert some protagonists to their peril, and many get more than one wake-up call. The protagonist in *Fight Club* gets three phone calls in his kitchen, and the protagonist in *The Art of War II* (2008) gets three calls in his apartment. A classic title for a cheesy neo-noir movie could be *The Cell Phone Rings Thrice*.

The recurrent calls and answering-machine messages from Jenn keep reminding Jesse of his largely unpacked personal "baggage," as Officer Molly Crane puts it in *Stone Cold*. These troubling entanglements of love, sex, and gender roles are Jesse's principal shares in the continuing, systematic concern of the Stone movies for patriarchal politics of sex and family. Across the eight movies, Stone also receives many calls, directly at home or passed through a dispatcher at work, to alert him to specific crimes impending, ongoing, or over but only then detected. *No Remorse* foregrounds difficulties in landline and cell phone access to his house, and the details of these troubles are rich in political as well as psychological symbolism. Jesse also gets a few of his wake-up calls from dreams, a device familiar from many neo-noir films, and from other communication media such as letters.

The Paradise Police seem to know in principle or intuitively that sleeping on the job, even figuratively, is an insidious danger for police. Especially in *Sea Change*, but also in the surrounding movies, there is insistent attention to coffee, coffee-making, and cappuccino. In *Sea Change*, Stone has no coffee to make at home. Then there is no coffee for Rose Gammon to make at the police station. Then Stone reads a newspaper item about a man arising after many months from a "coma in Italy," even as Simpson continues comatose from injuries in the previous film. Crane, Gammon, and Stone have been taking turns at reading and talking for hours on end to Simpson, as they try to spur his brain into awakening his body. Later Simpson sits suddenly bolt upright and barks "cappuccino," to the horror of a candy striper. Then Leeann Lewis offers coffee to Stone, forgets it's there, and starts making some anew. Will he awaken to who she is and what she's done? Does she want him to?

Simpson turns out to awaken with a new-found "coply intuition" of his own, to rival or trump the capacity that Stone has named and claimed before. Simpson's new talent for sensing key conditions and information, along with his new attunement to cappuccino, might suggest a categorically greater awareness of what's happening. On the other hand, Stone and the police station being recurrently out of coffee might parallel Stone's poor instincts for the two cases at issue in this film. Simpson's new "coply intuition" seems to compensate for Stone's momentary incapacity for it. The series interest in awakening Stone to the larger system of troubles in Paradise even produces lame, intermittent jokes about the availability and responsibility at the police station for providing the coffee that might make Jesse (and others) more alert. The coffee motif in several of the Stone movies plays with the neo-noir conventions of sleepers and wake-up calls.

Yet two of the most telling riffs on the convention of the wake-up call in the Stone movies are the ones that sidestep it. When alarming, awakening information is most crucial, it usually gets delivered to Stone in person and in private by a police officer, a councilman, or particularly by Captain Healy of the State Police. With Healy, this device is probably meant to make camera time for a popular character who otherwise would be too easy to keep offscreen (somewhat like Jenn). Nonetheless it carries important political implications, indicating early and insistently that Paradise police need outside resources, and especially that Paradise crimes are embedded in much larger systems.

The other Paradise play on the convention of the wake-up call is when it's notably missing. (Compare the dog that didn't bark for Sherlock Holmes.[25]) Then something terrible happens abruptly, without warning to Stone or viewers. Talking in a car parked in the rain in *Thin Ice*, Stone and Healy get shot from a side window by an ambusher who turns out to be Teddy Leaf (Fulvio Cecere). To begin *Benefit of the Doubt*, Chief Butler and Officer D'Angelo pull their cruiser onto a little lookout at the side of a coastal road; then the car explodes into flames. And to end that movie, Stone walks to meet Hathaway, when a shot from assassin Art Gallery misses Jesse's head—only because he flinches in holding onto a coffee cup that happens to slip accidentally in his hand. (Jesse Stone's luck is pretty good in his Paradise.) When bad things happen to Stone without warning in Paradise, it's because he's stayed deaf and blind to the corrupt systems that encompass him. Or we might recognize these sudden assaults as wake-up calls, for neo noirs do so when such attacks awaken protagonists rather than put them permanently to sleep. Wry tongues are frequent results; and in neo noir, we might say, whatever doesn't kill you makes you smarter.

Erupting gestures, especially abrupt acts of violence like the three just evoked, are common in neo noirs. This helps make neo noirs comfortable fits with thriller and horror conventions. Aside from the dramatic advantages of shock and suspense in holding viewers, surprise moves that radically disrupt lives can symbolize the unfathomable preponderance of power that corrupt systems typically have over any and all of their participants but especially their sleepers. The defense mechanisms of these systems are particularly attuned to aiming bolts from the blue at resisters, who often have a diffuse sense that doom approaches but do not anticipate exactly what threats loom where. Throughout the Stone movies, violent acts are often sudden and surprising. Seldom do viewers, let alone characters, expect most of the shots, physical assaults, or dead bodies to be seen in a Stone show.

Systems monitor their processes and units, especially potential resisters. Awakening to resistance of a corrupt system, the neo-noir protagonist has strong reason to monitor right back. This makes **surveillance of sins** a familiar motif of neo noir. In the early Stone movies, Jesse cracks that he's the police chief, so he knows everything. Even so, the main surveillance involves how people in the small town of Paradise keep eyes on one another, gossip, and thus know most sins of their neighbors, past or ongoing. Every one of the movies has Stone tailing suspects and criminals tailing victims. *No Remorse* uses grainy black-and-white surveillance videos of parking-structure murders and convenience-store robberies, not only to solve those crimes but also to make the movie more visibly noirish.

The *No Remorse* videos help Stone's detection in two different ways: with the robbery videos, the key is who he sees twice; with the murder videos, the key is who doesn't appear. This leaves the movie's alignment of the videos peculiar, strange, tense, and even transient in that the parallels are productive but they yield no principle of inference. Such strange and telling alignments are "syzygies," from the ancient Greek word for "spouses."[26] That history has special resonance for the Stone series, with its tense and transient alignment of Jesse and Jenn as well as its persistent focus on patriarchal disorders of family, gender, and sexual relations. The neo-noir take on systematic corruption is that it generates **sinister syzygies**. To discern and resist a corrupt system, let alone escape or defeat it, can depend in part on spotting its sinister syzygies or even turning them against the system.

American television loves dramas with several plotlines that complement each other to evoke a show's topic or theme. The Stone series is standard for police and detective TV in investigating two or three crimes that align, sometimes surprisingly, to reveal a social trouble. Then the Stone movies treat the trouble as systemic, even (sometimes especially) in Paradise. Startling alignments that betray systemic corruption are signs of neo noir. In *Stone Cold*, for example, the high-school boys who rape Candace Pennington (Alexis Dziena) are led by an advantaged and bored "football hero." He and his friends parallel the Lincolns as a rich and bored couple who cope with the meaninglessness of their lives by murdering people on a lark. The more Stone looks into the Lincolns, the clearer it becomes to him and us that their killings arise from many of the same sexualized power plays that spur the high-school rape. This is a surprising alignment because the murder targets had seemed maddeningly whimsical, even random. We learn that the very prosperity of Paradise leaves it vulnerable to sexual power plays, and *Death in Paradise* connects its three patriarchal crimes to economic conditions too.

Innocents Lost constructs two strikingly different sets of troubles for Cindy Van Aldan (Eileen Boylan) and Charles Morris (Ben Watson). It makes her a victim and him a predator. Then, however, it brings their cases into momentary alignment as the justice system rushes to judgment in both. As a detector of systemic, underlying troubles, Stone does not settle for the surface appearances. He is able and willing to face the roiling complications and implications that lurk beneath easy impressions. Again he makes himself a thorn in the system's side by taking personal responsibility for seeing through its disguises for (sexual and family) disorders pervasive in his community. Detecting misconceptions and cover-ups in the Van Aldan case, he looks harder for them in the Morris case. Then he learns the deeper resonance of the two. Spotting a sinister syzygy has enabled Stone to open a door into sexual politics in Paradise.

Another convention of scenes for neo noirs is the appearance of whirling machines such as fans, helicopters, or a tape recorders. As figures, these seem to fit neo noirs because their operations enact symbolically the circular, self-sustaining operations of a system. When we see a still fan, with blades not spinning, the neo-noir implication is that some system is not working smoothly or at all for the moment. Tape players and recorders are especially telling, for they appear in interrogation rooms, on answering machines, as videocassette equipment, and otherwise involved in producing and reproducing confessions, testimonies, and similar messages crucial to dramas of detection. In homage to the great musical theme (and figure) for *The Thomas Crown Affair* (1968 and 1999), I think of these tropes as **windmills of the mind**.

Jenn's telephone exchanges with Jesse are sometimes like interrogations, and they increasingly involve the whirling tape recordings of Stone's answering machine. Twice inside the building for the Paradise Police, *Death in Paradise* shows us a wire-enclosed fan on a tall pole in the background; and the fan is not turning. These are times when the police are not moving effectively to stop or solve the movie's focal crimes of patriarchy. *Thin Ice* offers a conventional scene of neo-noir interrogation and narration when Greenstreet uses, then turns off, a double-reeled recorder in a glass-walled room with Venetian blinds. She is questioning Stone about his recent shootings on the job. Just after Stone returns to work as police chief in *Benefit of the Doubt*, we see an old table fan sitting still in a box in his recently former office: it might symbolize how Stone in particular and the Paradise justice system in general has been disabled and sidelined when Stone has been "retired" as chief.

Scenes of **self-making and self-masking** are also conventional for neo-noir movies. In political terms, arguably, this is because a protagonist develops in awakening to a corrupt system and has urgent reasons for concealment in resisting it. Such scenes are especially memorable in most of the super-noir films, which meld neo noirs with superhero sagas. Usually there is a self-making scene or two when the lead character acquires special powers and revels in them, and frequently there is a self-masking scene or two when that character acquires a masked costume, then experiences implications of wearing—or losing—the mask. Self-making is crucial to Stone's project in moving to Paradise, but we might think that Stone is distinguished by a principled refusal of self-masking. From the first movie onward, some of the more amusing scenes show Stone pointedly acting as he sees fit when he knows this isn't what's wanted. Yet Jesse's talks with Jenn and especially his psychiatrist insistently show a man trying out new attitudes in struggling to remake himself. In many movies, masking a police officer involves his working undercover, with a fake identity. Stone does none of that, and he seldom takes much care to stay concealed when tailing suspects. Still he seems mightily masked from himself, and his scenes with the psychiatrist show them investigating this. It seems likely that self-masking is endemic, even intrinsic, to especially hard-boiled detectives: their thick shells *are* masks, in relation to the self as well as the world.

Stone's psychotherapist used to be a policeman. This helps him serve as a sounding board for Stone. But Dix is skilled, too, at the same intrusive and provocative techniques of investigation that Stone practices especially well. Thus the psychiatry scenes often show the two investigators trying to learn about Stone by spurring him to changes as well as replies. Classical detectives analyze clues to solve crimes already completed; hard-boiled detectives intervene into the midst of crimes to detect and disrupt them. When corruption is systemic, but the detective doesn't know it, the intervention is apt to go awry: probably serving the system rather than resisting it. That's what happens with Jake Gittes in *Chinatown*, and so memorably that its title names one of the seven kinds of plots conventional for neo noir. Whatever the kind of neo-noir plot, though, any neo-noir project of detection is likely to be hard-boiled; and therefore neo noirs often include scenes of **provocative detection**. These have investigators leak or falsify information to spur telling responses—on the spot or soon enough—from possible criminals, sinners, or other opponents who might serve the corrupt system being detected or resisted. Stone does this so much and with such relish that Healy often scolds him playfully for "stirring the pot," and that might be an even better name for this neo-noir convention in potboiling thrillers.

As mentioned, seven kinds of **overarching plots** dominate neo noirs to date. There are **Hamlet Dramas**, where the protagonist's challenge is to become his own man, or not.[27] There are **Chinatown Tales** where the protagonist is slow to learn and so stays dominated to the end by a corrupt system that eludes him. There are **Faust Myths**, where the protagonist becomes his own cautionary tale by going beyond his abilities to seek beauty, charisma, fame, fortune, power, or the spider woman, then failing in some disastrous way.[28] There are **Payback Plots**, where protagonists become caught in systematizing vengeance.[29] There are **No-Exit Narratives**, where corrupt systems give awakened resisters *No Way Out* (1987).[30] There are even **Superhero Sagas**, where superpowers enable protagonists to escape corrupt systems or at least liberate other people from them. (Keep in mind that neo noirs often twist away from their fated ends—to spare nearly half the protagonists the doom or damage that they have earned.) And there are **Quixote Quests**, where well-meaning protagonists ill-attuned to their situations wreak havoc as well as justice.[31] Put into Paradise an LA cop with deep and persistent troubles, and the best we could expect from him are Quixote Quests. So it is no surprise that these are exactly what we get from the series as a whole and from each of its movies considered individually.

Five endings for protagonists bring neo noirs to their conclusions. When corruption becomes systematic, any great success in resistance becomes unlikely. The protagonist seems fated to fail in any effort to free the whole society from the corrupt system, escape from it, or even sustain much resistance. Neo noirs often foreshadow **doom**, and doom is what some of their protagonists soon suffer. Rare is the neo-noir protagonist whose resistance soon ends in death yet still gains that person a new and better sense of **meaning** for a life experienced earlier as insignificant. A peculiar ending for the title character (Keira Knightley) in *Domino* makes her a protagonist in point. When a protagonist awakens to systematic corruption and resists it to the end, which can be his death, he earns recognition for the **resistance**. In neo noirs, though, protagonists sometimes **escape** the clutches of the system. Occasionally they even flee with the formerly deadly females (or males), who've become ready to depart the system. This is what happens to end the first release of *Blade Runner* (1982), when Deckard (Harrison Ford) and Rachael (Sean Young) fly from the gloomy future of LA into the green countryside beyond. Typically it takes special powers or resources to free a whole populace from a corrupt system, but such **liberation** is the outcome of many super noirs and a few other neo noirs as well. Plainly Stone neither liberates Paradise nor escapes from it, but his resistance to its corrupt systems is long and distinguished.

Neo-Noir Conventions of Setting

The setting of a work for cinema, television, or theater is the look, sound, components, and significance of its places. These provide the surroundings and presentations for a work's characters and their actions. Consequently a popular genre is also defined by its conventions of setting. If a film's setting is not neo-noir, the genre is much more likely to be a thriller.

Classic noirs have been known in important part for low-key lighting that displays faces in strong contrast to deep shadows. The images feature chiaroscuro—as pronounced, often intricate patterns of light and dark—from shadows cast by Venetian blinds, fans, grills, stairwells, and such. The camerawork includes exotic and estranging angles reminiscent of horror. Some classic noirs use "subjective cameras" for long looks at what a character sees rather than the character himself. The black-and-white film for classic noirs ranges from grainy to glossy, depending on how gritty or garish the aesthetical and political realism is to be. All these devices draw many a classic noir close to a "realistic" form of horror.

Neo noirs are inspired by classic noirs, but technologies and tastes have changed since the middle of the twentieth century. Cinema is now more likely to favor 3D than grayscale, and even television might be going that way. In forming a popular genre, neo noirs have been almost certain to sideline black-and-white movies in favor of conventionalizing other looks in color. New kinds of cameras and devices for moving them have made exotic angles more common for most genres, and computer graphics have done the same in every way for more exotic images. Technical advances in sound effects and "surround sound" also shift the ambitions and boundaries of genres. Yet the generic interests of neo noir still include looks and sounds consonant with aesthetic sophistication, moral ambiguity, and political realism.[32] Developing neo noir as a popular genre has involved intriguing experiments with bleaching, saturating, or even oversaturating colors, with computer editing and graphics, but especially—along with hard-boiled detection in literature—with reworking tropes and politics when the settings move from big cities to suburbs or small towns, to swamps or prairies or deserts, to lands of snow or midnight sun, and so on. Likewise neo noirs have explored amalgamations with many other popular genres—from fantasy and science fiction to martial arts and epics.

Notwithstanding their epic setting in the small town of Paradise, the Stone movies are also unmistakably neo-noir in their looks, sounds, and other elements of setting. **Chiaroscuro** continues to be conventional for noir as a popular genre. Many interiors of the Stone movies are dominated by complex patterns of light and dark, often from sunlight through Venetian blinds. As in many neo noirs, this holds especially for law-enforcement settings. A derelict ship that serves two of the Stone movies as a port equivalent of the **mean streets** and alleys used for **gritty or garish realism** by other noirs becomes a chiaroscuro feast for the eyes. In less urban settings, neo noirs replace mean streets with roads stretching ahead to horizons or unspooling almost endlessly, whether before or behind the protagonist. The Stone series uses *Night Passage* to put those roads behind Jesse for good, and it sidelines the **auto eroticism** that sometimes fills neo noirs with fancy cars. As the series proceeds, its exteriors increase their chiaroscuro from grills, stairwells, and the like. The videos and dreams in some shows even go grainy black-and-white to yield classically noirish chiaroscuro. Thus *Stone Cold* features the grainy, jittery videos by Andy Lincoln as noir snippets, often strikingly in grayscale.

Framing as a prominent device of neo-noir plots finds visual reinforcement in neo-noir shots that pointedly "frame" key characters in doorways and other enclosures. These **frames** force perspectives on the characters and confine them in ways similar to totalizing systems. The Stone movies have generic shares of such shots, sprinkling them throughout the series.

Neo-noir dynamics of social alienation, self-making, and self-masking suggest settings with glasses, mirrors, ponds, and other objects for **reflections**

or refractions. Mirrors and reflections are prominent in presenting Stone in every movie but *Death in Paradise*. It turns instead to refracted images of Norman Shaw that hint at his sexual exploitation of adolescent writers. In many of the Stone movies, Jesse uses rearview and side-view mirrors of cars to help in tailing suspects; and he does the same to help detect when he is being tailed. He uses reflections in storefront windows for the same purposes. In the violent coda to *Sea Change*, Jesse leans over his mantle to straighten a treasured photograph of Cardinal shortstop Ozzie Smith—whereupon Jesse spots the reflection of a mobster aiming to shoot him. Alerted to this threat, Stone is able to duck and dive to safety, before returning fire to kill the assassin. More often in his house by the shore, Jesse seems to try to find himself in the bathroom mirror.

The Stone movies are usual for neo noirs in using some **estranging cameras**, especially for establishing shots and scenes of violence. The **subjective cameras** occasional in neo noirs are occasional in the first five Stone shows as well. Yet they are important for *Innocents Lost* and crucial for *No Remorse*, when Stone is using his imagination to reconstruct or project the murders at issue. In neo noirs, **sounds of sophistication and turbulence** are conventional for the soundtracks. As already remarked, the Stone patter is plenty ironic; and the Stone music is pure noir: bluesy, brooding, and potboiling across its several themes.

Purging rain is prominent in the looks and sounds of neo noir. In fact, rain is rare in Los Angeles as the **big-city** home of classic noir. Worse, rain in New York does not so much wash away scum (the *Taxi Driver*'s forlorn hope) as coat the oil and other spills to make that city's **mean streets** into a shimmering wonderland of reflections, distortions, and distractions. See *Conspiracy Theory* (1997). So the noir notion that its rain can arrive reliably to climax and symbolize the cleansing of streets, cities, or souls is a blatantly artificial conceit. It is a trope of moral and political idealism in a genre that announces itself as an opposing realism.

Possibly all the more because they are set in Paradise, at least seven of the eight Stone movies include a purging rain or a neo-noir equivalent. (*Sea Change* is the exception, but neo noir set in boats or ports that has protagonists leaping into the water to escape tight spots is apt to treat the immersions as symbolizing prospects of redemption.) The one rain in *Night Passage* is during Jesse's cross-country trek. Just as a downpour begins, he calls Jenn from a booth. This hints that distance from her could help heal Jesse, but won't help much as long as he's walled off from the rest of the world—and protected from pain by drinking booze. The one rain in *Stone Cold* occurs with Abby in Jesse's bed, just before a phone call alerts him to a second man murdered by the serial killers. It implies that Jesse's friendship with Abby, consummated by sex, starts to cleanse him a bit of his LA marriage and other baggage. But *Death in Paradise* is when Jesse's corner-turning becomes concerted—as an assault on the patriarchy in Paradise and in himself. *Death in Paradise* begins with sights and sounds of a gathering storm. A rush of rain ensues; then driving rain stays intermittent in the movie's first half, as Stone tries mightily but fails badly to purge some Paradise families of patriarchal corruption. Meanwhile his visions of young Billie Bishop (Carolyn Fitzgibbons) floating in the lake almost demand that Stone purge Paradise after her exile by her father and her seduction by Norman Shaw, let alone her murder by Lovey Norris (Brendan Kelly) and Leo Finn. *Sea Change* extends the Stone campaign against patriarchal exploitation and punishment of women. Apparently its potentially purging water is almost all around, but ineffective with Jesse and others still at sea.

Rain is dense and sustained for much of *Thin Ice* too. The opening scene pours rain onto the "stakeout," when Teddy Leaf tries to assassinate Healy and Stone. Stone later accosts Leaf in a restroom stall and plunges his head into the toilet, implying that even its water could be cleansing by Leaf's low standards. But Teddy doesn't turn over a new leaf, so Stone eventually stages a talk with Simpson in a drenching rain. That lets Leaf as Stone's tail mistake Simpson for an informant whom Leaf must kill. Then Stone follows Simpson out of the rain and into an apartment building, where Stone waits to coldcock Leaf and frame him for breaking and entering. This is a third felony for Leaf, enabling the justice system to purge Paradise for decades of another murderous man who mistreats women for a living.

The only rain in *No Remorse* is at the end: a drizzle at the family funeral for a woman murdered capriciously by a killer trying to obscure the motive for another murder. Already having provoked a mob murder of the killer, Stone observes the funeral from a distance. The ending drizzle might mark how cleansing or consolation is little, late, and largely insufficient, even in Paradise. By contrast, rain suffuses *Innocents Lost*, perhaps symbolizing how Stone's forced retirement as Paradise Police Chief puts him into purgatory. But he's soon back on the job in *Benefit of the Doubt*, where it rains on Jesse driving, just after his reinstatement early in the movie. It also rains midway through the movie, as Reggie, the adopted dog, first climbs onto Jesse's bed to tighten their bond and as Jesse's thinking improves on the latest murders. A little grace is his.

Not exactly in a nutshell, that's how the Stone movies are popular noir. Still my account omits many telling details of the Stone movies and of neo noir as a popular genre. Eight movies or television shows are inclined to contain multitudes of interpretable particulars, many packed with implications of genre and therefore politics. Any popular genre of cinema or television soon includes hundreds of works, many with twists for the genre's conventions. This does not mean that most viewers recognize any interest in most of the conventions, let alone their political connections. But watching popular cinema and television for personal enjoyment involves making decent sense of them; and that depends on using genre conventions to spot and understand what's happening with whom, when, where, how, and why.[33] Politics are readily available at these levels of myth, which is to say, story and symbolism.[34] In this way, people can and do learn lots of political patterns, principles, expectations, and explanations.[35]

Epic

Already we've started to see how the Paradise movies are epic and how that ties to television, but it's time to be more systematic about it.[36] When writing develops, oral stories start becoming literature.[37] (*Myth* is from the ancient Greek for a *story uttered by the mouth*.[38]) Most of the earliest myths that endure are the epics or sagas of gods, heroes, and humans that say who we are, whence we've come, and sometimes where we're going. Early epics of the West include *The Iliad, The Odyssey, The Aeneid, The Bible, The Song of Roland, The Poetic Edda, The Prose Edda, Le Morte D'Arthur*, and many more. Epic is arguably the first literary form in Western civilization and some other civilizations too. Thus epic is a (maybe *the*) major source of all later literary forms in the West. If Shakespeare's *Hamlet* is the Ur plot for neo noir as a popular genre, epic might be the Ur literature for all popular genres. But a literary form need not begin as a popular genre nor become one. Even in literature, no popular genre is more than a few centuries old. So *Hamlet* antedates all noir, and classic noir precedes the gradual conventionalization of neo noir into a popular genre. Likewise early epics long predate the emergence of epic as a popular genre. Still the popular genre of epic existed for the earliest moviemakers, who foregrounded it—let alone the earliest television producers, who didn't.

All this probably reinforces an initial impression that any link of "epic" to the Paradise movies is likely to be distant, weak, or misleading. In ordinary talk, after all, *epic* is apt these days to mean *spectacular* and *portentous*: *bigger than big* in whatever ways matter most. With movies and events, *epic* calls to mind a cast of thousands making world history. The Paradise series is none of that. Like most American television, its scope is modest, its cast is concise, and its subjects seem to stop well short of world-historical. Even so, the Paradise movies participate amply in the conventions of epic as a popular genre. Epic conventions arise from setting the movies in Paradise, plotting them as Quixote Quests, and suiting the series to American TV.

As a genre, epic is especially prominent and popular in recent films from Hollywood. At least seven epics débuted in 2012: *Cloud Atlas*, *Django Unchained*, *Les Misèrables*, *Life of Pi*, and *Lincoln*, plus initial episodes of *The Hobbit* and *The Hunger Games*. All seem categorically more daring, showy, and momentous than the Paradise movies. Yet all join the Paradise series in featuring many conventions of epic as a popular genre. Likely the grandest epic among the series current on American TV is HBO's *Games of Thrones* (2011–).[39] Again its popular conventions of epic surface with surprising prominence and power when we take a further look at the Paradise movies. As a result, more obvious epics share much political mythmaking with the Paradise series. Together they can teach us about the present and practical relevance of epic politics to ordinary people in their everyday lives. May we say in consequence that political theorists have epic reasons to analyze episodic series on television?

Epic Conventions of Setting

Epic conventions in the Paradise series start with its setting. As the movies construct it, the setting of Paradise, MA plainly lacks the grand scale conventional for epics. In Western civilization, though, paradise is epic in character and significance, whatever the scale. This holds from the holy books of monotheisms in the beginning, to canonical visions of Dante and Milton in the middle, to our popular cultures in the present. The Paradise novels treat Stone's new home as his little piece of heaven in principle or potential, then they develop the idea in concept and dialogue. The Paradise movies do the same while adding epic tropes of editing and cinematography. As a popular genre, epic features **settings that ache with beauty or plenty, deprivation or devastation, fresh starts or thrilling consummations**, and so on. In cleverly contained ways, the Paradise series attends to this set of conventions in every movie.

Many of the exterior establishing shots in the Paradise series overflow with beauty. The editing often sustains them in order to steep viewers in the visual pleasures of the town, with its quaint streets, the neighboring shores and waters, the spectacular sunsets, the autumns of New England, and the like. For the camera, all this *is* Paradise. Film epics are generally vivid in cinematography, with **sweeping vistas** and **fully or overly saturated colors**. Paradise vistas are seldom vast, save for the ocean. But it's the community and the intimacy of Paradise, not the horizons, that are to be epic for Stone. Moreover the Paradise colors and exteriors are exceptionally vivid and idyllic for network television in the United States. These departures from neo noir are striking, because most Paradise images contrast categorically with the gritty or garish realism generic for noir. The catch here is that some directors do experiment with strongly saturated colors as neo-noir codes for their movies. Tony Scott showed keen interest in such cinematography for neo noir—along with hand-cranked cameras, jazzy editing, and even playful labels on the screen. Partly as a result, Scott's *True Romance* (1993), *Spy Game, Man on Fire, Domino*, and *Déjà Vu* make for a terrific run of neo-noir films. But the Paradise scenery and colors clearly stay epic because they do not link at all to neo-noir experiments in camera movement, editing, or computer processing of footage after it's shot.

Another neo noir noted for strident colors is *Blue Velvet* (1986). It comes to mind all the more because it's notorious for finding noir in small-town, increasingly exurban realms of motley houses with tidy yards and a white picket fence or two. 'Twas nasty in *Blue Velvet* to discover noir in such a setting, notwithstanding the purity and power of the colors. In 1999, *American Beauty* and *The Matrix* both took noir suburban, the first literally though not the second, but they have left Middle America ripe for noir ever since. Noir did begin in and about the Big City.[40] Our new century knows noir in many settings, however, making it ready for Paradise—not only as a bedroom and vacation community, but especially as a site for epic. Classic noirs occasionally complement the Big City with an exotic hinterland, like Mexico in *Touch of Evil* (1958 and 1998), the Orson Welles effort later returned to his editing intentions for rerelease. Nonetheless it's useful to recognize in neo noirs a more sustained interest in the politics of corrupt systems outside big-city settings.

The Paradise series loves opening and other long gazes at the natural beauties of the coastal setting in Massachusetts. It dwells on sunrise and sunset silhouettes of Stone's house near the shore. It prizes the small town's motley palette of colors posed against bright skies. It thrills to rainstorms gathering themselves, thumping down on inlets and trees and streets, then sweeping out to sea. For all the corruptions in it, noirs have throbbed to scenes of cities being built and undone by their own machinations; and this fits the constructivist politics of films determined to parse and punish the ambitions of would-be builders who lack the sense or skill to master urban(e) ways. Neo noirs often teach needs for better, fuller constructivism. But popular epics find counters to such corruptions in natural virtues of the kinds that loom large in Aristotelian philosophy and republican politics.[41] Then these epics find them in the "nature" that humans have distinguished from themselves and located outside the big city. The Paradise movies (unlike the novels) connect this sort of **naturalism** to an outdoorsy type of **environmentalism** that shows Stone enjoying the scenery and protecting the idyllic beauty of Paradise as little more than a quaint, somewhat wealthy village on the sea.

To explore corrupt systems in an epic, idyllic, or at least **idealized community** is not unprecedented or sharply surprising for generic noir. Ironically, if not sarcastically, we might say that even the top cops and crime bosses collaborate constructively in Paradise. Is this what makes it so? Lou Carson's collaboration with Hasty Hathaway is corrupt outright, to be sure. But we should not miss that Carson seems to have done a fairly good job of policing Paradise, save for turning a profitably blind eye toward the various crimes for money by Hathaway. Stone's policing reveals that Paradise keeps most of its organized crime visible only at arm's length, in Boston. The inference worth considering is that the best, or at least the most pleasant, settings available to us merely keep most of their corruption out of sight. From Hathaway's standpoint, the advantage is that out of sight is out of mind, which can make crime a comfortable (if limited) business in Paradise. From Stone's viewpoint, the advantage is that the location and focus of Gino Fish in Boston, rather than Paradise, lets those two men work out a cordial (if wary) cooperation that holds through the seventh movie. Fish helps Stone solve and even prevent crimes in Paradise. This makes policing about as good as it can get for Stone, for he knows with Fish and Hathaway that no place—no matter how good—stays long without crime that can become severe.

Presumably, superior policing will out, however, with Stone discerning by the middle of the eighth show that Paradise's own Hathaway is actually the area's top crime boss. Then Hathaway escapes Stone at the end of the eighth episode. There goes that noir ambiguity again, even in the midst of Paradise! Like Sidney Greenstreet of Internal Affairs for the Boston Police, we also do well to notice the noir fact that killings skyrocket with Stone in Paradise. Hard-boiled detectives in literary series operate in specific, often recurring locales. Often those detectives use their local knowledge to detect crimes and combat criminals. This makes detectives and their locales almost one. These detectives mostly stay put, save for occasional novels about them as fish out of water; and booksellers index the resulting book series not only by author and detective names but also by the detection places. Other hard-boiled detectives take jobs throughout the country or around the world. Then each crime investigation just is a setting investigation: it is how detectives and readers learn a lot about what holds together a place (city, culture, institution, etc.) or practice (banking, building, bookmaking, etc.)—and makes it tick. The first kind of investigator knows the place and tries to improve it by intervening to disrupt its crimes. The second kind learns the place by intervening to disrupt its crimes, and he might or might not learn it to be a setting he could or should try to improve. Can either kind of noir policing make Paradise better or even leave it as good, that is, as Paradise?

Stone and his setting seem skillfully constructed to split the difference between these two templates of hard-boiled detection, just as Stone and his new home seem clearly intended to interrogate the easy opposition between noir and paradise. In Georg Simmel's sense, as the one who comes to stay, Stone is truly a "stranger in Paradise."[42] The Stone questions are how he changes Paradise in the process, or doesn't, and how it changes him—or not. Does Stone bring noir to Paradise, or was it (always?) already there for him to find? Does Stone disrupt the patriarchal crimes he investigates in Paradise, and start to undo the perverse system of gender oppression and exploitation that seems to have defined Paradise from the beginning; or does Stone reinforce the Paradise patriarchy by policing only some of its worst excesses? Feminist critics of Christianity might see the Stone movies (even more than the novels) as watching a recovering patriarch stumble into the Garden of Eden, only to face some of the most brutal origins and products of the very sexism he has started to undo in himself.[43] Can he undo that corrupt system in Paradise and himself at the same time? Will he succumb to his situation and learn to fit right in? Or will he merely smooth the sharpest edges of patriarchy in his setting and himself? Well...what moves does epic as a genre encourage him to make?

Epic Conventions of Action

By convention, generic epics feature **warrior politics.**[44] The genre typically configures these as the nomadic politics of warlords and their tribal conclaves, or it civilizes them as the imperial politics of great kings and their courts.[45] Most often, however, epics make these into platforms for the heroic politics of liberating incipient peoples from corrupt tyrants. All three routes lead epics into the politics of **defining communities.** By genre, epics focus accordingly on community founders, destinies, exemplary deeds and heroes, crucial virtues and vices, plus dynamics of oppression and exploitation on the one side as well as liberation or at least resistance on the other side. As this hints, the politics of taking sides also loom large in epics.

The conventional scenes of action associated with these epic politics are legion in the Paradise movies. To spot and interpret them, however, we need to trace the twists in each convention that translate it from settings with literal warlords, emperors, and liberators to their epic equivalents in a Paradise specified instead by a town council, a police department, a high school, a car dealership, a bank, a marina, the nearby metropolis of Boston, and so on. Many of the translations are fairly easy. The **assassinations, ambushes, and battles** familiar from epics become the shootings that warn, wound, and kill in Paradise, where some happen in every episode. Yes, gun battles with at least two on a side might be closer equivalents to wars against thousands of enemy combatants, especially if political implications depend on strategic or tactical deployment of multiple fighters on each side. And admittedly, there are few gun "battles" in Paradise. (Again that's part of how it *is* Paradise.) Yet much of what other epics do politically with battles in war is still done with shootings in the Paradise series. Many a generic epic puts its hero into a (premodern) single combat, a (modern) duel, or a (postmodern) face-off; and the Paradise shootings often seem straightforward instances of those variants of the epic convention of armed assaults or other struggles to the death.

Scenes of **enemy deception**—to show the "good guys" misdirecting the "bad guys" or vice versa—need even less adjustment from wars and courts to crimes and town councils. In the Paradise series, there are several handfuls of such scenes. But it might be telling that they almost exclusively present Stone and other police contriving the deception of criminals rather than the other way around. For the most part, the Paradise episodes plot and present action from police perspectives. Thus police and viewers alike learn of deception by criminals more from inferences than observations. The only Paradise movie that shows us criminals as they plan and conduct their crimes is *Stone Cold*. In Paradise, apparently, the sources of crime are so mundane and familiar—greed, favoritism, and patriarchy, for example—that they are easy to infer. The boredom and caprice of the Lincolns in *Stone Cold* might need to be seen directly to be believed, because these motives seem perverse beyond what could be included in a humanly achievable paradise. (In fact, the Lincolns are merely seasonal residents of Paradise, and soon to be moving on.) Or maybe at most a town that claims the name of Paradise can keep everyday sins offstage.

Prophecies are a staple of epics, whereas they are unusual in crime shows. Neo noirs do use a range of fateful devices to foreshadow doom for their protagonists, but noir senses of realism seldom make room for acts of clairvoyance. Without being mystical about it, Paradise movies treat "coply intuition," guesses, hunches, even predictions in ways akin to prophecies. These come principally from Stone and Simpson but occasionally from others. Even though Stone is gently ironic about his own foresight and Simpson's, while Healy openly ribs Stone about his vaguely oracular pronouncements, the plots mostly fulfill these prognostications. The epic convention is to make good on prophecies—yet to do so in punning or other ways that frustrate ill-conceived but concerted attempts to prevent them from coming to pass. Even that aspect of prophecy holds in the Stone movies. In *Thin Ice*, the mother of a newborn abducted long ago from Arizona comes to Massachusetts seeking police help to track her child. Listening to the mother, Gammon is sure in her bones that the nationally famous "Baby Blue" has gone to Paradise.

After brain trauma in an earlier episode, Simpson preternaturally "knows" that the child has died. In an epic mode, both of these "prophecies" prove right, and in several senses.

Speaking of **listening**, it's another scene standard for epics. Their generic wisdom is that listening carefully to others—in the sense of paying close attention to their ideas, logics, and motives—is a skill and thus a mark of the astute leadership that a community requires. The first episode in the second season for *Game of Thrones* virtually starts with young Bran Stark (Isaac Hempstead Wright) being taught by his aged advisor why and how to listen to others. This is not an interrogation that pressures somebody reluctant to be truthful or forthcoming. Interrogation is a stock scene for police procedurals and hard-boiled detections but not epics. When Stone grills a football player about a rape, we witness a scene of interrogation, not listening. But when Stone invites police and visitors into his office to talk with him, we see scenes of listening; and there are one or two important examples in just about every episode. It's suggestive that Niccolò Machiavelli's primer for realism in politics analyzes listening—in addressing advisors. Yet the nicely updated rules for realist success in politics formulated by Christopher Matthews neglect listening.[46] Epics know better. And it's telling that, as the host for many years of national television talk shows, Matthews is not exactly renowned for his listening.

A **conference** is a further convention of epics. It involves antagonists talking directly to each other on behalf of their communities, and its overt ambition is a deal to stop bloodshed or other loss by arranging some kind of cooperation. Of course, a conference can be a ruse to cover a different agenda; yet epics treat conferences as important preliminaries, interludes, or conclusions for epic struggles. Such a conference could be a (premodern) parley, a (modern) negotiation, or a (postmodern) facing. A conference is an occasion for listening, yet an epic conference can include many additional dynamics of politics familiar to courtiers and realists. When Gino Fish appears as system boss, Stone confers with him, although they also meet at other times for one side simply to inform or question the other, without attention to a new bargain. As noted in considering the Stone movies as noir, politics in Paradise don't avoid shooting or even murder; but they do feature moral, constructive cooperation between the police chief and a nearby crime boss. From the realist perspective of noir on Paradise as an ideal community, police and criminals can collaborate to limit crime in severity and perversity, but not eliminate it: after all, humans live there.

Community is the political preoccupation of epic, and communication is the gist of community.[47] To scenes of listening and conferring, epics add **speeches to rally communities** for great efforts. As William Wallace in

Braveheart (1995), Mel Gibson appeals passionately to fight for Scotland. As US president in *Independence Day* (1996), Bill Pullman makes a ringing call to defend humanity from alien invasion. Without girding for war, can a police chief rally his town or even his officers? Even in Paradise? None of the Paradise movies is the kind of thriller that assaults an entire town or otherwise puts its survival at stake. Yet it's at least arguable that Stone spurs rallies more modest in size and emotion. Does he? Not exactly...but sort of...well, it's hard to say. True, Stone never talks to Paradise as a whole. Still he does rally other members of his police community with effective words of pep and support. These go to one and two officers at a time. So if we see these as twists on epic addresses, we see his police colleagues as emblems of the larger community of Paradise. It's debatable whether to do this.

Less iffy are some connected scenes that cut two ways at once in conventional epics. Scenes that demonstrate **pecking orders** and scenes that turn on **paying tribute** both show power dynamics of warrior politics that connect them to courtly styles of personal conduct.[48] Epics use pecking-order and paying-tribute scenes to specify who asserts and who accepts what claims of obedience, deference, and respect by whom. Accordingly they also use these scenes to spotlight who rejects or deflects such claims, how, and to what effect. Both sorts of scenes are prominent throughout the Paradise movies. These use pecking-order scenes to show how Stone understands Paradise government and society in particular as well as patriarchal order in general. He is selective but not grudging in obedience, deference, and respect. He is not, in other words, the kind of "maverick hero" beloved for half a century in American movies for spurning rules and hierarchies.[49] Stone heeds and even defends some authorities, he is clever about circumventing orders from others, and he openly defies a few. Seldom, though, does Stone pay tribute to anybody about anything. This contrast in how Stone treats these closely related conventions of epic politics suggests that Paradise is a place with power and authority—but also a place where everybody is due (and should insist on) the fundamental respect and functional independence that strongly limits deference, let alone rank obedience.

In epics, scenes of **celebration** or **commemoration** conventionally become emblems of the specific communities at issue. These scenes are sometimes rites and sometimes syzygies, but the syzygies are seldom sinister in the noir sense. The rites (with practiced repetition) and the syzygies (with surprising fortuity) gather nearly the whole community in ways that testify to its virtue and vitality. Epic rites include weddings, feasts, festivals, funerals, parades, and parties. The opening wedding in *The Godfather* (1972) and the closing wedding in *The Return of the King* (2003) work thus, as do the ceremonial coda for *Star Wars* (1977) and the ghostly coda for *Titanic* (1997).

Furthermore the ending feast for *Return of the Jedi* (1983) includes the dead as well as the living. Epic syzygies are more miscellaneous. *O Brother, Where Art Thou?* (2000) pivots on a campaign dinner that just happens to have the whole company of players crossing paths at a crucial moment in the film. *Places in the Heart* (1984) shows a long string of emblematic moments in a Southern community's struggle through the Great Depression; then it culminates in a church service where a camera slowly scans the pews to show again all the community's people, living and dead, as its places in the heart. The final episode of *Scrubs* (2001–2010) shows the focal Dr. Dorian (Zach Braff) walking down a corridor to leave the hospital as he sees (one after another, on both sides) virtually every person (living and dead) who has crossed his path during that long television series.[50] *Love Actually* (2003) opens and closes with scenes at Heathrow Airport, where the film's myriad lovers converge accidentally and momentarily—unknowing the first time but greatly heartened the second.

The Paradise movies show no regular conclaves of police, as with the beloved opening roll call in episodes of *Hill Street Blues* (1981–1987). Nor do they show any ritual or syzygous gatherings for the town. Instead they rely on irregular gatherings of Jesse with two or three others in his band of police. Sometimes these are unplanned, with the Paradise police converging on crime scenes. Often, though, they're scheduled in advance—with Simpson or (once) Stone bringing donuts to sites that shift throughout Paradise rather than favoring the police station. Do these amount to a movable feast? They seem to split the difference between rites and syzygies, and this could be seen as another case of noir sensibilities inflecting epic alternatives in politics.

Might splitting the difference between epic conventions emerge as a winning strategy for noir in Paradise? In scheduling and subject, the police meetings in Paradise respond for the most part to developments that threaten the integrity of the Stone-led band of police. The donuts mark these gatherings as celebrations of this small community, seemingly emblematic (especially for Jesse) of Paradise as a whole. Yet these are working sessions as well—reaching beyond merest affirmations of the community toward further actions that seek to save and advance it. That turns out to be equally true of rites and syzygies that grace many other epics. Important projects launch from the weddings in *The Godfather* and *The Lord of the Rings*. The syzygies in *Love Actually* spark then fan many of its romances.

If we ask what plot seems most epic, the answer is the **quest**. In an epic quest, a hero seeks something of great significance to himself and his community, surmounts great troubles to attain it, learns along the way that its meaning is other and greater than has been thought, then graces his community with both the attainment and the learning. In *Gladiator* (2000), General Maximus Decimus Meridius (Russell Crowe) gets stripped of his calling, his family, his freedom, his fortune, and his health. He is laid low as a slave in Africa, forced to fight as a gladiator merely to live another day. Eventually he quests for revenge against the corrupt emperor of Rome who engineered this. Surviving many battles, temptations, and treacheries, he learns that defeat of the emperor can defeat the empire and restore the Roman Republic. Maximus kills the emperor but dies from a poisoned blade, reuniting him in the Elysian Fields with his family, and ridding Rome of his charisma as an obstacle to re-forming the republic.

Along our way, we have learned that each of the Paradise movies, like the series as a whole, is plotted as a Quixote Quest. This twists the epic convention to make the quester a fool who mistakes the obstacles or even the object of his quest. In some tales, he's a holy fool; in others, a damn one. In some dramas, he's benighted; in others, he's fortunate. And so on. (Numerous permutations of human folly are available to inflect an epic hero and his quest.) Hung up on Jenn, Stone is a fool for love; and this visibly warps his judgment in several movies. Maybe worse, Stone is fooled for far too long, far into the eighth movie, by Hasty Hathaway. Stone's overarching objects are to defeat organized crime and undo violent patriarchy. Yet he misconceives Leo Finn then Gino Fish as the area crime boss, and his noir sensibility misses that organized crime is centered under his nose in Paradise rather than in the big city of Boston. As a neo-noir fool for the love of a spider woman, Stone even misjudges in many cases the momentum of patriarchal oppression, exploitation, and violence. He sends many "messages" to deter patriarchs from further violence; but most of his threats, beatings, and investigations work only too late or too little. On the other hand, Stone helps undo several patriarchs and punish others, to protect many women. Eventually he even chases away Hasty Hathaway.

The Quixote Quest is peculiar as a conventional plot, because it participates more or less equally in epic and neo noir. It's another way for Stone in Paradise to split the difference between counterposed conventions of epic and noir as popular genres. Outside noir, though, the Quixote character is genuinely heroic, if quirky or misguided. He is flawed in judgment, and the flaws can even be fatal for the Quixote figure. (Hence we might wonder whether to recognize as a fool the hero of ancient Greek tragedy, whose signal excellence is also his fatal defect.) Nevertheless an epic Quixote is pure of heart and noble in character, whereas a neo-noir protagonist is mixed in motives and morals as well as performance. Whatever Stone has become for a while in LA, where he seems to have fallen pretty far from morally admirable or even professionally competent, he climbs slowly, laboriously back toward some heroism in Paradise. The movies show him hitting at least a couple of kinds of bottoms in *Night Passage*, when he seems to consider suicide in Santa Monica, then drinks himself stupid for the job interview in Massachusetts. From his hiring onward, however, Stone gets better in almost every way, albeit raggedly and with relapses. As the name has promised, Paradise proves good for Stone. By the end of the eighth movie, he's still far short of newspaper—let alone epic—heroism. But he's getting better than your average protagonist, at least in neo noir.

Epic Conventions of Character

By this point, we're well into analyzing Stone in Paradise as the Quixote character in epic. Generic epic includes other families of conventional acts, plots, settings, and characters. But from here, the shortest road home is to stick with the Cervantes template, since it seems the best epic fit to Stone in Paradise. By noir inflection, Stone is not only an idealistic fool but also an alcoholic, an obsessive, and a violent vigilante. Yet the Quixote figure still suits him. The Paradise movies *are* made for American television, after all, and their star *is* Tom Selleck. While we might get the fateful feeling that Stone is bound to fail in some important ways, we don't really feel that he'll die a failure, much less in the movie of the moment. 'Tis television too, and not epic or paradise alone, that helps Stone split the difference between a noble hero and a benighted protagonist. In epic terms, Stone is a **lonely, foolish champion of justice**.

Epic threats are not mere dangers, and epic villains are not just opponents. Typically epic **enemies** of the hero and his community are mortal sins personified; often they are social atrocities and political travesties naturalized into storms, swamps, pests, plagues, quakes, deserts, droughts, or other relentless troubles; sometimes they are community dooms made literally monstrous. Quixote is infamous for tilting at windmills that he mistakes for enemy knights, marauding giants, and menacing monsters. For this and his romancing of a mostly imaginary woman, we think him insane: no longer in the most minimal touch with practical realities. With admiration as well as sympathy and impatience, Panza shares this sense of Quixote for most of the saga, only to lapse into insanity himself toward his epic's end. Because Quixote fights for classical virtues, however, we should pause to recognize that windmills were a leading edge of the modern industry that continues to eclipse classical cultures almost the world over. In his own folly, Stone mistakes some of the system minions for crime bosses, and he alienates town councilors one after another. Still we should pause to note that his campaign for justice manages along the way to help avenge, protect, or even liberate quite a few women in Paradise and Boston. Maybe Jesse is better attuned than we might suppose to the more insidious monsters around.

Cervantes has Don Quixote speak of the main female figure in his quests as Dulcinea. As his **idealized love**, she is his radically romanticized vision of a local peasant girl, who has a different name and character than he imagines for her. Quixote does not know or speak to her, and he glimpses her only in passing. She stays almost entirely offstage in the novel, but she is still the shining star of his adventures. According to Quixote's sidekick, "Dulcinea" is in fact a tall, strong, loud, and lusty woman, with a lively, slashing sense of humor. The Paradise movies (even more than the novels) likewise keep Jenn offstage. From what we hear of the phone conversations between Jenn and Jesse, his noirish knowledge of her human flaws and betrayals coexists with his idealizing love of her feminine beauties, needs, and possibilities. Like Dulcinea to Quixote, Jenn's actual talents and ambitions probably seem more assertive and masculine than the residually macho imagination of Stone can readily face. As a spider woman, Jenn does focus at times on manipulating Jesse, whereas Dulcinea attends not at all to Quixote. On the other hand, Dulcinea inhabits an ironical epic only, whereas Jenn is a neonoir character as well.

Jenn can manipulate Jesse in important part because he wants to see her as an epic **Damsel in Distress**. Then Jesse can become the **St. George** who rescues her from the **Dragon**. Jenn, too, likes this fantasy, up to the point when it impinges on her autonomy, aka power. Quixote also seems drawn in the abstract to such epic possibilities, although the real woman at the edges of his stories does nothing we know to lure his imagination in these directions. In Paradise, Jesse stays attracted to treating Jenn that way, as long as their geographical and professional gap keeps him just talking about it rather than acting on it. (The novels differ, bringing Jenn all too soon to Boston.) As we meet him in the movies, Jesse is trying to leave his St. George aspiration behind with Jenn in LA. In Paradise, he takes care to pick women who've known the distress of divorce but who've come through it with flying colors. Abby Taylor, Sidney Greenstreet, and Thelma Gleffey seem to be successful, self-sufficient females.

It's possible to read Parker's novels about Stone as a psychosexual exploration of the hard-boiled detective. Jesse's principal defect is said to be how "obsessive" he is about Jenn, and the movie's psychiatrist implies that Stone is unduly possessive of her. Even though the books endorse monogamy from male and female perspectives where marriage is concerned, they also insist on adult sexual freedom outside marriage. Moreover they seem to insist on adult psychological freedom—from obsession and possession—inside marriage. The novels leave this principle carefully poised between patriarchal wish-fulfillment and an incipiently feminist exploration of how women want the independence and respect that Jesse struggles to give Jenn. According to the novels, Stone is remarkably tough but also sentimental; and he's loved for both. The movies show the same, yet they feature Stone as a vigilante foe of the most obnoxious operations of patriarchy. This aspect of Stone is available in the Parker novels, but their keener interest in friendly and recreational sex for men and women leaves them seeming more macho. Therefore the movies arguably go beyond the Parker novels in developing some elements in the Paradise politics of female (not just sexual) liberation.

Once Quixote slides into divine folly and turns to questing, Sancho Panza becomes his squire and **sidekick**. Readers love Panza for his practical outlook, his earthy sense of humor, his debunking commentary on Quixote's deeds and ideas, yet his staunch loyalty to the noble but deluded knight. Panza is well into adulthood when he enters Quixote's service, and Panza sustains a full family life of his own to counterbalance Quixote's questing. In all these respects, he's the model for the police officers who work—usually three at a time—with Chief Stone in Paradise. They stay in better, more practical and realistic, touch with the town and its council than does Stone. Like Panza in la Mancha, Crane, Gammon, and Simpson, if not exactly D'Angelo, are clever and fast learners. Moreover their priorities are mostly in the right places. But like Quixote, Stone is the knight, the one who knows most about quests and adventures.

By convention, the neo-noir protagonist is notoriously a *lone* knight of justice. In epic improvement on that desperate condition, Paradise gives Jesse Stone a mentor, partners, even a "sister." All these figures join Jesse on (some of) his quests for justice and women's liberation. Hence they act in important respects as epic sidekicks. All these figures are somewhat ironic in outlook and wry in speech, even as they admire and share aspects of Jesse's idealism. Notwithstanding their many individual differences, which make for more enjoyable TV, they seem individually and collectively modeled on Panza. They are epic but earthly (and earthy) companions and helpers for the hero, with every potential star in the firmament of community memory likely to need them, especially insofar as he is a fool. What's fascinating is that neo noir, too, has lately branched out to conventionalize mentors, partners, even sisters. It's been doing so as it forms such hybrids as superhero noir (or super noir, for short) and martial-arts noir (or eastern noir, for short, from comparing martial-arts films to westerns). In light of the feminist (or at least anti-patriarchal) politics that emerge in the Paradise series, it's particularly telling that all three of these kinds of characters are important to recent experiments in feminist noir.

As epic coalesces into a popular genre, Carl Jung's archetype of the Wise Old Man becomes its conventional character of the **mentor**.[51] Think of Ben "Obi-wan" Kenobi (Alec Guinness) and Yoda (Frank Oz) as mentors for Luke Skywalker (Mark Hamill) in *Star Wars*, Old Ptolemy (Anthony Hopkins) as mentor for the title character played by Colin Farrell in Oliver Stone's *Alexander* (2004), or Dr. King Schultz (Christoph Waltz) as mentor for the title figure played by Jamie Foxx in *Django Unchained*. In Paradise, Stone's mentor becomes Dr. Dix. Not only is Dix a Wise Old Man who serves Stone personally as psychiatrist, but Dix is a former cop who mentors Stone professionally in police procedure and crime psychology. As mentor, Dix is sometimes a sounding board to help Stone think through his own ideas. At other times, Dix answers questions or even volunteers suggestions about particular cases. It seems easier for Stone to accept mentoring from Dix because Stone himself mentors Officers Simpson and Gammon.

A **partner** or more emerges from the sidekick when popular epics engage democracies. A mentor is a senior disciplinarian who drills the potential hero in epic virtuosities. Then the mentor advises the pupil after he's graduated from training adventures to full-fledged quests. A partner is a colleague who shares actively in some of those quests. To the Paradise Police, Stone adds further partners: Captain Healy of the State Police, Detective Greenstreet of the Boston Police, and Dr. Peter Perkins (John Beale) as the medical examiner for Paradise, which he continues to serve as a pediatrician. In epic as a popular genre, quests are not just for lonely heroes anymore; quests are for **bands of adventurers** too. And in epic noirs such as the Stone movies, the help makes the quests more successful than outcomes for other kinds of neo noirs.

With their defeat or doom amply foreshadowed, and with corrupt systems closing in on them, the best that noir protagonists often can do is resist with some virtuosity and leave the rest of us with their cautionary tales. Classic noirs are notorious downers, their endings seldom light. Less than half of neo noirs since 1980 have happy endings of escape, meaning, or liberation; and some 40 percent of these upbeat conclusions trace directly to ways that superpowers in super noirs, super-technologies in sci-fi noirs, or even magic in fantasy noirs enable neo-noir protagonists to elude realistic likelihoods of doom readied throughout their movies. Yet feminists noirs, which feature female protagonists to undo the misogyny conventional for classic and neo noirs, manage happy endings more than three-fourths of the time. Implicated in this stunning reversal of fortunes is the support typically available to female champions for justice. More than half have male mentors or partners to help the lead females, and fully half have a **sister** who doubles the female lead to enable feminist strategies of "sisterhood."[52]

All these function in part as extra unto superpowers or epic helpers for neo-noir's female protagonists, who remain relatively few—but numerous enough define a new hybrid or subgenre of neo noir.

In Stone, the Paradise series has a male protagonist; but he's working through therapy and policing to undo his own and his society's dynamics of patriarchy. In Paradise, noir can overcome its misogyny; or at least, that is the epic hope of the Stone movies. They provide a striking, amusingly over-the-top kick in this direction by giving Jesse something of a feminist "sister." Like Stone, she particularly defends young women from ravages of patriarchy; and she doubles his efforts in a different orbit that intersects his. Sister Mary John is a nun who runs a shelter for runaway, abused, and otherwise troubled girls. In four of the Paradise movies, she provides crucial help to Stone. In one, they even have something like a dinner date, suggesting strong mutual attractions. Yet Stone seems especially unsure what to make of this. Neither quite knows how or whether to proceed, while the movies encourage us viewers to chuckle gently and sympathetically at their perplexity. This subplot plays a bit like the "romance" between Luke Skywalker and Princess Leia (Carrie Fisher) in *Star Wars*. Still the political lesson is that, in this epic Paradise, noir gets less lonely, bleak, and sexist.

A Coda on Television

Detailed attention to genre politics in the Jesse Stone series of television movies can tell us about politics that are important to comprehend yet hard to fathom in other ways. These are the politics of stories, symbols, and styles rather than ideologies, institutions, and policies. In their everyday lives, few people are strongly attuned to ideologies, institutions, or policies that they associate with governments and politics. By contrast, stories, symbols, and styles are the very stuff of everyday interaction, information, entertainment, and more. They are the cultures in which we swim as ordinary people, and they are thoroughly political. Stories are crucial to political memory and community, symbols to political meaning and reasoning, and styles to political identity and action. Stories, symbols, and styles readily lead and turn into each other; taken together, they comprise the cultural politics of myth and mythmaking. To study popular genres of novels, movies, musics, video games, and TV shows is come to terms with the myths by which we live and politick.[53] This is one good set of reasons to study the politics implicit in popular entertainment by "mass media."[54] Our popular cultures are where much of our political mythmaking proceeds.

When the focus falls instead on ideologies, institutions, or policies, it is less clear that analysis of popular entertainment in cinema or television can be highly helpful. Political ads and news are primary events for political ideologies, institutions, even policies: overtly and directly, we produce and receive ads and news as political acts of ideology, institution, and policy. Few other kinds of shows on television and films in theaters work that way. At best, they are secondary events for ideologies, institutions, or policies. Even when entertainments dramatize happenings in government institutions, the events are fictional, parasitic on what occurs in other arenas.

The question becomes why we should study fictions to understand realities. Why not focus directly and exclusively on the realities themselves? The supposition is that fictions are distortions: that they are bound (if not always designed) to mislead about realities. But even if we reject the premise, and we should, issues remain. Imagine that some writers, directors, producers, and such can make dramas that show at least a little of what we did not already know about political realities. Why not have the fictionalizers share their knowledge in facts and theories that tell it in terms as clear, direct, literal, evidenced, and truthful as possible? Yes, facts and theories might themselves be "fictions," by root meaning, because they must be "made or invented." But shouldn't theories at least learn as directly as they can from realities and facts—not indirectly from novels, movies, and television series? We who would improve theories of politics by analyzing dramas, musics, or narratives do well to confront these challenges.[55]

What advantage is there even in scrutinizing recent entertainments on Washington politics, such as *The West Wing* (1999–2006) or *Scandal* (2012–)?[56] If we want to learn about ideologies of liberals and conservatives, institutions like Congress and the Presidency, or policies for banking and health care, we could expect to do better by interviewing the likes of Aaron Sorkin, Shonda Rhimes, and Lawrence O'Donnell. Then we could go directly for their knowledge of ideologies, institutions, and policies; then their devices of dramatization could not distort or distract. When we concentrate on how people make and live political myths, however, we can see primary and important politics in the dramatization and its devices.

Theory and philosophy present ideas in argument; drama and story feature characters in action. Even when cinema, television, or other dramatic forms develop ideas and pursue arguments, as they sometimes do more expressly than others, their particulars and qualities come primarily from who does what, when, where, and why. Accordingly dramas do not merely reproduce any explanations of action that might inform them so much as test, twist, extend, or confound those logics. Interactions of characters to engage us can cohere in ways that exceed philosophies of their own dramatists, let alone theories of contemporary analysts. Hence political theorists can learn from fictional dramas and stories in ways that exceed their learning possible from scientific reports, factual histories, or participant testimonies about our political ideologies, government institutions, and public policies. By analyzing specific works and popular genres of cinema, television, or other entertainment, political theorists can learn directly about the political mythmaking that pervades the everyday lives of ordinary people.

But why television? Well...what's television? For purposes of political implications, especially, technologies alone do not take us far in defining media. Technologies alone are too plastic in their development and flexible in their use to determine all that much about media. To contrast cinema and television by screen size, storage technology, or projection device no longer can work as it did only a decade ago. Cultural forms matter for differentiating media, even though some cultural constructs—such as popular genres—cross many media. So here let's ask more specifically, if less comprehensively: Why focus on American televised dramas rather than the feature-length films from Hollywood? Or for related purposes: What politics come to the fore when we focus on Hollywood TV? In answering these questions, we should learn about the implicit politics that are especially significant in televised dramas, the reasons for that significance, and the possible contributions of these lessons to our theories of politics.[57]

As neo noir became a popular and prominent genre in American cinema, toward the end of the twentieth century, it still did not prosper in American television. It isn't especially difficult to do technically on television, but noir series remain rare. The idea here is that this recommends a neo-noir series for comparing political mythmaking in American television to Hollywood movies, and the CBS series of movies with Jesse Stone in Paradise seems suitable to compare with neo-noir films in English since 1980. So what do the comparison particulars suggest about political mythmaking in dramas on American TV?

A first inference is that American television resists realism as a philosophy and a style of politics. The Paradise series works energetically, self-consciously, and skillfully to blend its noir conventions with a contrary idealism implicit in epic conventions. The apparent scarcity of noir series on American television suggests that the medium includes an elective, cultural reluctance to pursue the genre's politics of either existentialism or realism. Yet American TV has lots of dramas focused on existentialist politics, including attention to social systems. So there's little doubt that the distaste is for sordid aesthetics, preemptive violence, whatever-it-takes morals, and routinely downbeat endings: in short, political realism.

Does the resistance to realism arise in important part from a penchant of American television for the politics of idealism? In the Paradise series, idealism seems a major dynamic in limiting the noir realism of Jesse Stone. The idealism comes from the series commitment to conventions of epic as well as noir. Do American TV dramas have some formal but elective affinity for epic conventions, thus epic politics, especially idealist politics?

Any noir is unusual in American television, but epic noir is rare even in Hollywood movies. Aside from the Stone series of movies for television, epic noir runs no higher than 2 percent of neo-noir films in English after 1980. My firm nominees would be only three: *Magnolia* (1999), *Crash*, and *All the King's Men* (2006). Of the noir hybrids I've noticed, epic noir is rivaled in rarity only by fantasy noir, which also seems conventionally inclined to leaven noir realism with strong doses of political idealism (table 4.3).

I should add that there is double-counting, for these hybrids overlap at least a little: *Edward Scissorhands* is horror noir and sci-fi noir, *Catwoman* (2004) is super noir and feminist noir, etc. The only noir hybrids that offset their noir affinity for realist politics with a second affinity for idealist politics are epic noir and fantasy noir. This, too, is decent—not conclusive—evidence that American TV dramas have cultural inclinations toward political idealism, probably in important part through elective dispositions toward epic form.

Another reason to think these links likely is a strong formal connection between epics and episodes. 'Tis a tie of time. A phrase like "epic time" brings to mind epochs, even eons; it evokes origins and destinies, beginnings and ends; thus it connotes founding, foundering, collapse, or apocalypse. In time, too, epics are somehow vast and momentous. Yet the how is sometimes surprising, because the temporal units of epics can be small and intimate. These units are episodes. An episode is a component occurrence that stands mostly as an emblem of the entire, encompassing, typically epic complex of events. It is not mainly a chronological step meaningful for getting us from

Table 4.3   Noir hybrids

Noir hybrid	*Portion of neo noir*
Epic noir	1–2%
Fantasy noir	1–2%
Gangster noir	2–3%
Martial-arts noir	2–4%
Spy noir	2–3%
Horror noir	7–10%
Sci-fi noir	10–13%
Super noir	13–16%
Feminist noir	12–15%

the previous step to the next one in a longer march from start to finish: that's for history instead. Early epics tell of communities and their heroes in a string of stories, each tale complete in itself but sharing some characters, settings, or concerns with some other tales in the series. Conflicting particulars across the component tales keep them from an order that can be strictly chronological. The motley narratives of an early epic find a close equivalent in the episodes of a generic epic, which can be enjoyed one after another but out of any originally presented order because each is a decent microcosm of the whole series.

In American television, most programs (even news, I'd argue) are primarily episodic. This is to say that the seriality of American television is not historical in the Darwinian sense of one brief instant after another, with larger patterns appearing only in retrospect. From *Hill Street Blues* onward, many TV series in the United States have featured story arcs longer than an episode, some as long as whole seasons of shows. Yet most of these series continue to include many one-off, stand-alone episodes; and most of these series continue to overlay the longer narratives onto shows still viewable as independent episodes.[58] *M*A*S*H* (1972–1983) fans can enjoy its shows rerun in almost any order, and *CSI* or *Law & Order* watchers have been able to dip intermittently but enjoyably into the several concurrent series run or rerun from those prosperous franchises, even though they typically rely in part on longer story arcs.

Instead the seriality of American television is historical in a Hegelian, teleological way. Seldom is this telos Aristotelian: viewable all along as developing in readily recognized stages from acorn to oak, with the end clear almost throughout. Hoping for long success over many seasons, not even showrunners for American television usually know in advance detail when or how their series are to end, let alone how get to there. Complications of commerce and production prevent Aristotelian teleology.[59] Each TV series in America tends rather to gain overall shape and potential as it proceeds, with its trajectory affected along the way by the viewer disposition to see individual shows and the longer dramatic arcs as emblems of an emergent whole formed by the full series. By a similar logic, political theorists already know where I'm going with this: Hegelian philosophy and politics are idealist, so even the familiar seriality of American TV gives advantages to idealism over realism and other political styles.

A scarcity of neo-noir series, a Hegelian kind of seriality, and a penchant for episodes all reveal cultivated inclinations of American television for idealist rather than realist politics. These TV dispositions to idealism arise in important part from a structural bias toward epic. TV times are subtly epic in preferring episodes and series. On top of that, TV characters are incipiently epic in favoring archetypes over individuals who develop realistically in historical and psychological terms. The claim is not that characters usual for American television fail to change at all across their shows or seasons; it is that they gradually reveal characteristics that stay consistent with their mythic templates rather than showing traits that change their types altogether. Rather than present personalities as trajectories of changes that transform major characters, American TV tends to keep focal characters within their kinds: its Gandalfs stay gray rather than sometimes turning white, whether abruptly or gradually, on-screen or off.[60]

Because Western civilization is teleological, the contrast between archetypal characters gradually detailed and historical characters realistically developed can be difficult to call in practice. Few viewers fail to see Marshal Matt Dillon (James Arness) in *Gunsmoke* (1955–1975) as an epic, archetypal hero. Like Chief Stone, Marshal Dillon is the strong, silent type made more approachable. But how should we view Al Swearengen (Ian McShane) in *Deadwood* (2004–2006)? The Western drive is to see unfolding consistency as oneness of character.[61] This discerns in retrospect how Al's acts and traits cohere as a ruthless but loyal man who adjusts to rapidly changing circumstances. Yet viewers in my circle of conversants more often see Swearengen as a man pushed by loyalty, illness, and opponents toward more cooperative politics than before, "growing" him from a ruthless villain into someone with redeeming virtues.[62]

Likewise the first three seasons of *The Killing* leave unclear, at least to me, whether Sarah Linden (Mireille Enos) is changing in character even as we watch or is merely revealing her complications to us through an exceptional string of twists and turns. Nor can I tell from those seasons whether *The Killing* is taunting us with repeated recontextualizations of slowly accumulating information about a secretive but enduring character in Stephen Holder (Joel Kinnaman). Instead it might be developing his character as a cop coming through crises of addiction, career, marriage, and maybe more that are remaking him. Don't forget, though, that *The Killing* is noir, inclining it toward realism in ways and degrees unusual for dramas on American television. In any event, the punch line is familiar. Some cases might be hard to classify, yet the overall proclivity of American TV for archetypal over historical characters is another of its affinities for epic, which more readily yields idealist than realist politics.

Note that Linden is not a *lone* knight of justice. She has a policing partner in Holden, although she doesn't always want him. Each episode in the Paradise series gives Stone three to five collaborators, and most of them repeat from one movie to the next. This helps satisfy an apparent American craving in the last half-century for regular casts of characters in TV comedies and dramas. Anthology series such as *Playhouse 90* (1956–1960), with different casts for disconnected productions from one week to the next, have been as rare as neo-noir series. Instead American TV loves small networks of friends; and in epic terms, these are bands of adventurers rather than lonely questers (even with sidekicks). They are how American TV can give us crabby, gabby, or needy leads more often than strong, silent, self-sufficient types. The stark reserve and objectivity of early epic heroes like Achilles is closer to the wry stoicism of hard-boiled detectives like Stone than to the bantering of bands of brothers and sisters on most American dramas of detecting, policing, litigating, doctoring, educating, and so on. Gangster series such as *The Sopranos* (1999–2007) and *Boardwalk Empire* (2010–) might resemble noirs in many other ways, but continuing gangs as regular casts of colorful characters who chat cleverly within the group give gangster shows a generic advantage on TV over neo noirs with lone champions of justice. Give a lone resister of corrupt systems a sidekick, and those two ease toward Quixote conventions and the epic politics of idealism. Give a lone resister of corruptions a team, and it morphs toward an epic band of adventurers on idealist quests.

One of the simplest truths about dramas on American television is that viewers prefer happy endings. It's one of the most powerful truths about dramas on American television, because it's a big part of what "everybody knows" in Hollywood.[63] This doesn't distinguish American television from American cinema, of course, because Hollywood also knows that its filmgoers prefer happy endings. Yet many genres popular in American movies rely more on endings that thrill, chill, outrage, terrify, ironize, or even help cleanse sadness by catharsis that has viewers wallowing for a while in grief and despair. Half the time and more, endings for neo-noir films are downers; and these have been doing well for Hollywood. But neo-noir TV with conventional endings has not. The ending of *Twin Peaks* is not so much depressing as weird, but it certainly isn't happy. The season resolutions for *The Killing* are coy, downbeat, and disappointing to many viewers. The *Sarah Connor Chronicles* are stuck from the start with a sad ending, in the sense that they lead into the grim conclusion for the third film in the *Terminator* series. So the TV series ends with an apocalypse to reframe the rest; and it lingers on an image at once mysterious, threatening, and thrilling. For that moment, the sensibility is much less neo noir than sci-fi-horror.

Notable are the television series that depart from noir even though they are inspired by successful neo-noir films.[64] *Blade* (2006) keeps the horror and hard-boiled detection of the original film (1998); but after its feature-length pilot, Spike's television version makes few gestures toward neo noir.[65] *La Femme Nikita* (1990) and *Point of No Return* (1993) blend cinematic noir with romance and the spy thriller; but USA's *La Femme Nikita* (1997–2001) usually settles for the last two, while CW's *Nikita* (2010–) likes neo-noir looks more than neo-noir sounds, stories, and characters.[66] Still it might be telling that neo noir adapted to American television favors femmes focales—my name for noir protagonists who are females—far more than does American cinema. Of the six television series noted in these last two paragraphs, only *Twin Peaks* features a male protagonist.[67] Even *Blade* used its pilot to introduce not only a new actor (Sticky Fingaz) for its title character but also Krista Starr (Jill Wagner) as a second day-walking vampire to serve sometimes as neo-noir protagonist (yet more as horror heroine and intervening detective). And as we've seen, the Paradise movies have Jesse Stone as their male protagonist pursue insistently, if modestly, feminist politics.

Especially of late, horror has been doing much better than noir on American television. Horror films from Hollywood are rampant; they've prospered and proliferated for decades. Some of these play with happy resolutions, yet their codas typically hint that the monsters stir anew. Otherwise resolutions for horror movies in recent decades are mostly, emphatically "unhappy." Does this undercut the diagnosis that noir is too depressing for American television? Not exactly, for television horror often ends upbeat, however briefly. Even when it doesn't, it seems arguable that American television viewers find dark-and-scary better than bleak-and-depressing. One way or another, though, the conventional wisdom about happy endings dominating American TV seems to have at least some merit. Even news shows tend to end with upbeat items of "human interest."

Let's end this essay into noir in Paradise by asking what the conventional demand or expectation for happy endings might mean for the politics we can learn from American TV. And let's notice that happy endings, as Americans see them, need not promote idealist politics. From Machiavelli to Matthews, political realism projects happy endings for virtuosos in the crafts of force, fortuna, fraud, and other public relations. The realist recommendation to do whatever it takes to endure and prevail comes with a realist expectation that the ends will justify the means. Neo noir might be regarded as idealist in the end because it so insistently shows realist politics by resisters of corrupt systems coming to bad ends. Neo noir might be seen as idealist in the end because it so often shows how means become ends, condemning rather than justifying realist endeavors. Or neo noir might be treated as idealist in the end because it sometimes grants resisters the late escape that usually comes as grace and redemption. Yet an ending note of idealism, in criticism of realism throughout, does not suffice by itself to make a drama's ending "happy" in the American sense. Ending "happiness" turns out to be a more global property than the label might imply. It participates in the pervasive ethos of a drama; and when that's realist, so is the ending, most of the time. Happy endings have no special tie, not even loose and elective, to idealist politics—or to popular epics, for that matter. Happy endings do not a paradise make.

Yet happy endings have encouraged the development of neo noir as a Hollywood genre. Realist and existentialist politics admit of happy endings, but just not in classic noirs. In part, those films were selected in the first place for clustering and naming because they depart from the happy endings otherwise prominent even in the Hollywood movies of the 1940s and 1950s. As a group, classic noirs were not particularly popular in the United States when initially released. Some did very well, some didn't, and many were "B" releases made on the cheap by the standards of the time—hence not even expected to make out like bandits at the box office. Neo noirs gradually made much, much more room for happy endings; and this enabled noir to conventionalize itself into a popular genre. It's hard to become a popular genre in America if few works of the kind at issue become popular, and it's hard to become a popular genre of movies in America if next to none of the movies at issue can be anticipated to end happily. It's intriguing that ending happily almost half the time hasn't made neo noir more welcome on American television, even as that shift seems to have helped make neo noir prominent in Hollywood films.

Arguably the audiences differ more than the media.[68] Even in America, significantly different sets of people focus on TV and film—with overlap, of course. Even shared viewers bring different expectations to television than cinema, and these help construct each medium. By definition, to be sure, media never operate in themselves, apart from their communicators or communicants. And the first principle of the rhetorical analysis practiced in these pages is to start with the audiences. A great advantage in exploring the political mythmaking in uses of conventions by popular genres is that we audiences—we ordinary people—are makers of these conventions, these genres, these myths. To start with the politics in popular genres of television or cinema is to start, in part, with their viewers. To study the politics of interest in happy endings and other aspects of popular entertainments is to make sense of them in terms of the whole works, genres, media, and cultures where the devices appear. For us at the moment, the main implications of happy endings for American television spring from this recognition: TV devices depend on larger myths and styles, those are political, and they are why analysts should be working frequently with television. It can help us comprehend our political mythmaking as a popular mode of political theorizing. Isn't this a happy ending?

CONCLUSION

Unsettling Idealism versus Realism: Perfectionism in Two Classics of Neo Noir

(Featuring *Hannibal* and *No Country for Old Men*)

We used to measure movies by how far they were from our lives.[1]
—Sidney Pollack

Pollock's point is that Americans long looked to popular cinema for great stars who enact grand lifestyles in events of historical significance on a world stage. This echoed the Hollywood love, at least intermittent, for epics. Yet epics were far from the only genres of popular cinema that grew more engaging with increasing distance from ordinary people in their everyday lives. The desire for distance and contrast came from a popular sense that moving pictures exalt us more as they remove us further from mundane existence. Even in comedies and satires, stardom and spectacle loomed larger, more magical, and altogether more satisfying as they left behind familiar realities in favor of figures that we viewers first idealized then idolized.[2] Hollywood glamorized American criminals as gangsters, politicians as statesmen, wars as crusades, westward expansion as manifest destiny, and almost anything at all as musicals. Throughout much of the twentieth century, popular movies were the premier entertainment in America because glimpses of the greats on the big, silver screen could ennoble and inspire us regular folks.

This sensibility is not gone from American cinema, but it no longer dominates as it once did, and its symbolic sites have shifted toward other shores. Its epitomes of late include India's Bollywood; China's Yimou Zhang of *Ju Do* (1990), *Raise the Red Lantern* (1991), *Hero* (2002), *House of Flying Daggers* (2004), *Curse of the Golden Flower* (2006), *The Flowers of War* (2011), and the Beijing Olympics in 2008; Britain's Danny Boyle of *Trainspotting* (1996), *28 Days Later...* (2002), *Millions* (2004), *Sunshine* (2007), *Slumdog Millionaire* (2008), *127 Hours* (2010), *Trance* (2013), and the London Olympics in 2012; or even Australia's Baz Luhrmann of *Strictly Ballroom* (1992), *Romeo + Juliet* (1996), *Moulin Rouge!* (2006), *Australia* (2008), and *The Great Gatsby* (2013).[3] American cinema continues to make room for such movies full of spectacle and sentimentalism—and idealism; but it also generates down-to-earth or even debunking aesthetics for biopics, satires, thrillers, war movies, noirs, and other films that feature more realist politics.

By the middle of the last century, classic noir already was contributing to a Hollywood turn from hyper idealisms to complementary, stylized realisms. In 1950, in as acclaimed a noir as has ever been released, Billy Wilder's *Sunset Blvd.* has its down-and-out screenwriter (played by William Holden) tell its star, "You're Norma Desmond. You used to be in silent pictures. You used to be big." As delivered by Gloria Swanson, the retort has become justifiably famous: "I *am* big. It's the *pictures* that got small." This says it in a nutshell. It foreshadows and laments the Hollywood shift from transcendent stars to accessible celebrities. It heralds yet ridicules the cinematic drift from grandeur toward grind house. It redoes but undoes the cultural rift between idealism and realism.

Accordingly Pollock's implication is that Americans are now as likely to seek senses of intimacy, familiarity, and reality from their movies. At times, they value gloominess, grittiness, and other aspects of what we sometimes see as realism. Yet the recent prominence of epics and other kinds of movies inclined toward political idealism shows that popular cinema in America still prizes dynamics of idealism as well. It also shows that we do not experience idealism as simply incompatible with realism. Therefore it's fair to infer that our popular cinema no longer endorses—if it ever did—a Western antinomy of idealism versus realism. Recent movies in America do not present idealism and realism as necessarily antagonistic or mutually exclusive— let alone mutually exhaustive of our political styles.

Hence it's useful to explore how our popular cinema shows interest in other aesthetics and philosophies. Some of these political styles simply operate to the side of battles between idealism and realism. Other styles show specific interests in unsettling such Western alternatives. Perhaps the premier example of such a postwestern political style is perfectionism, especially the sort that springs from Ralph Waldo Emerson and Friedrich Nietzsche in the nineteenth century.[4] To be sure, totalitarian ideologies, movements, and regimes already taught us in the twentieth century all too much about political perversions of Nietzschean perfectionism.[5] Even so, the twenty-first century continues to experiment in popular culture with everyday politics of this sort.

Pretty much paradoxically, since perfectionist politics often condemn the merely human and celebrate the transcendent genius, Nietzschean aphorisms of perfectionism have become popular watchwords in American culture. In quotation or paraphrase, they can be heard at times in Hollywood films.

There are no facts, only interpretations.
Without music, life would be a mistake.
That which does not kill us makes us stronger.
Whoever has a why to live for can bear almost any how.
You must have chaos within you to give birth to a dancing star.
Whoever fights with monsters should be careful lest he thereby
    become a monster. And if you gaze long into an abyss, the abyss
    will also gaze into you.

Such sayings reverberate at frequencies similar to those in *Forrest Gump* (1994): "shit happens," "stupid is as stupid does," and "life is like a box of chocolates: you never know what you're going to get." Even (or sometimes especially) when we misinterpret them, several of Nietzsche's most perfectionist phrases are mainstays in the cultural repertoire of Americans: "beyond good and evil," the death of God," "human, all too human," "twilight of the idols," and "the will to power."[6] Among the most familiar advertising slogans of our times is the eminently perfectionist "Just Do It" from Nike.[7] And could we come to good terms with current conditions if we were to lack such perfectionist concepts as aestheticism, charisma, cult of personality, eternal return, monumental history, moralized memory, nihilism, perspectivism, or truths as tropes?[8]

Perfectionism often confounds the Western politics of idealism versus realism. For one thing, perfectionism as a style of action in everyday life takes itself to outdo both idealism and realism, individually and as antinomies. For another, it claims to trump each in its own terms—as well as each in the other's terms. Perfectionism out-idealizes idealism and out-realizes realism, even as it out-realizes idealism and out-idealizes realism. Or so it suggests; and it's clear enough that idealists and realists often feel flummoxed, debilitated, and outdone by perfectionists. For all their "genius," the leaps of logic, feeling, and action by perfectionists seldom seem sound by standards of Western civilization, although it's apparent that perfectionists somehow leave many laws and other limits behind. For this reason, there's little doubt that perfectionists can be extraordinarily creative, and in our times that could be more than useful. For the same reason, though, there's little doubt that perfectionists in our times can be extraordinarily dangerous.

Hence Hollywood has been pitting perfectionists against idealists and realists to see what we might learn. As preceding chapters establish, neo noir is one of the popular genres that lately test the morality and practicality of realism versus idealism. So far as I can see, in fact, neo noir has become our primary arena for seeing how perfectionism unsettles idealism and realism. It's where we experiment too with ways for idealism, realism, and other styles to evolve in response. So let's conclude this consideration of idealism and realism as political styles in popular movies, novels, and television by looking briefly at their confrontations with perfectionism in two classics of neo noir. *Hannibal* (2001) pits a perfectionist against two idealists plus another two realists, and *No Country for Old Men* (2007) sets a perfectionist against an idealist and three realists. Unsurprisingly the perfectionists prevail; yet one idealist survives in *Hannibal*, as one realist does in *No Country for Old Men*. What can we join the survivors in learning from their confounding encounters with perverse perfectionists?

Political theorists including Max Weber, Albert Camus, and Hannah Arendt could see the strangely "idealist" yet "realist" politics of perfectionism in some twentieth-century states and movements. So Weber tried desperately to come to terms with an "ethic of ultimate ends" fit at times for statesmen and charismatics.[9] Camus reimagined the Roman Emperor Caligula ruling by the ruthless idealism of an ideological fanatic.[10] And Arendt argued that totalitarian leaders such as Adolf Hitler and Josef Stalin idealized an empty, vicious ruthlessness into relentless logics of biology or history.[11] Still academic theories of politics seldom face such perfectionist politics in our everyday lives. Fortunately *Hannibal* and *No Country for Old Men* can help us do just that.

Where Only Manners Remain

Pure idealists might sense some kinship with the sheer extremity, the impulsive purity, of a Nietzschean perfectionist; but they're bound to be unsettled by the perfectionist's cool leaps to success. It's disconcerting to even ironic idealists of great subtlety and great experience when a seemingly self-involved sociopath proves more refined and responsible—if also more rigid and ruthless—than they could have imagined.[12] One way or the other, such a strange sort of "realist" claims to outdo the idealists at their own missions of "morality" and "justice," albeit of inhuman brands and without any belief in "morality" or "justice" by our more usual meanings.

This is evident in *Hannibal*.[13] It's the sequel to *The Silence of the Lambs*, which even as a horror movie won every major Oscar: Best Picture for 1991, Jonathan Demme for Best Director, Ted Tally for Best Adapted Screenplay, Jodie Foster for Best Actress, and Anthony Hopkins for Best Actor. Hopkins returned as Dr. Hannibal Lecter to play the sequel's title role, but Julianne Moore replaced Foster as FBI Special Agent Clarice Starling. Moreover Ridley Scott as director worked with screenwriters Thomas Harris and David Mamet to make *Hannibal* more playful than the Harris novel of that name or the preceding film, then they infused *Hannibal*'s horror with neo noir. On release, enthusiasm for the film was modest, probably in part because of its shifts in cast and tone. But *Hannibal* has since become a cable favorite, and it's been gaining appreciation as a terrific movie.

How is Lecter a perfectionist? His intelligence, temperament, and physical prowess in dexterity and strength seem off the charts for us humans. Hannibal is an aesthete, a dandy, who seems to think of himself as effectively superpowered and virtually a species beyond humans. His cannibalism and other forms of contempt for us rude, inept, and fallen humans is just about boundless. His "principles" are that the strong and creative are laws unto themselves. In other words, his ideal is power—to do and become—with others never to obstruct. If their manners keep them out of the way or at least respectful, Lecter won't go out of his way to trouble them. For Lecter, like Nietzsche, art is the enactment of genius and thus beyond the capacities of most people. But Lecter also seems to see manners as the embodiment of art more generally available, and he insistently treats style as the perfection of manners.

Hannibal takes care to show that its title character appreciates Clarice in important part for her sense of style. To perfect Clarice, he gives her a special perfume, style advice on a catalog page, beautiful shoes, an elegant gown for dinner, and more. For Lecter, style is how Starling's purity of principle enters by impulse and sensibility into action. From selecting shoes and cars to saving lambs and citizens, often from themselves, Starling's idealism seems to Lecter just a leap or two shy of potential perfection. Yet as an idealist still, she isn't there yet, and Hannibal would have to help Clarice hollow out her ideals of justice in order to get there. Only this could streamline her instincts for perfectionist exercises in sheer style. And only then could Clarice join Hannibal in reveling beyond the horizons of civilization, at least of a Western sort, enjoying territories where laws and goals have been left behind and where only manners or styles remain. Perfectionists in the manner of Friedrich Nietzsche take themselves to leap beyond good and evil as well as plans and strategies. This is a reason that Lecter presses so hard in *The Silence of the Lambs* to learn about Starling's impulsive flight from her uncle's gelding of sheep. When the chips are down, Starling is preternaturally, by family trajectory, ready to spring into action on the spur of the moment: perfectionists "Just Do It," as Nike says. Action is what counts; and it succeeds when it arises from vital, more or less biological impulses preternaturally attuned to the situation. Unlike realists, perfectionists do not (pretend to?) hate and denigrate words and images as mere, manipulative illusions. Unlike idealists, perfectionists do not expect words and images to remake realities. Unlike realists *and* idealists, perfectionists are not foundationalists, either metaphysical or political, because perfectionists acknowledge no grounds for morality or givens for science. Instead geniuses remake realities—many of them, leaving the perfectionist likes of Hannibal perspectivist in ethics, epistemics, and politics.

For perfectionists such as Lecter, guilt and regret are weakness. So are justice, history, and memory. Civilization is a gambit for the mediocre to tame the great. Better to stay savage instead, and that's the perfectionist significance of Hannibal's cannibalism. Nietzsche regarded civilization as a scheme by women, worshippers, and such to weaken and enslave men. But Lecter does not share in such misogyny. Instead he seems to admire purity and power as perfection in whatever form they're found—although Lecter does not seem to imagine that a (mere) woman, not even Starling, could subdue or defeat him. This starts to explain Hannibal's peculiar interest in Clarice as a pure idealist of daunting integrity, resourcefulness, and personal strength. But it also starts to explain how a perfectionist can seem realist in prizing power and success, can seem idealist in embracing impulse and purity, yet can stay strangely singular: "a pure psychopath," as psychiatrist Frederick Chilton (Anthony Heald) labels Lecter in *The Silence of the Lambs*.

As neo noir, *Hannibal* has two protagonists, a male and a female; and both try to subdue the title figure. Italian Police Inspector Rinaldo Pazzi (Giancarlo Giannini) enacts a Faust Myth, and the FBI's Clarice Starling pursues a Quixote Quest. This makes *Hannibal* one of the fairly few feminist noirs to date, with Starling a femme focale even more than a femme fatale. Both these protagonists are detectives, and both have begun their careers in law enforcement as idealists. Pazzi is from a long-established family in his home city of Florence, whereas Starling has been poor white trash orphaned early from a policing family in West Virginia. In different ways, their idealisms stem in part from coming to adulthood with family identities to live down—disgrace for Pazzi and poverty for Starling—as well as family destinies to fulfill in the honorable service of justice. These trajectories help make each of them idealist, at least initially.

Pazzi is a senior figure who seems to have been scapegoated and demoted when an earlier investigation of serial killings ran into corruption and trouble. He now has a beautiful young wife who's used to the finer things in life. Pazzi seems to have stayed true to his ideals of justice, but he's compensating for his career disappointment and disillusionment by focusing on his wife. Unfortunately he's learning that his reduced income is not sufficient for her desires. All this eats away at his idealism; and when he recognizes Hannibal Lecter, hiding under an assumed identity in Florence, Pazzi seeks a private reward to aid personal revenge rather than seeking community justice for this notorious serial killer, who's prominently listed among the FBI's "Most Wanted."

Starling began her career in an awkward collaboration with Lecter, then incarcerated as a criminally insane killer who's eaten parts of his victims. Calling him "Hannibal the Cannibal," the media have made him a renowned fugitive and Starling ("little star") a celebrity, too, as his FBI nemesis.[14] But now she's entering mid-career. She's learned a lot about FBI hardball as well as misogyny and other patriarchal corruption throughout the Department of Justice and politics of the United States. In fact, Lecter has defended her against some of this macho realism and tried to teach her about it. Yet she's still an idealist who seeks protection for the innocent and justice for the violated; and she still addresses others, whether virtuous or vicious, with respect as well as courage. In *Hannibal*, we learn that Lecter admires not only her incorruptible idealism and excellent style but also her careful manners. He has pledged not to assault her, even though she's pursuing him. For as Lecter explains, he finds the world a more interesting place with her in it. And as we also learn, Lecter eats only his enemies, whom he regards as the "free-range rude."

As an idealist who lately despairs of public justice, Pazzi makes his private bargain with a realist victim of Hannibal's named Mason Verger (Gary Oldman). (If many a neoconservative is a liberal who's been mugged, many a realist is an idealist who's been disillusioned.) Verger is in league with another realist, Paul Krendler in the Department of Justice. Both corrupted long ago, the two arrange to derail Starling's career in order to draw Lecter out of hiding. They recognize that Lecter is fascinated with Starling and apparently wants to protect her. But otherwise they don't know what kind of fellow Lecter is, what sorts of things he'll do, or why. His perfectionism stymies their understanding, then it also dooms them and their minions. Hannibal kills them one by one.

Yet Pazzi is no better at comprehending Lecter. Warned repeatedly that Lecter is far too dangerous and unpredictable to pursue by himself, Pazzi has this reinforced by one disaster after another as he tries to demonstrate Lecter's identity and finger him for Verger's henchmen to haul back to America. These disasters get Pazzi assistants killed by Lecter. Still Pazzi has become too desperate, foolish, and obsessive to face the fact that he's out of Lecter's league—and doesn't even know what league's at issue. Hannibal escapes Italy to return to America on his own, but not before he taunts, guts, and hangs Pazzi in the public plaza already notorious to Pazzi's family from the similar death there of its most famous ancestor.

Lecter comes back to the United States in part to deal with Verger. It's not clear whether Lecter wants revenge against Verger or simply an end to him as a threat. Neither in the novel nor in the movie does Lecter himself kill Verger, although he suggests it in each case to an individual (different in the film from the novel) with personal reasons to hate Mason and stop his incessant puppeteering. Verger has paid considerable money for Lecter memorabilia in a concerted effort to get a better sense of his character and conduct. Yet Verger dies almost as much out to lunch about Lecter as when Hannibal got the young Mason high and had him slice off his face to feed to his dog. Is being fed entirely to pigs any better? There's poetic justice in it for Verger, since it's the end that he had readied for the elusive Lecter.

The other reason for Lecter's return is to deal with Starling. Although she's been trying to track him for the FBI, his project is to protect her—not just from Verger, Krendler, and the media, but especially from the hardball realism rampant in the FBI and from her uncompromising idealism in the pursuit of justice. Clarice seems rivaled only by Barney Matthews (Frankie R. Faison), an asylum attendant, in starting to understand Lecter; and he knows it. Yet Hannibal feels more excited than endangered by this. He travels back to the corrupt heart of American politics primarily in order to educate, rescue, and perhaps recruit—or at least seduce—Clarice.

In horror terms, Hannibal is a monster—and more specifically a cannibal or a vampire. But who is Hannibal in noir terms? By one of the special conventions for feminist noir, he's a mentor for Clarice. At the FBI, she's had other male mentors, especially Jack Crawford (Scott Glenn) in *The Silence of the Lambs* and apparently John Brigham (Peter Shaw) before the events in *Hannibal* begin, when Brigham's shot to death during the later film's opening ambush in a public market. Crawford is a moral and successful realist, making him arguably a more dangerous nemesis than Starling for Lecter. The novel about *Hannibal* hints that Brigham might be an idealist, and he briefly became Starling's lover, but we learn little more about him. There is no doubt, however, that Hannibal is by far the most advanced and ambitious of Clarice's male mentors. Their mutual attunement is particularly acute, and his tutoring of her as we move to the climax of *Hannibal* is especially adventurous.

But even in the novel, let alone the movie, there remains distance and tension between Lecter and Starling. As unmitigated horror, the novel ends in an evil too appalling for popular cinema. As neo noir too, the movie lets Hannibal escape from the custody of Clarice, through a turn more grisly than we might have imagined, then adds a playful coda where he winks at us all. The perfectionist still takes the purest and most resourceful of idealists by surprise. For Western politics in the twenty-first century, a signal trouble can be that the most moral and resourceful of realists fare no better in facing the strange politics of perfectionism.

When Chance Comes to Call

Verger and Krendler, the figures who begin *Hannibal* as realists, have long been corrupt through and through. For the title perfectionist, this makes them easy meat (pun needed). In *Hannibal*, it's the two main idealists who are both moral and capable, notwithstanding their flaws and sins; so we've focused on their attempts to fathom and tame the title perfectionist. In *No Country for Old Men*, by contrast, the one idealist who claims much of our attention simply condemns the film's perfectionist then succumbs to him. Yet this later movie also shows three realists who are fairly moral and exceptionally resourceful in their various human ways. All three struggle to make sense of the movie's perfectionist in order to defeat—or at least survive—him.

Yet only one of them survives in body, and arguably none in spirit. It's disconcerting to clever realists of good sense and good will when a person of "principle" proves more cunning and effective—but also more brutal and arbitrary—than they could have imagined. Such a peculiar kind of "idealist" can outdo the realists at their own game of playing the hardest ball, with no-holds-barred. This is how the realists in *No Country for Old Men* experience its perfectionist, whose similarities to Hannibal Lecter are striking. These realists have keen talents for strategy and survival, but none is a match for his strange challenge. *No Country for Old Men* confronts a borderland where perfectionist politics disrupt our realities and ideals with increasing frequency and severity. Again let's venture just enough analysis to show how the film uses a perfectionist along with other characters and scenes conventional for popular noirs. Then we can trace how it twists them to unsettle the Western shootout between political realism and political idealism.

Have you seen *No Country for Old Men*? I'm among many who prize it as one of the best movies ever made. It won Ethan and Joel Coen three Oscars each for Best Adapted Screenplay, Best Direction, and Best Motion Picture of 2007. Critics usually see it as a modern Western, like its source in the terrific novel of the same name by Cormac McCarthy.[15] Coming from the Coen brothers, though, it can't surprise us that this film also fits the popular genre of noir.[16] Of 15 feature-length films by the Coens through 2012, fully a third of them share this recently popular form: *Blood Simple* (1984), *Fargo* (1996), *The Big Lebowski* (1998), and *The Man Who Wasn't There* (2001) are noir too. At least two of these are outstanding movies as well. *Fargo* could have been named the best movie in English for its year of release. Yet *No Country for Old Men* still stands out, not only as a Coen film but as an American great. Its perspectives on the long-running debate between idealism and realism are especially unsettling. Less as a Western than as a noir, *No Country for Old Men* shows how the perfectionist style that coalesces in the last couple of centuries can challenge the political coherence of idealist and realist styles.

As a genre, noir is renowned for aesthetic realism full of grainy, gritty details. When *No Country for Old Men* leaves cities and small towns for the countryside of Texas, we do not get the majestic, sometimes austere vistas of many earlier westerns.[17] Instead we see Llewelyn Moss (Josh Brolin) hunting antelope on dry and dusty plains that offer little concealment from sun or bullets. His a hard land, but we sense that Moss knows its ways. In noir parlance, he's the primary protagonist, who propels the movie's main action, but who lacks the virtue to be a hero. Tracking a wounded animal, Moss finds remnants of a major drug deal gone bad, where buyers and sellers have massacred each other. One Mexican still lives, but not for long without water and treatment. Moss leaves him and the drugs, but finds the money and takes it back to town. He hides the money under his trailer home, then tells his beloved wife—the film's lone idealist—to get ready to disappear with him on the morrow. As a realist, Moss knows that they need to flee, because the drug dealers will soon send killers to investigate and take back the money as well as the drugs. Yet the money is a chance for Moss to live in decent style with his wife, and he goes for it. Llewelyn is a tough, skillful little guy. But he has a conscience; and a few hours later, he goes back with water for the dying man. Of course, the killers arrive, almost murder Moss, and follow him back to town. Now his wife goes to her mother's, and he's on the run.

This plot for Llewelyn Moss is a Faust Myth, one of the seven stories conventional for noir films. Despairing of his ability to make it otherwise, he symbolically sells his soul to the Devil for riches to buy him and his wife the good life. (Other Faustians want power, beauty, fame, knowledge, and such.) In *Hannibal*, we see Rinaldo Pazzi as a much older man who has many scenes in the movie (plus many earlier years) of acting in good faith as an idealist, and only later does he gradually fall into his deal with the Devil. In *No Country for Old Men*, Llewelyn Moss begins his own fall almost from his first frame in the film. This is why we may see Pazzi as an idealist who eventually falls into despair, whereas we may see Moss as a realist who spots and leaps at his big, once-in-a-lifetime, but immoral and outrageously dangerous opportunity. Their kinship is still telling, though, and it suggests how idealism and realism can turn all too readily into each other. Like Faust and Pazzi, Moss thinks he knows what's at stake. But actually, he's in way over his head; and soon the Devil comes to collect. In *No Country for Old Men*, the Devil is a strangely principled fellow named Anton Chigurh; and playing him won an Oscar for Javier Bardem.

Chigurh has been hired to recover the money, and he's the deadly male standard for noir as a popular genre. But the movie has several deadly males: maybe Moss; surely Carson Wells (Woody Harrelson), who's called in to corral a Chigurh gone rogue; and equally Sheriff Ed Tom Bell (Tommy Lee Jones), who's honor-bound to protect potential victims like Carla Jean Moss (Kelly Macdonald) and even her husband from alpha predators like Chigurh and Wells. How does Chigurh stand out in this deadly company? From Chigurh's standpoint, he is an "idealist" facing a bunch of realists. Realists expect to dominate idealists by out-thinking, out-toughing, out-working, if need be out-savaging them.[18] But Chigurh's "idealism" prevails. As a radical, arguably inhuman "idealism," his perfectionism trumps the human, plainly more humane, realism shared by Bell, Wells, and Moss. From the start, as we've been noticing, noir protagonists seem fated to come to bad ends. Smart, humorless, merciless, inexorable: Chigurh personifies fate, destiny, and even death on the prowl for Moss and the others.[19] Chigurh tracks down and kills his employer, Wells, Llewelyn Moss, then Carla Jean Moss for good measure. Only Bell manages a narrow, demoralizing escape into retirement. Paying the piper can be worse than expensive.

What's the setting for this limiting case in the continuing contest between realist and idealist politics? The politics of popular noir have the protagonist awakening to resistance of a corrupt system. By kind, these politics are principally existentialist, so that the system and its corruptions can vary widely from one film to the next. Thus a noir way to specify settings is to identify the social system at issue. So what's the corrupt system in *No Country for Old Men*?

One answer is the drug trade and America's war on it. Toward the end of the movie, the El Paso Sheriff (Rodger Boyce) talks with Bell about the shooting death of Llewelyn Moss in the Desert Sands Motor Hotel. He worries that the times have been changing—with kids wearing Mohawks, while drugs and money make people wild. Bell agrees in part; and as the novel has him say earlier in the story, "If you were Satan and you were settin around tryin to think up something that would just bring the human race to its knees what you would probably come up with is narcotics."[20] Furthermore the drug war has helped systematize the drug trade, while addiction and money have corrupted the system thoroughly. *No Country for Old Men* makes this clear enough, yet it gives much less attention to the operation and corruption of the drug system than do other noirs: *Traffic* (2000) and *Savages* (2012), for instance. Bell and his film suggest that drugs are just symptoms of a larger, more encompassing and pervasive, disease.

Hence a better answer might be that the movie's corrupt system is Western civilization. *No Country for Old Men* is a western as well as a noir; and by genre, westerns focus their politics less on the American West than the virtues, vices, and devices of Western civilization. If so, the corruption would seem to be modernization. From the Renaissance and Reformation onward, the West has been constructing human individuals as rational self-managers who pursue self-interest as a kind of self-indulgence. This can be said of Llewelyn Moss, the drug operatives, Carson Wells, and many young people lamented by the movie's old sheriffs for indulging in Mohawks, nose bones, and particularly nasty crimes. Modernization and self-development seem gradually to degrade human capacities for charity, solidarity, sympathy, even decency. Likewise they leave many people defenseless against degenerative addictions to drugs, money, and more.

Yet the modern West isn't exactly the source of Bell's distress, at least not as he tries to diagnose it. Even later in the film, Bell visits his Uncle Ellis (Barry Corbin), now disabled as a sheriff; and they rehearse how Mac in their family of sheriffs had died many years before. One evening, Indians came, shot Mac in the lung, then sat on their horses, and watched him take hours to die. The inhumanity that unmans Bell is not unique to modern or Western civilization. What's at issue is its increase in what supposedly civilized people do to one another. Noir films often include voice-overs for narration or reflection, and these go more often than not to protagonists. Bell is the film's secondary protagonist. He's another realist who's done hard, bad things in minimizing the violence and other harms to his people. Yet his world-weary voice-over begins the movie with deep perplexity at this cold new world:

> I always liked to hear about the old-timers, never missed a chance to do so. You can't help but compare yourself up against the old-timers, can't

help but wonder how they'd operated in these times. There's this boy I sent to the electric chair in Huntsville a while back: my arrest and my testimony. He killed a fourteen-year-old girl. The paper said it was a crime of passion, but he told me there wasn't any passion to it. Told me he'd been plannin to kill somebody for about as long as he could remember. Said if they turned him out, he'd do it again. Said he was goin to Hell: be there in bout fifteen minutes. I don't know what to make of that; I surely don't. The crime you see now, it's hard even to take its measure. It's not that I'm afraid of it. I always knew you had to be willin to die even to do this job. But I don't want to push my chips forward, and go out and meet somethin I don't understand. A man'd have to put his soul at hazard; he'd have to say, "Okay, I'll be part of this world."[21]

As best he can tell, Bell finds himself somehow facing a Faustian situation. Unlike Moss, he's not sure how that's happened. But he fears how it must turn out, and he suspects he's not up to the bargain. The film's events bring no clarity to Bell, just more killing and more trouble for his soul. Then in the end, a retired Bell tells about his dreams the night before:

Two of em: both of em, my father in em. It's peculiar. I'm older now than he ever was, by twenty years. So when you see us, he's the younger man. Anyway the first one I don't remember too well, but it was about meeting him in town somewheres, and he give me some money. I think I lost it. The second one, it was like we was both back in the older times. And I was a-horseback, goin through the mountains for the night, goin through this pass in the mountains. It was cold, an there was snow on the ground. And he rode past me and kept on goin: never said nothin goin by, just rode on past. He had his blanket wrapped im and his head down. When he rode past, I seen he was carryin fire in a horn, the way people used to do. And I, I could see the horn from the light inside of it, bout the color of the moon. And in the dream I knew that he was goin on ahead, and he was fixin to make a fire somewhere out there in all that dark and all that cold. And I knew that, whenever I got there, he'd be there. And then I woke up.[22]

Does the first dream echo the Biblical parable about squandered talents? Bell might feel such a weight of judgment from his father's own work as a sheriff, dying in the line of duty. Is the second a dream of death, with his father "goin on ahead?" Even if so, the dark and cold of that wintry realm might well awaken Bell, just because he suddenly recognizes that it's the condition he's already coming to know in this world, where his father's also gone ahead with only a small fire to light the way. It's the cold of casual cruelty inflicted almost unfelt—from a chronic itch, a momentary whim, or an inhumanly high ideal. It's the dark of nothingness, randomness, chaos, lack of meaning. In the nineteenth-century nightmare intruding into the realities of centuries to follow, it's the nihilism of human aspiration come to naught but pain.

The second dream is a wake-up call to Bell, whose name implies he may be something of a human wake-up call for the rest of us. The wake-up call is a noir event that summons a sleeping protagonist, so far participating unaware, to recognize a corrupt system and resist it. When the wake-up call comes only at the end, the protagonist has been a dupe of the system throughout the film. He's never quite figured out what he's doing, let alone facing. I think of this as a Chinatown Tale, because that's the plot for protagonist Jake Gittes (Jack Nicholson) in Roman Polanski's superlative noir of that name (1974). In the course of the Coens' film, Moss gets several wake-up calls; and in his case, these are literally telephone calls, as happens often in noirs. By contrast with Bell, in other words, Moss knows during most of the movie what kind of drama he's enacting. Yet Moss does not know what kind of menace he's facing. Wells has a better sense, although not good enough for even a minimal defense against Chigurh. Bell suspects, and he joins Wells in trying to warn Moss. Even Chigurh tries to tell Llewelyn, but to no avail. So Wells dies, Moss dies, his wife dies, and Bell is psychologically and morally disabled. Again literally, he seems de-moralized by how Chiguhr and others act. The only way for Bell not to "go out and meet somethin [he doesn't] understand" is not to go out at all, because he does not in fact understand Chigurh's style, Chigurh's politics; and that's the mark of a Chinatown Tale.

But Bell's a realist: by all evidence, he's been tough, shrewd, and discerning for many decades. Realists earn the name by facing even the hardest realities with composed calculation. How or what can Bell, as a courageous and experienced realist, somehow not comprehend? The general way I've been putting it is: our cold new world. The noir equivalent, as the genre's name suggests, is: our dark new world. In Bell's dream, the Coen film—like the McCarthy book—embraces both formulations. Yet a more specific version is: our world with the likes of Anton Chigurh in it.

Who *is* Chigurh? In noir terms, he's not just a deadly male but a system fixer. If a corrupt system is threatened by resisters or even by dangers in its ordinary dynamics, the system boss summons an outside, independent character to save the system with force and judgment that it can't manage on its own. There are risks, especially because resort to a fixer shows system weakness and because a fixer could turn against the system or at least its boss.

A fixer is apt to command more resources for undoing the boss or the system than could be generated by any sleeper recently aroused to resistance.

Carson Wells is a system fixer too. When killers from the American cartel fail to get the drug money or the escaping Moss, the respectably corporate crime boss behind this side of the drug deal hires Chigurh to clean up the mess and retrieve the money. But then Chigurh makes it a personal point of honor (and safety) to kill Moss and others for their defiance of his will. Thus Chigurh warns the crime boss, "I have no enemies. I don't permit such a thing."[23] Still Chigurh's killing campaign threatens to expose the crime syndicate's hidden position behind the scenes. So this system boss has called in Wells to take out Chigurh. Wells seems to be the movie's one realist who mostly knows what he's facing in Chigurh, for Wells keeps cautioning others that they don't recognize their jeopardy from Chigurh. Yet not even Wells comprehends Chigurh enough to resist him even momentarily. (Moss does much better.) Chigurh soon learns of the extra threat and promptly kills Wells plus the boss. What could have possessed Wells to pit himself against Chigurh? Neither the movie nor the novel says, leaving us to wonder if Wells is demonstrating the self-destructive hubris of realists that idealists sometimes cite when they claim superior success in practice.

If there's a corrupt system that Wells intends to defend, it would be the criminality in drugs and other addictions that bedevil America. Sheriff Bell's reflections suggest that Wells, whether he knows it or not, could also be acting to protect Western civilization from Chigurh. Yes, civilization in the West suffers many corruptions; but crimes might be far preferable to the scourge of Chigurh's annihilating "idealism," his nearly nihilistic perfectionism.

From our Western perspective, Chigurh is an "agent of chaos."[24] Hollywood films have become fascinated with this predatory, destructive "idealist." Thus *The Silence of the Lambs, Hannibal*, and *Red Dragon* (2002) led the American Film Institute in 2003 to name the Anthony Hopkins version of Lecter as the premier movie villain of the previous one hundred years.[25] *The Dark Knight* trilogy from Christopher Nolan foregrounds at least one agent of chaos in each of its films: Henri Ducard as Ra's al Ghul (Liam Neeson) in *Batman Begins* (2005), the Joker (Heath Ledger) and District Attorney Harvey Dent as "Two-Face" (Aaron Eckhart) in *The Dark Knight* (2008), then Bane (Tom Hardy) and Talia Ducard as Miranda Tate (Marion Cotillard) in *The Dark Knight Rises* (2012). For playing the Joker in 2008, Ledger joined Hopkins and Bardem as winners of the Oscar for Best Actor. And we need to note that Tim Burton had paved the way with his notion of the Joker (Jack Nicholson) as "the world's first fully functioning homicidal artist" in *Batman* (1989). At least in such super-noir movies,

Sheriff Bell and Cormac McCarthy have lots of company in their dread for the future of humanity or at least its Western branches.

To the extent that he thinks about it, Chigurh seems to see himself as an idealist. But I've kept his self-conception in scare-quotes until now, because the idealist reasons for disputing this are many. Knowing Chigurh to be vastly different from themselves, though, the realists are apt to see him as an idealist; and there are decent reasons to agree. More literally and seriously than most individuals, Chigurh holds—with idealists like G. W. F. Hegel—that, "There's a reason for everything."[26] Realists have trouble relating to this, as Wells tries to explain to Moss: "You cant make a deal with him...Even if you gave him the money he'd still kill you. There's no one alive on this planet that's ever had even a cross word with him. They're all dead. These are not good odds. He's a peculiar man. You could even say that he has principles. Principles that transcend money or drugs or anything like that."[27] As with an idealist, Chigurh finds self and strength in hewing rigorously to his "principles."

When Carla Jean Moss as a religious idealist pleads with him to set his principles aside and spare her, Chigurh's response is that of an idealist more pious—or at least rigid—but also more defensive than she: "You're asking that I make myself vulnerable and that I can never do. I have only one way to live. It doesnt allow for special cases. A coin toss perhaps."[28] Ordinarily in the West, at least until late in the nineteenth century, such principles would make someone an idealist and probably a monotheistic one. But lately, as Camus once narrated, they sometimes make such a somebody into a "stranger."[29] (Similarly Christopher Nolan has his Joker, another agent of chaos, twist the iconic, ironic quip from Friedrich Nietzsche to say, "What doesn't kill you simply makes you stranger.")

When he comes to kill her, Chigurh taunts Carla Jean with his principles. She is the one major character in the film who's been an idealist without qualification, although she might have "suffered a loss of faith" from recent events.[30] And it's telling that she doesn't accept at all that Chigurh is any kind of "idealist." To her, he's more like an über realist, manipulating situations and people to have his way with them. "Get real!" is what she seems to hear in his explanation that his course—and therefore her end—cannot be altered. "Even a nonbeliever might find it useful to model himself after God. Very useful in fact...But what's done cannot be undone."[31] So is Chigurh a "realist" instead of an "idealist?" More unsettling still, is Chigurh a "realist" at the same times and in some of the same ways as he's an "idealist?"

Well, what about that "coin toss?" Like Harvey Dent after he's been led into despair by the Joker in *The Dark Knight*, Chigurh sometimes has potential victims call coin flips to see if he will kill them. Early in the film, he rattles a gas station proprietor (Gene Jones) just as badly as he does Bell by subjecting that poor soul to this strange rite of chance, change, chaos, fortune, luck, whim, call it what you will. But like Bell, the gas guy has "good luck" and goes free, if tormented ever after. Chigurh tells Carla Jean, "None of this was your fault . . . You didnt do anything. It was bad luck."[32] Then he has her call a toss, incorrectly.

> *Carla Jean*: You make it sound like it was the coin. But you're the one.
> *Chigurh*: It could have gone either way.
> *Carla Jean*: The coin didnt have no say. It was just you.
> *Chigurh*: Perhaps. But look at it my way. I got here the same way the coin did . . . I had no say in the matter. Every moment in your life is a turning and every one a choosing. Somewhere you made a choice. All followed to this. The accounting is scrupulous. The shape is drawn. No line can be erased. I had no belief in your ability to move a coin to your bidding. How could you? A person's path through the world seldom changes and even more seldom will it change abruptly. And the shape of your path was visible from the beginning . . . Yet even though I could have told you how all of this would end I thought it not too much to ask that you have a final glimpse of hope in the world to lift your heart before the shroud drops, the darkness.[33]

Godlike, Chigurh claims to be nothing but principles *and* nothing but consequences. As he observes to Carla Jean, "Most people dont believe that there can be such a person."[34] Ere he shoots her, Carla Jean calls Chigurh "crazy."[35] And in the Jesse Stone movies examined in the previous chapter, that realist detective in an idealized place observes that a textbook name for a figure similar to Chigurh is a "sociopath."[36] Sociopath or psychopath, there can be political methods to the seeming madness of perfectionists; and strangely it can clarify the contests between idealism and realism by confounding them. This can enable us to detect limits and dangers for realism and for idealism in our politics. It also can empower us to face everyday challenges for action in our changing world.

A Coda on Kinds of Formalism

Admittedly the method of political analysis in these pages is formal. We've sought to illuminate contrasts between idealism and realism as forms of art, culture, inquiry, and especially politics. We've even sought insights principally in specific uses of the conventions that define such popular forms as genres, media, and cultures, plus ideologies, movements, and styles. The postmodern principle is that style is substance, medium is message, form is content.[37] Given the cultural history of Western civilization, the postmodern question about what we've been doing becomes: Is there an elective affinity of formalism in analysis for idealism in politics? In other words, does a focus on popular genres of cinema, literature, and television bias the analysis to promote idealism as the most self-consciously formal of political styles?

As we've been learning, realists often distrust forms as misleading representations of what could and should be encountered as unvarnished realities. Hence realists often debunk formal analysis of politics as mistaking (pretty or tidy) ideas about realities for the (disorderly and unpleasant) things in themselves. How could a formal analysis of politics appreciate the rough-and-tumble takes of realists on traditions, institutions, or actions? How could a formal analysis of politics help but favor political idealism instead? Especially if you're a realist, but even if you're an idealist, you're probably wondering about these possibilities.

As we've also been glimpsing, perfectionists turn away from self-conscious reflection of almost any kind. The bone-deep intuition is that self-awareness, let alone self-criticism, impedes the instinctive attunement of bodies and deeds to situations that can generate successful leaps of genius. The somehow pure, aestheticist practice of style and manners essayed by perfectionists such as Hannibal Lecter, the Joker, and Anton Chigurh unsettles idealists and realists in part for its instinctive resistance to self- and sustained analysis. Perfectionists can and do analyze, just as realists can and do work with words and images. Still the temperamental distrust of analysis by perfectionists is like the abiding distrust of language and illusion by realists: It tends to redirect, distract, and eventually disrupt the activity. Thus in *The Silence of the Lambs*, Clarice Starling razzes Lecter by daring him to analyze himself. "You see a lot, Dr. Lecter. But are you strong enough to point that high-powered perception at yourself? How about it...? Look at yourself and write down the truth. Or maybe you're afraid to." Averse to self-analysis, Hannibal does not take the bait. This is one way to suggest why Emersonian and Nietzschean perfectionists might share the suspicion of realists that formal analysis of their politics as styles is inclined to discredit them in comparison to idealists.

Such challenges deserve decent responses. They can spotlight further limits and lessons of the analysis at hand. So let's end quickly with four. First, elective affinities are not necessary, obligatory, or correct connections. Instead they are conventional: we make them, we make sense with them, we can ignore or violate them to make other sense, and we can remake them.[38] As Hayden White has demonstrated, some of our most insightful and influential connections are intentionally, creatively unconventional.[39] If analyzing politics into styles, genres, or other forms were to favor idealism in particular or any political alternative, the challenge could be simply to ignore or violate the familiar affinities in order to pursue different links. This is something we do intermittently. Eventually we might even seek to consolidate some exceptional connections into different conventions. In this respect, challenges to elective affinities involved in formal analysis of politics can be challenges to action.

A second response is that recognizing and respecting everyday politics as styles of action is one of the better, more favorable ways to appreciate them. This holds even for realism as an antistyle. Among the least plausible aspects of realism are its antistyle pretenses to escape spin, avoid illusion, and eliminate emotion. To treat realism as a political style is to drop such poses or rework them into points of style. For example, realism can become plain speech or blunt talk, with looks and sounds from news or neo noir, and with commitments to calculations that are cool or presentations that are calm. This approach can respect or even improve perfectionism, too, as simultaneously a super-style yet supposedly a nonstyle—or at least a non-self-conscious style. Among the less admirable features of perfectionism are its nonstyle fantasies of simple sincerity, total transparency, and preternatural attunement to the times.[40] Reconfigured as a perfectionist style, such non-style features can morph toward the super-style devices of engaging theatricality, prompt response, and minute attention to detail. Even if formal analysis of politics were to favor idealism in some ways, always elective and probably subtle, it still can make other politics better in substance and more appealing in prospect by appreciating them more adequately as styles.

Like all forms, moreover, styles are intrinsically plural and open to proliferation. Neither idealism nor any other form stands long alone, especially in politics. This is because forms are defined by (networks of) conventions, and conventions have meaning as comparisons. The noir protagonist coheres as a conventional character in comparison to the epic hero, the satirical fool, and leading characters in other genres as well as other characters in noir. The noir femme fatale is meaningful not only in relation to other noir figures but also in comparison to the epic damsel in distress, the gangster moll, and the western schoolmarm. The spider woman in noir also needs the matriarch in family drama, the Mata Hari in spy thrillers, and the bawdy woman in satire in order to mean and do what's needed by noir as a genre or by any of its individual works.

192 • Popular Cinema as Political Theory

Consequently a third response is that formal analysis tends to recognize further forms as legitimate options rather than discredit them. Formal analysis often promotes the perspectivism that respects many forms rather than privileging one. The more styles of politics we acknowledge and analyze, the less we seek one style to suit all people and situations. Instead we consider how to move and choose among diverse styles of politics. Some political styles we differentiate by settings: autocratic, bureaucratic, business, courtly, democratic, feminist, environmentalist, idealist, legalist, liberal, militarist, pacifist, realist, republican, socialist, totalitarian styles, etc. Others we distinguish by genres: disaster, fantasy, horror, news, noir, romance, science fiction, sports, westerns, and the like. Formal analysis of politics can incline toward appreciating many forms far more than any one of them, idealism included.

All these considerations suggest in turn that there are not just many forms but many kinds of forms, even many kinds of political forms: genres, media, institutions, ideologies, movements, styles, manners, mores, conventions, cultures, ideas, logics, tropes, topics, representations, and so on. More to the point, there are also many kinds of formalism. As the previous chapter sketches, Plato's idealism differs significantly from Hegel's; and each of these is a formalism that differs from the noumenal analysis of Immanuel Kant.[41] Kant's formalism contrasts significantly with the analysis of symbolic forms by neo-Kantians such as Ernst Cassirer.[42] Their sort of formalism departs from Kenneth Burke's analysis of literary forms as invoked in the second chapter.[43] And still another sort of formal analysis surfaced earlier in this chapter, with Hayden White applying Northrop Frye's analysis of Romance, Comedy, Satire, and Tragedy as meta-genres to match with Kenneth Burke's four master tropes, Karl Mannheim's four modes of politics, and similar typologies.[44] The key point is that some of these formalisms show elective affinities for idealist politics, as we discovered with Plato and Hegel, but some don't.

The kind of formalism practiced in these pages is a kind that doesn't implicate idealism in aesthetics, ethics, or politics. If anything, it's perspectivist or even perfectionist instead, though weakly so. Here we've been analyzing conventions from popular forms of cinema, literature, television, and politics. This brand of formal analysis traces back from Stanley Cavell to Ludwig Wittgenstein thence to Friedrich Nietzsche. Its principal inspiration is Wittgenstein's analysis of forms of life and language.[45] Of the three, only Nietzsche's philosophy is—for the most part—perfectionist. Yet all three philosophies are perspectivist, and none is partial to idealist politics. In these analyses of art, inquiry, and action, forms are cultural, tropal, and practical rather than ideal—or otherwise perfected.[46]

Accordingly a fourth response is that there are diverse kinds of formal-ism, just as there are numerous styles in politics, with the kind of formal analysis in this book leaning toward perspectivism rather than idealism in politics. Among the perspectives we've explored, the most prominent—and favored—have been epic, noir, and satire as well as idealism and realism. The epistemic and political bias has been to use each for interrogating the others and itself. This is as fair and revealing a method as I know.

APPENDIX A

Classic Film Noir According to Critical Consensus

Scarlet Street
Uncle Harry
The Woman in the Window
1946 *The Big Sleep*
The Blue Dahlia
Crack-Up
The Dark Corner
The Dark Mirror
Deception
Fallen Angel
Gilda
The Killers
Notorious
The Postman Always Rings Twice
A Stolen Life
The Strange Love of Martha Ivers
The Stranger
Suspense
1947 *Body and Soul*
Boomerang
The Brasher Doubloon
Brute Force
Crossfire
Dark Passage
Dead Reckoning
Framed
The High Wall
Johnny O'Clock
Kiss of Death
Lady in the Lake
The Locket
The Naked City
Nightmare Alley
Out of the Past
Possessed
Railroaded
Ride the Pink Horse
They Won't Believe Me
The Web
1948 *The Big Clock*
Call Northside 777

Cry of the City
The Dark Past
A Double Life
I Walk Alone
Key Largo
Kiss the Blood Off My Hand
The Lady from Shanghai
The Night Has a Thousand Faces
Road House
Sorry, Wrong Number
T-Men
They Live by Night

1949 *The Accused*
The Bribe
Champion
City Across the River
Criss Cross
He Walked by Night
House of Strangers
The Reckless Moment
The Set-Up
The Third Man
The Undercover Man
White Heat
The Window

1950 *The Asphalt Jungle*
Caged
Convicted
D. O. A.
Dark City
The File on Thelma Jordan
In a Lonely Place
Night and the City
Panic in the Streets
711 Ocean Drive
The Sleeping City
Sunset Blvd.
Union Station
Where Danger Lives
Where the Sidewalk Ends
Woman on the Run

1951 *Appointment with Danger*
   The Big Carnival
   Cry Danger
   Detective Story
   The Enforcer
   The Mob
   The Prowler
   Strangers on a Train
1952 *Beware My Lovely*
   Clash by Night
   The Narrow Margin
   On Dangerous Ground
1953 *Angel Face*
   The Big Frame
   The Big Heat
   The Blue Gardenia
   City That Never Sleeps
   The Class Web
   I, the Jury
   Niagara
   Pickup on South Street
1954 *Blackout*
   Human Desire
   The Long Wait
1955 *The Big Combo*
   The Big Knife
   I Died a Thousand Times
   Killer's Kiss
   Kiss Me Deadly
   Mr. Arkadin
1956 *Beyond a Reasonable Doubt*
   The Harder They Fall
   The Killing
   A Kiss Before Dying
   Nightmare
   While the City Sleeps
   The Wrong Man
1957 *The Brothers Rico*
1958 *Touch of Evil*
   Vertigo

APPENDIX B

Some Interim Noir Films According to Commentators

1959	*Odds Against Tomorrow*
1960	*Psycho*
1961	*Blast of Silence*
	Underworld U. S. A.
1962	*Cape Fear*
	Experiment in Terror
	The Manchurian Candidate
1963	*Shock Corridor*
1964	*The Killers*
	The Naked Kiss
1965	*Brainstorm*
1966	*Harper*
1967	*Point Blank*
1968	*The Detective*
	Lady in Cement
1971	*Chandler*
	Dirty Harry
	Klute
	Shaft
1972	*The Getaway*
1973	*The Long Goodbye*
	Serpico
1974	*Chinatown*
	Death Wish

The Parallax View
Thieves Like Us
1975 *The Drowning Pool*
Farewell, My Lovely
Night Moves
1976 *Taxi Driver*
1978 *The Driver*
Who'll Stop the Rain
1979 *Apocalypse Now*

APPENDIX C

Neo-Noir Films According to Nelson

1981   *Body Heat*
        Eyewitness
        The Postman Always Rings Twice
1982   *Blade Runner*
        Dead Men Don't Wear Plaid
1983   *Breathless*
1984   *Against All Odds*
        Blood Simple
        The Terminator
1985   *To Live and Die in L. A.*
1986   *Blue Velvet*
        The Morning After
        Nomads
1987   *Angel Heart*
        No Way Out
1988   *D. O. A.*
        Who Framed Roger Rabbit?
1989   *Batman*
        Johnny Handsome
1990   *After Dark, My Sweet*
        Desperate Hours
        Edward Scissorhands
        The Hot Spot
        Narrow Margin
        Rainbow Drive
        The Two Jakes

Mulholland Falls
Trade Off
1997 *Batman and Robin*
City of Industry
Conspiracy Theory
Face/Off
Fallen
Incognito
L. A. Confidential
Lost Highway
The Sweet Hereafter
This World, Then the Fireworks
Twilight
1998 *American History X*
Babe: Pig in the City
The Big Lebowski
Blade
Brown's Requiem
Caught Up
Croupier
Dark City
Palmetto
A Simple Plan
1999 *American Beauty*
Bangkok Dangerous
The Boondock Saints
Fight Club
Forever Mine
The General's Daughter
In Too Deep
Magnolia
The Matrix
Mumford
Payback
The Thirteenth Floor
2000 *Boiler Room*
The Crow: Salvation
Gangster No. 1
Innocents [*Dark Summer*]
Memento

Panic
Pilgrim
The Pledge
Reindeer Games
Shaft
Traffic
2001   *After Image*
The Caveman's Valentine
The Deep End
Donnie Darko
From Hell
The Glass House
Hannibal
The Man Who Wasn't There
Mulholland Dr.
The Score
Soul Assassin
Spy Game
Swordfish
Training Day
Unbreakable
Vanilla Sky
Who Is Cletis Tout?
2002   *The Badge*
City by the Sea
Confessions of a Dangerous Mind
Femme Fatale
Impostor
Insomnia
Minority Report
Murder by Numbers
One Hour Photo
Ripley's Game
Road to Perdition
The Salton Sea
2003   *Confidence*
Daredevil
The House of Sand and Fog
The Human Stain
I'll Sleep When I'm Dead
Kill Bill: Volume 1

Levity
The Limit [Gone Dark]
Paris
The Singing Detective
Terminator 3: Rise of the Machines
The Tesseract
21 Grams
Wonderland

2004 *The Butterfly Effect*
Catwoman
Collateral
Eternal Sunshine of the Spotless Mind
I, Robot
Kill Bill: Volume 2
Layer Cake
Man on Fire
Never Die Alone
November
Out of Season
The Punisher
Seven Times Lucky
Sky Captain and the World of Tomorrow
Suspect Zero

2005 *Batman Begins*
Brick
Crash
The Crow: Wicked Prayer
Derailed
Domino
Dot.Kill
Hostage
Jesse Stone: Stone Cold
Kiss Kiss, Bang Bang
Shadowboxer
Sin City
Stay
Where the Truth Lies

2006 *All the King's Men*
Basic Instinct 2
The Black Dahlia
The Butterfly Effect 2

Crank
Déjà Vu
Even Money
The Good German
The Good Shepherd
Hollywoodland
The Illusionist
Inland Empire
Inside Man
Jesse Stone: Death in Paradise
Jesse Stone: Night Passage
Lonely Hearts
Lucky Number Slevin
The Net 2.0
Played
A Prairie Home Companion
The Prestige
Renaissance
A Scanner Darkly
16 Blocks
V for Vendetta

2007   *The Air I Breathe*
Awake
Cherry Crush
Cleaner
Death Defying Acts
Eastern Promises
First Snow
Flawless
He Was a Quiet Man
Hitman
The Hoax
In the Valley of Elah
Jesse Stone: Sea Change
Love Lies Bleeding
Michael Clayton
No Country for Old Men
The Number 23
Sleuth

2008   *The Art of War II: Betrayal*
Bangkok Dangerous

Appendix C • 207

Babylon A. D.
The Dark Knight
In Bruges
Max Payne
The Narrows
Punisher: War Zone
Redbelt
Righteous Kill
Seven Pounds
The Spirit
The Square
Street Kings
21
Twilight
Vice
Wanted
What Doesn't Kill You
2009 *The Bad Lieutenant: Port of Call—New Orleans*
Beyond a Reasonable Doubt
Daybreakers
Give 'em Hell, Malone
In the Electric Mist
Jesse Stone: Thin Ice
Killshot
The Missing Person
Powder Blue
Push
Red Riding: 1974
Red Riding: 1980
Red Riding: 1983
Watchmen
Wrong Turn at Tahoe
2010 *Animal Kingdom*
Brooklyn's Finest
Dylan Dog: Dead of Night
Inception
Jesse Stone: No Remorse
Kick-Ass
The Killer Inside Me
London Boulevard
Love Ranch

The Next Three Days
Repo Men
Twelve
2011 *The Big Bang*
Catch .44
Drive
In Time
Jesse Stone: Innocents Lost
The Ledge
Limitless
Mysteria
Rampart
Restitution
The River Murders
Road to Nowhere
Seeking Justice
Source Code
Street Kings 2: Motor City
Sucker Punch
Unknown
2012 *Assassin's Bullet*
The Courier
The Dark Knight Rises
Deadfall
Dredd 3D
End of Watch
The Factory
Freelancers
Jesse Stone: Benefit of the Doubt
Lockout
The Paperboy
Savages
Tomorrow You're Gone
Total Recall

Notes

Introduction   Doing Political Theory with Popular Films: Styles in Action in Everyday Life

1. Stephen Colbert, "Interview of Kathryn Bigelow," *The Colbert Report*, MSNBC, January 22, 2013.
2. See Joseph Campbell, *Myths to Live By*, New York, Viking Press, 1972; Henry Tudor, *Political Myth*, New York, Praeger, 1972; H. Mark Roelofs, *Ideology and Myth in American Politics*, Boston, Little, Brown, 1976; James Oliver Robertson, *American Myth, American Reality*, New York, Hill and Wang, 1980; Dora C. Pozzi and John M. Wickersham, eds., *Myth and the Polis*, Ithaca, NY, Cornell University Press, 1991. Also see Geoffrey Hill, *Illuminating Shadows: The Mythic Power of Film*, Boston, Shambhala, 1992; John Izod, *Myth, Mind and the Screen: Understanding the Heroes of Our Time*, Cambridge, Cambridge University Press, 2001.
3. See Phillip L. Gianos, *Politics and Politicians in American Film*, Westport, CT, Praeger, 1998.
4. See Stanley Cavell, *Pursuits of Happiness: The Hollywood Comedy of Remarriage*, Cambridge, MA, Harvard University Press, 1981.
5. See Kiku Adatto, "Mythic Pictures: The Maverick Heroes in American Movies," *Picture Perfect*, New York, Basic Books, 1993, pp. 124–166; John Izod, *Myth, Mind and the Screen: Understanding the Heroes of Our Time*, Cambridge, Cambridge University Press, 2001.
6. See Laurence A. Rickels, *The Vampire Lectures*, Minneapolis, University of Minnesota Press, 1999.
7. Gore Vidal, "Reel History," *New Yorker* 73, no. 34, November 10, 1997, pp. 112–120, on p. 115.
8. See Gore Vidal, *Screening History*, Cambridge, MA, Harvard University Press, 1992. Also see Gore Vidal, *The Narratives of Empire*, New York, Random House: *Burr*, 1974; *1876*, 1976; *Lincoln*, 1984; *Empire*, 1987; *Hollywood*, 1990; *The Golden Age*, 2000.
9. See John S. Nelson, "Conspiracy as a Hollywood Trope for System," *Political Communication* 20, no. 4 (October–December 2003): 499–503.

10. See John Fiske, *Reading the Popular*, Boston, Unwin Hyman, 1989; John Fiske, *Understanding Popular Culture*, New York, Routledge, 1989.
11. See Joseph Campbell, *The Hero with a Thousand Faces*, New York, World, 1949.
12. See G. R. Boynton and John S. Nelson, "Orchestrating Politics," *Hot Spots: Multimedia Analyses of Political Ads*, Urbana, University of Illinois Press, 1997, third chapter of a videocassette.
13. See Dan D. Nimmo, *Popular Images of Politics*, Englewood Cliffs, NJ, Prentice-Hall, 1974; Dan D. Nimmo and James E. Combs, *Subliminal Politics: Myths and Mythmakers in America*, Englewood Cliffs, NJ, Prentice-Hall, 1980; Dan D. Nimmo and James E. Combs, *Mediated Political Realities*, New York, Longman (1983), 2nd ed., 1990; Geoffrey Hill, *Illuminating Shadows: The Mythic Power of Film*, Boston, Shambhala, 1992; Michael Parenti, *Make-Believe Media: The Politics of Entertainment*, New York, St. Martin's Press, 1992; Michael Parenti, *Land of Idols: Political Mythology in America*, New York, St. Martin's Press, 1994.
14. See John S. Nelson, *Tropes of Politics: Science, Theory, Rhetoric, Action*, Madison, University of Wisconsin Press, 1998, pp. 115–204.
15. See Barry Keith Grant, ed., *Film Genre Reader*, Austin, University of Texas Press, 1986.
16. See Jane Gaines, ed., "Film and TV Theory Today," *South Atlantic Quarterly* 88, no. 2 (Spring 1989): 321–539; Elizabeth Ezra and Terry Rowden, eds., *Transnational Cinema*, New York, Routledge, 2006.
17. Niccolò Machiavelli, in *The Prince*, Robert M. Adams, ed. and trans., New York, Norton (1975), 2nd ed., 1992, p. 42.
18. See Thomas More, in *Utopia*, Robert M. Adams, ed., New York, Norton (1975), 2nd ed., 1992.
19. See Isadore Traschen, "Pure and Ironic Idealism," *South Atlantic Quarterly* 59, no. 2 (Spring 1960): 1673–170.
20. See Kenneth Burke, "Realism and Idealism," *Dial* 74 (1923): 97–99.
21. See Roman Jakobson, "On Realism in Art (1921)," in *Language in Literature*, Krystyna Pomorska and Stephen Rudy, eds., Cambridge, MA, Harvard University Press, 1987, pp. 19–27. Also see Nelson Goodman, "Realism, Relativism, and Reality," *New Literary History* 14, no. 2 (Winter 1983): 269–272; W. J. T. Mitchell, "Realism, Irrealism, and Ideology: After Nelson Goodman," *Picture Theory*, Chicago, University of Chicago Press, 1994, pp. 345–362.
22. See Lois Parkinson Zamora and Wendy B. Faris, eds., *Magical Realism: Theory, History, Community*, Durham, NC, Duke University Press, 1995; Maggie Ann Bowers, *Magic(al) Realism: The New Critical Idiom*, New York, Routledge, 2004; Wendy B. Faris, *Ordinary Enchantments: Magical Realism and the Remystification of Narrative*, Nashville, Vanderbilt University Press, 2004.
23. See Roberto Mangabeira Unger, New York, Cambridge University Press, 1987: *False Necessity: Anti-Necessitarian Social Theory in the Service of Radical Democracy*, 1987; *Social Theory: Its Situation and Its Task*, 1987; *Plasticity into Power: Comparative-Historical Studies of the Institutional Conditions of Economic*

and Military Success, 1987. Also see David Graeber, *Debt: The First 5,000 Years*, Brooklyn, Melville House, 2011; David Graeber, *The Democracy Project: A History, a Crisis, a Movement*, New York, Random House, 2013.

24. See Fredric Jameson, *The Political Unconscious: Narrative as a Socially Symbolic Act*, Ithaca, NY, Cornell University Press, 1981.

25. See Robert Hariman, *Political Style: The Artistry of Power*, Chicago, University of Chicago Press, 1995; Dick Hebdige, *Subculture: The Meaning of Style*, London, Routledge, 1979; Stuart Ewen, *All Consuming Images: The Politics of Style in Contemporary Culture*, New York, Basic Books, 1988; Barry Brummett, *A Rhetoric of Style*, Carbondale, Southern Illinois University Press, 2008.

26. See John Dunn, *Western Political Theory in the Face of the Future*, Cambridge, Cambridge University Press, 1979, pp. 1–27; Nelson, *Tropes of Politics*, pp. 150–179.

27. See Nelson, *Tropes of Politics*, pp. 205–230.

28. On Hollywood films as popular movies for Americans, see Richard Maltby, *Hollywood Cinema: An Introduction*, Oxford, Basil Blackwell, 1995.

29. See J. P. Telotte, *Science Fiction Film*, Cambridge, Cambridge University Press, 2001. Also see John S. Nelson, "Political Mythmaking for Postmoderns," *Spheres of Argument*, in Bruce E. Gronbeck, ed., Annandale, VA, Speech Communication Association, 1989, pp. 175–183.

30. See Olaf Stapledon, *Odd John*, New York, Garland (1936), 1975; Olaf Stapledon, *Star Maker*, Middletown, CT, Wesleyan University Press, 2004. Also see Doris Lessing, *The Four-Gated City*, New York, Knopf, 1969; Doris Lessing, *Briefing for a Descent into Hell*, New York, Knopf, 1971; Doris Lessing, *Canopus in Argos: Archives*, New York, Knopf: *Shikasta*, 1979; *The Marriages Between Zones Three, Four, and Five*, 1980; *The Sirian Experiments*, 1980; *The Making of the Representative for Planet 8*, 1982; *The Sentimental Agents*, 1983.

31. See John G. Cawelti, *Adventure, Mystery, and Romance: Formula Stories as Art and Popular Culture*, Chicago, University of Chicago Press, 1976.

32. See Rikke Schubart, "Passion and Acceleration: Generic Change in the Action Film," in *Violence and American Cinema*, J. David Slocum, ed., New York, Routledge, 2001, pp. 192–207; Eric Lichtenfeld, *Action Speaks Louder: Violence, Spectacle, and the American Action Movie*, Middletown, CT, Wesleyan University Press (2004), expanded edition, 2007.

33. See Machiavelli, *The Prince*; Harvey Mansfield Jr., *Machiavelli's Virtue*, Chicago, University of Chicago Press, 1966; Martin Fleisher, ed., *Machiavelli and the Nature of Political Thought*, New York, Atheneum, 1972; Michael Ledeen, *Machiavelli on Modern Leadership*, New York, St. Martin's Press, 1999.

34. See Max Weber, "Bureaucracy," in *From Max Weber: Essays in Sociology*, H. H. Gerth and C. Wright Mills, eds. and trans., New York, Oxford University Press, 1946, pp. 196–244; Hannah Arendt, "Race and Bureaucracy," *The Origins of Totalitarianism*, New York, Harcourt Brace Jovanovich (1951, 1958), 4th ed., 1973, pp. 185–221; Robert Hariman, "A Boarder in One's Own Home: Franz Kafka's Parable of the Bureaucratic Style," *Political Style*, pp. 141–176.

35. See John S. Nelson, "Prudence as Republican Politics in American Popular Culture," in *Prudence: Classical Virtue, Postmodern Practice*, Robert Hariman, ed., University Park, Pennsylvania State University Press, 2003, pp. 229–257.
36. See Darko Suvin, *Metamorphoses of Science Fiction: On the Poetics and History of a Literary Genre*, New Haven, Yale University Press, 1979, pp. 1–15; Samuel R. Delany, "About Five Thousand Seven Hundred and Fifty Words," *The Jewel-Hinged Jaw: Essays on Science Fiction*, New York, Berkley Books, 1977, pp. 21–37; Mark Rose, *Alien Encounters: Anatomy of Science Fiction*, Cambridge, MA, Harvard University Press, 1981, p. 20.
37. See Mark Rose, ed., *Science Fiction: A Collection of Critical Essays*, Englewood Cliffs, NJ, Prentice-Hall, 1976.
38. Tom Godwin, "The Cold Equations," in *Approaches to Science Fiction*, Donald L. Lawler, ed., Boston, Houghton Mifflin, 1978, pp. 232–252.

1 An Epic Comeback? Postwestern Politics in Film and Theory

1. Anthony Lane, "Miles to Go: *The Way Back* and *Biutiful*," *New Yorker*, 86, 46, January 31, 2011, pp. 82–83, on p. 82.
2. See Peter Toohey, *Reading Epic: An Introduction to the Ancient Narratives*, London, Routledge, 1992.
3. See Franco Moretti, *Modern Epic: The World-System from Goethe to Garcia Marquez*, trans. Quinton Hoare, London, Verso, 1996; Margaret Beissinger, Jane Tylus, and Susanne Wofford, eds., *Epic Traditions in the Contemporary World: The Poetics of Community*, Berkeley, University of California Press, 1999; Dean A. Miller, *The Epic Hero*, Baltimore, Johns Hopkins University Press, 2000.
4. See Robert D. Kaplan, *Warrior Politics: Why Leadership Demands a Pagan Ethos*, New York, Random House, 2002.
5. See Hannah Arendt, *The Human Condition*, Chicago, University of Chicago Press, 1959; Hannah Arendt, *Between Past and Future*, New York, Viking Press (1963), expanded edition, 1968. Also see John S. Nelson, "Political Foundations for Rhetoric of Inquiry," in *The Rhetorical Turn: Invention and Persuasion in the Conduct of Inquiry*, Herbert W. Simons, ed., Chicago, University of Chicago Press, 1990, pp. 258–289; John S. Nelson, "Commerce among the Archipelagos: Rhetoric of Inquiry as a Practice of Coherent Education," in *The Core and the Canon*, L. Robert Stevens, G. L. Seligmann, and Julian Long, eds., Denton, TX, University of North Texas Press, 1993, pp. 78–100.
6. See Robert E. Nisbett and Dov Cohen, *Cultures of Honor: The Psychology of Violence in the South*, Boulder, CO, Westview Press, 1996.
7. See Thomas Malory, *Le Morte D'Arthur*, Norman Lorre Goodrich, ed. (1485), 1963; T. H. White, *The Once and Future King*, New York, Putnam, 1939.
8. See Guy Debord, *Society of the Spectacle*, Detroit, Black and Red (1967), 1977; Hal Foster, *Recordings: Art, Spectacle, Cultural Politics*, Port Townsend, WA, Bay Press, 1985; Thomas Shevory, *Notorious H. I. V.: The Media Spectacle of Nushawn Williams*, Minneapolis, University of Minnesota Press, 2004; Eric Lichtenfeld,

Action Speaks Louder: Violence, Spectacle, and the American Action Movie, Middletown, CT, Wesleyan University Press (2004), expanded edition, 2007.

9. See Barry Keith Grant, ed., *Film Genre Reader*, Austin, University of Texas Press, 1986; Rick Altman, *Film/Genre*, London, British Film Institute, 1999.

10. See John S. Nelson and G. R. Boynton, *Video Rhetorics: Televised Advertising in American Politics*, Urbana, University of Illinois Press, 1997.

11. See John S. Nelson, "Horror Films Face Political Evils in Everyday Life," *Political Communication* 22, no. 3 (July–September 2005): 381–386.

12. See Nelson and Boynton, *Video Rhetorics*, pp. 27–86.

13. See John S. Nelson, "Conspiracy as a Hollywood Trope for System," *Political Communication* 20, no. 4 (October–December 2003): 499–503.

14. See Lee Clark Mitchell, *Westerns: Making the Man in Fiction and Film*, Chicago, University of Chicago Press, 1996; Will Wright, *The Wild West: The Mythical Cowboy and Social Theory*, Thousand Oaks, CA, Sage, 2001; Robert B. Pippin, *Hollywood Westerns and American Myth: The Importance of Howard Hawks and John Ford for Political Philosophy*, New Haven, Yale University Press, 2010.

15. See Peter A. French, *The Virtues of Vengeance*, Lawrence, University Press of Kansas, 2001.

16. See Robert Goldman and Stephen Papson, *Nike Culture: The Sign of the Swoosh*, Thousand Oaks, CA, Sage, 1998.

17. See John S. Nelson and G. R. Boynton, "Arguing War: Global Television against American Cinema," in *Arguing Communication and Culture*, G. Thomas Goodnight, ed., Washington, DC, National Communication Association, 2002, pp. 571–577.

18. See Tzvetan Todorov, *The Fantastic: A Structural Approach to a Literary Genre*, Richard Howard, trans., Ithaca, NY, Cornell University Press (1970) (1973), 1975; W. R. Irwin, *The Game of the Impossible: A Rhetoric of Fantasy*, Urbana, University of Illinois Press, 1976; Christine Brooke-Rose, *A Rhetoric of the Unreal: Studies in Narrative and Structure, Especially of the Fantastic*, Cambridge, Cambridge University Press, 1981.

19. See Stephen King, *Danse Macabre*, New York, Berkley Books, 1981; Douglas E. Winter, *Faces of Fear*, New York, Berkley Books, 1985, p. 62; Darryl Jones, *Horror: A Thematic History in Fiction and Film*, London, Arnold, 2002; Stephen Prince, ed., *The Horror Film*, New Brunswick, NJ, Rutgers University Press, 2004.

20. See Nelson, "Horror Films Face Political Evils in Everyday Life."

21. See John S. Nelson, "Popular Rhetorics for Non-Linear Politics: Movements, Styles, Systems, and More," in *Concerning Argument*, Scott Jacobs, ed., Washington, DC, National Communication Association, 2009, pp. 572–579.

22. See David Worcester, *The Art of Satire*, New York, Russell and Russell, 1940; Alan Reynolds Thompson, *The Dry Mock*, Berkeley, University of California Press, 1948.

23. Mock epics from Mel Brooks include *History of the World: Part I* (1981), *Spaceballs* (1987), and *Robin Hood: Men in Tights* (1993). Mock epics from Monty Python include *Monty Python and the Holy Grail* (1975), *Life of Brian* (1979), *The Meaning of Life* (1983), and *The Adventures of Baron Munchausen*

(1988). The recent surge in epics is the satirical target of *Epic Movie* (2007) from Jason Friedburg and Aaron Seltzer.

24. See Dan Nimmo and James E. Combs, *Subliminal Politics: Myths and Mythmakers in America*, Englewood Cliffs, NJ, Prentice-Hall, 1980; Bruno Bettelheim, "The Art of Moving Pictures: Man, Superman, and Myth," *Harper's Magazine* 263, 1577, October 1981, pp. 80–83; Geoffrey Hill, *Illuminating Shadows: The Mythic Power of Film*, Boston, Shambhala, 1992.

25. See Hendrik Hertzberg, "Upset Victory: *Primary Colors* Triumphs Over the Old Politics of Hollywood," *New Yorker* 74, no. 5, March 23, 1998, pp. 86–90.

26. See Thomas Hobbes, in *Leviathan*, C. B. Macpherson, ed., New York, Penguin Books (1651), 1968; Thomas Hobbes, in *Man and Citizen*, Bernard Gert, ed., Garden City, NY, Doubleday, 1972. Also see Thomas A. Spragens, *The Politics of Motion: The World of Thomas Hobbes*, Lexington, University Press of Kentucky, 1973; Quentin Skinner, *Reason and Rhetoric in the Philosophy of Hobbes*, Cambridge, Cambridge University Press, 1996; Ted Miller, *Mortal Gods: Science, Politics, and the Humanist Ambitions of Thomas Hobbes*, University Park, Pennsylvania State University Press, 2011.

27. See John Locke, *Two Treatises of Government*, New York, New American Library, revised ed., 1963. Also see Joyce Appleby, *Liberalism and Republicanism in the Historical Imagination*, Cambridge, MA, Harvard University Press, 1992; Philip Pettit, *Republicanism: A Theory of Freedom and Government*, Oxford, Oxford University Press, 1999.

28. See Margaret Canovan, *Populism*, New York, Harcourt Brace Jovanovich, 1981; Michael Kazin, *The Populist Persuasion: An American History*, Ithaca, NY, Cornell University Press (1995), revised ed., 1998; Ernest Laclau, *On Populist Reason*, New York, Verso, 2005; Charles Postel, *The Populist Vision*, New York, Oxford University Press, 2007.

29. See Friedrich Nietzsche, *The Birth of Tragedy* and *The Genealogy of Morals*, Francis Golffing, trans., Garden City, NY, Doubleday, 1956; Friedrich Nietzsche, *Ecce Homo*, R. J. Hollingdale, trans., Baltimore, Penguin Books, 1979; Friedrich Nietzsche, *Thus Spake Zarathustra*, R. J. Hollingdale, trans., Baltimore, Penguin Books, 1961; Friedrich Nietzsche, *Twilight of the Idols* and *The Anti-Christ*, R. J. Hollingdale, trans., Baltimore, Penguin Books (1889 and 1885), 1968; Friedrich Nietzsche, *On the Advantage and Disadvantage of History for Life*, Peter Preuss, trans., Indianapolis, Hackett, 1982; Friedrich Nietzsche, *The Will to Power*, Walter Kaufmann, ed., Walter Kaufman and R. J. Hollingdale, trans., New York, Random House, 1967. Also see Tracy B. Strong, *Friedrich Nietzsche and the Politics of Transformation*, Berkeley, University of California Press, 1975; Daniel W. Conway, *Nietzsche and the Political*, London, Routledge, 1997.

30. See Frederick M. Dolan and Thomas L. Dumm, eds., *Rhetorical Republic: Governing Representations in American Politics*, Amherst, University of Massachusetts Press, 1993.

31. See Michael Moorcock, *Wizardry & Wild Romance: A Study of Epic Fantasy*, Austin, TX, MonkeyBrain, 2004.

32. An especially provocative take on opera treats it as passionate speech; see Stanley Cavell, *A Pitch of Philosophy: Autobiographical Exercises*, Cambridge, MA, Harvard University Press, 1994.

33. See James Gleick, *Chaos: Making a New Science*, New York, Penguin Books, 1987; James Gleick, *Nature's Chaos*, New York, Basic Books, 1990. Also see N. Katherine Hayles, *Chaos Bound: Orderly Disorder in Contemporary Literature and Science*, Ithaca, NY, Cornell University Press, 1990; N. Katherine Hayles, ed., *Chaos and Order: Complex Dynamics in Literature and Science*, Chicago, University of Chicago Press, 1991.

34. See J. G. A. Pocock, *The Machiavellian Moment: Florentine Political Thought and the Atlantic Republican Tradition*, Princeton, NJ, Princeton University Press, 1975; Paul A. Rahe, *Republics Ancient and Modern*, Chapel Hill, NC, University of North Carolina Press, in three volumes, 1994; Philip Pettit, *Republicanism*, Oxford, Oxford University Press, 1997; Quentin Skinner, *Liberty Before Liberalism*, Cambridge, Cambridge University Press, 1998.

35. On postwestern settings and responses, see Glenn Tinder, *The Crisis of Political Imagination*, New York, Scribner, 1964; John Dunn, *Western Political Theory in the Face of the Future*, Cambridge, Cambridge University Press, 1979; David Morley and Kevin Robins, eds., *Spaces of Identity: Global Media, Electronic Landscapes, and Cultural Boundaries*, London, Routledge, 1995, pp. 187–228.

36. Even after the theatrical release, which seems to have received exceptional editing, even by Hollywood standards, Oliver Stone tried again with a director's cut, then later with a "final cut."

37. See John S. Nelson, *Tropes of Politic: Science, Rhetory, Rhetoric, Action*, Madison, University of Wisconsin Press, 1998, pp. 138–141.

38. See Mark Twain, *A Connecticut Yankee in King Arthur's Court*, New York, New American Library, (1889), 1963. When I point out that the 1949 movie stars Bing Crosby, you won't be surprised to learn that it makes no discernible effort to match the novel's epic sensibility.

39. See Christopher Matthews, *Hardball*, New York, HarperCollins, 1988; Christopher Matthews, *Life's a Campaign*, New York, Random House, 2007. Also see John S. Nelson, "Prudence as Republican Politics in American Popular Culture," in *Prudence: Classical Virtue, Postmodern Practice*, Robert Hariman, ed., University Park, Pennsylvania State University Press, 2003, pp. 229–257.

40. See Garry Wills, *Cincinnatus: George Washington and the Enlightenment—Images of Power in Early America*, Garden City, NY, Doubleday, 1984.

41. See Carl G. Jung, in *Psyche and Symbol*, Violet S. de Laszlo, ed., Garden City, NY, Doubleday, 1958; Joseph Campbell, *Myths to Live By*, New York, Viking Press, 1972; Janice Hocker Rushing and Thomas S. Frentz, *Projecting the Shadow: The Cyborg Hero in American Film*, Chicago, University of Chicago Press, 1995.

42. See Robin Morgan, ed., *Sisterhood Is Powerful*, New York, Random House, 1970; Robin Morgan, ed., *Sisterhood Is Forever*, New York, Washington Square Press, 2003.

43. See Murray Edelman, *Constructing the Political Spectacle*, Chicago, University of Chicago Press, 1988; Robert Hariman, "No One Is in Charge Here: Ryszard Kapuscinski Anatomy of the Courtly Style," *Political Style: The Artistry of Power*, Chicago, University of Chicago Press, 1995, pp. 51–94; Adam Gopnik, "Display Cases," *New Yorker* 75, no. 9–10 (April 26 and May 1, 1999), pp. 176–184. Also see John S. Nelson, "All's Fair: Love, War, Politics, and Other Spectacles," *Poroi* 4, no. 2 (July 2005), http://inpress.lib.uiowa.edu/poroi/papers/nelson050701.html.

44. See Quentin Skinner, *The Foundations of Modern Political Thought*, Cambridge, Cambridge University Press, 1978, in two volumes; Jean-François Lyotard, *The Postmodern Condition*, Geoff Bennington and Brian Massumi, trans., Minneapolis, University of Minnesota Press (1979), 1984; Jim Collins, *Uncommon Cultures: Popular Culture and Post-Modernism*, New York, Routledge, 1989; Jonathan Bignell, *Postmodern Media Culture*, Edinburgh, Edinburgh University Press, 2000.

45. See Joseph Campbell, *The Hero with a Thousand Faces*, New York, World, 1949.

46. On contrasts among bourgeois, pagan, and Christian virtues, see D. N. McCloskey, "Bourgeois Virtues," *American Scholar* 63, no. 2 (Spring 1994): 177–191; D. N. McCloskey, *The Vices of Economists— The Virtues of the Bourgeoisie*, Amsterdam, Amsterdam University Press, 1996; D. N. McCloskey, *The Bourgeois Virtues: Ethics for an Age of Commerce*, Chicago, University of Chicago Press, 2006.

47. See Nelson, *Tropes of Politics*, pp. 141–143.

48. See Johann Wolfgang von Goethe, *Faust*, Louis MacNeice, trans., New York, Oxford University Press, 1951; Marshall Berman, "Goethe's *Faust*: The Tragedy of Development," *All That Is Solid Melts into Air*, New York, Simon and Schuster, 1982, pp. 37–86; Harry Redner, *In the Beginning Was the Deed*, Berkeley, University of California Press, 1982. See Thomas Mann, *Doctor Faustus*, H. T. Lowe-Porter, trans., New York, Random House, 1948. Also see John S. Nelson, "Toltechs, Aztechs, and the Art of the Possible," *Polity* 8, no. 1 (Fall 1975): 80–116.

49. Sheldon S. Wolin, *Hobbes and the Epic Tradition of Political Theory*, Los Angeles, University of California Press, 1970, p. 4.

50. See Dan Nimmo and James E. Combs, *Subliminal Politics: Myths and Mythmakers in America*, Englewood Cliffs, NJ, Prentice-Hall, 1980; Gerald Mast and Marshall Cohen, eds., *Film Theory and Criticism*, New York, Oxford University Press (1974, 1979), 3rd ed., 1985; David Bordwell, *Making Meaning: Inference and Rhetoric in the Interpretation of Cinema*, Cambridge, MA, Harvard University Press, 1989.

51. See Jack Goody, *The Domestication of the Savage Mind*, Cambridge, Cambridge University Press, 1977; Eric A. Havelock, *The Literate Revolution in Greece and Its Cultural Consequences*, 1982; Eric Havelock, *The Muse Learns to Write*, New Haven, Yale University Press, 1986; Walter J. Ong, *Orality and Literacy*, New York, Methuen, 1982.

52. See Kiku Adatto, "Mythic Pictures: The Maverick Heroes in American Movies," *Picture Perfect: The Art and Artifice of Public Image Making*, New York, Basic Books, 1993, pp. 124–166.

53. See Isadore Traschen, "Pure and Ironic Idealism," *South Atlantic Quarterly* 59, no. 2 (Spring 1960): 163–170; Elizabeth Markovits, *The Politics of Sincerity: Plato, Frank Speech, and Democratic Judgment*, University Park, Pennsylvania State University Press, 2008, pp. 47–122.

54. See John S. Nelson, "Stands in Politics," *Journal of Politics* 46, no. 1 (February 1984): 106–131.

55. See J. R. R. Tolkien, *The Lord of the Rings*, New York, Ballantine Books, 1965: *The Fellowship of the Ring, The Two Towers*, and *The Return of the King*. Also see Roger Sale, "Tolkien and Frodo Baggins," *Modern Heroism*, Berkeley, CA, University of California Press, 1973, pp. 193–240.

56. See Charles D. Elder and Roger W. Cobb, *The Political Uses of Symbols*, New York, Longman, 1983. Also see Murray Edelman, *The Symbolic Uses of Politics*, Urbana, University of Illinois Press (1964), 2nd ed., 1985; Murray Edelman, *Political Language: Words That Succeed and Policies That Fail*, New York, Academic Press, 1977; Murray Edelman, *Constructing the Political Spectacle; The Politics of Misinformation*, Cambridge, Cambridge University Press, 2001.

57. See John S. Nelson and Barbara J. Hill, "Facing the Holocaust: Robert Arneson's Ceramic Myth of Postmodern Catastrophe," in *Human Rights/Human Wrongs: Art and Social Change*, Robert Hobbs and Fredrick Woodard, eds., Seattle, University of Washington Press, 1986, pp. 189–209.

58. See Rushing and Frentz, *Projecting the Shadow*; Nelson, "Political Mythmaking for Postmoderns."

59. See David Denby, "Battle Fatigue: *Flags of Our Fathers* and *Babel*," *New Yorker* 82, no. 35, October 30, 2006, pp. 102–103; Louis P. Masur, "Suspended in Time," *Chronicle of Higher Education* 53, no. 12, November 10, 2006, p. B16.

60. Thus the philosopher of science Paul K. Feyerabend once urged, "Let's Make More Movies," in *The Owl of Minerva: Philosophers on Philosophy*, Charles J. Bontempo and S. Jack Odell, eds., New York, McGraw-Hill, 1975, pp. 201–210. In a different direction, the scholarly journal of *Philosophy and Literature* strives to treat literary works as philosophical contributions.

61. See Max Horkheimer and Theodor W. Adorno, *Dialectic of Enlightenment*, John Cumming, trans., New York, Herder and Herder, 1944; Max Horkheimer, *Eclipse of Reason*, New York, Seabury Press, 1947. Also see Jürgen Habermas, *Legitimation Crisis*, Thomas McCarthy, trans., Boston, Beacon Press (1973), 1975; Jürgen Habermas, "The Crisis of Late Capitalism and the Future of Democracy: An Interview by Angelo Bolaffi," Eleni Mahaira-Odoni, trans., *Telos* 39 (Spring 1979): 163–172. And see Martin Jay, *The Dialectical Imagination: A History of the Frankfurt School and the Institute of Social Research, 1923–1950*, Boston, Little, Brown, 1973; Morton Schoolman, *Reason and Horror: Critical Theory, Democracy, and Aesthetic Individuality*, New York, Routledge, 2001.

62. See Wolin, *Hobbes and the Epic Tradition of Political Theory*.

63. See Arendt, *The Human Condition* and *Between Past and Future*.

64. See Sheldon S. Wolin, *Politics and Vision*, Princeton, NJ, Princeton University Press (1960), revised version, 2004.

65. See John G. Gunnell, *Political Theory: Tradition and Interpretation*, Cambridge, MA, Winthrop, 1979; John G. Gunnell, *Between Philosophy and Politics: The Alienation of Political Theory*, Amherst, University of Massachusetts Press, 1986; John G. Gunnell, *The Descent of Political Theory: The Genealogy of an American Vocation*, Chicago, University of Chicago Press, 1993; John G. Gunnell, *The Orders of Discourse: Philosophy, Social Sciences, and Politics*, Lanham, MD, Rowman and Littlefield, 1998.

66. See Thomas S. Kuhn, *The Structure of Scientific Revolutions*, Chicago, University of Chicago Press (1962), expanded edition, 1970; Thomas S. Kuhn, *The Essential Tension: Selected Studies in Scientific Tradition and Change*, Chicago, University of Chicago Press, 1977; Imre Lakatos and Alan Musgrave, eds., *Criticism and the Growth of Knowledge*, Cambridge, Cambridge University Press, 1970.

67. See John S. Nelson, "Once More on Kuhn," *Political Methodology* 1, no. 2 (Spring 1974): 73–104.

68. See Sheldon S. Wolin, "Political Theory as a Vocation," *American Political Science Review* 63, no. 4 (December 1969):1062–1082.

69. See Robert Dahl, "The Behavioral Approach in Political Science," *American Political Science Review* 55, no. 4 (December 1961): 763–772; David Easton, "The New Revolution in Political Science," *American Political Science Review* 63, no. 4 (December 1969): 1051–1061; John A. Wahlke, "Pre-Behavioralism in Political Science," *American Political Science Review* 73, no. 1 (March 1979): 9–31.

70. See Heinz Eulau, *The Behavioral Persuasion in Politics*, Stanford, CA, Stanford University Press, 1963; George J. Graham Jr. and George W. Carey, eds., *The Post-Behavioral Era: Perspectives on Political Science*, New York, David McKay, 1972. Also see John S. Nelson, "Education for Politics: Rethinking Research on Political Socialization," *What Should Political Theory Be Now?* Albany, State University of New York Press, 1983, pp. 413–478; John S. Nelson, ed., "Political Theory as Political Rhetoric," *What Should Political Theory Be Now?* Albany, State University of New York Press, 1983, pp. 413–478.

71. See Sheldon S. Wolin, "Paradigms and Political Theories," in *Politics and Experience*, P. King and B. C. Parekh, eds., Cambridge, Cambridge University Press, 1968, pp. 125–152; Sheldon S. Wolin, "Political Theory: Trends and Goals," in *International Encyclopedia of the Social Sciences*, David L. Sills, ed., New York, Crowell Collier and Macmillan, 1968, vol. 12, pp. 318–330.

72. By genre, Wolin's *Politics and Vision* is intellectual history rather than epic theory, and the same goes for *Tocqueville between Two Worlds: The Making of a Political and Theoretical Life*, Princeton, NJ, Princeton University Press, 2001. Wolin engaged the politics of the day not only in *democracy* but also in books that defend of his sense of student politics of the sixties in *The Berkeley Rebellion and Beyond: Essays on Politics and Education in the Technological Society*, New York, Vintage Books, 1970, plus a volume edited with Seymour Martin Lipset on *The Berkeley Student Revolt: Facts and Interpretations*, Garden City, NY, Doubleday, 1965. Otherwise Wolin's articles and books strike me, at least, as works of critical—rather than constructive, let alone epic—theory: Sheldon S. Wolin, *The Presence of the Past: Essays on the State and the Constitution*, Baltimore, Johns

Hopkins University Press, 1989; Sheldon S. Wolin, *Democracy Incorporated: Managed Democracy and the Specter of Inverted Totalitarianism*, Princeton, Princeton University Press, 2008.

73. Wolin, *Hobbes and the Epic Tradition of Political Theory*, p. 4.
74. See Joseph H. Lane Jr., "Thucydides beyond the Cold War: The Recurrence of Relevance in the Classical Historians," *Poroi* 4, no. 2 (June 2005), http://inpress.lib.uiowa.edu/poroi/ papers/0506021.html.
75. See Malcolm Gladwell, *The Tipping Point: How Little Things Can Make a Big Difference*, Boston, Little, Brown (2000), enlarged edition, 2002.
76. On stands and stances, see John S. Nelson, "Stands in Politics," *Journal of Politics* 46, no. 1 (February 1984): 106–131. On movements, see Sidney Tarrow, *Power in Movement: Social Movements, Collective Action and Politics*, New York, Cambridge University Press, 1994; Jeff Goodwin, James M. Jasper, and Francesca Polletta, eds., *Passionate Politics: Emotions and Social Movements*, Chicago, University of Chicago Press, 2001; Davis S. Meyer, Nancy Whittier, and Belinda Robnett, eds., *Social Movements: Identity, Culture, and the State*, Oxford, Oxford University Press, 2002; Charles Tilly, *The Politics of Collective Violence*, New York, Cambridge University Press, 2003.
77. At the manifesto level, my call is to (Nelson,) "Political Theory as Political Rhetoric," *What Should Political Theory Be Now?* pp. 169–240. Many of my other essays invoked in these notes are attempts to invent aspects of its practice, but none is the least "epic," and movies remain more powerful by far for political mythmaking in current conditions.
78. From Reagan through the second Bush, so far, "right-wing Straussians" should get credit for going more amply into punditry but especially into the federal service of the United States. Because my politics differ, their effects seem mostly perverse and incipiently disastrous. Their rhetoric, sometimes sonorous and powerful, has flowed ironically from ideology increasingly inflexible and unresponsive to experience rather than practical wisdom. Unsurprising for any of us humans, it has showed more penchant for self-aggrandizement and personal enrichment than political virtue. Its oddly "foundational" alliance with the Chicago School of economics, to use a pun for the two notably opposed approaches feeding often from the same troughs, keeps its many would-be players near the arenas even when they are "out of power." Both networks of scholars include some who have learned in the American context to make potently populist appeals. Yet their practical accommodation also raises questions about whether both sides are selling their intellectual souls, while agitating fault lines that relentlessly fissure this elitist camp on the political right. Still this must remain a tale for another time.
79. See Judith N. Shklar, "Hegel's *Phenomenology*: The Moral Failures of Asocial Man," *Political Theory* 1, no. 3 (August 1973): 259–286; Judith N. Shklar, "The *Phenomenology*: Beyond Morality," *Western Political Quarterly* 27, no. 4 (December 1974): 597–623.
80. See Quentin Skinner, ed., *The Return of Grand Theory in the Human Sciences*, Cambridge, Cambridge University Press, 1985.

81. See John Dunn, *Modern Revolutions: An Introduction to the Analysis of a Political Phenomenon*, Cambridge, Cambridge University Press, 1972; John Dunn, *Dependence and Opportunity: Political Change in Ahafo*, Cambridge, Cambridge University Press, 1973; John Dunn, *West African States: Failure and Promise*, Cambridge, Cambridge University Press, 1978; John Dunn, *Setting the People Free: The Story of Democracy*, London, Atlantic, 2005. Also see John Dryzek, *Rational Ecology*, Oxford, Blackwell, 1987; John Dryzek, *Discursive Democracy*, Cambridge, Cambridge University Press, 1990; John Dryzek, *Deliberative Democracy and Beyond*, Oxford, Oxford University Press, 2000; and John Dryzek and Leslie Templeman Holmes, *Post-Communist Democratization*, Cambridge, Cambridge University Press, 2002; and others. John Dryzek and others, *Green States and Social Movements*, Oxford, Oxford University Press, 2003;

82. See Aldo Leopold, *A Sand County Almanac, with Essays on Conservation from Round River*, New York, Ballantine Books (1949, 1953), 1966; Wendell Berry, *The Unsettling of America: Culture and Agriculture*, San Francisco, Sierra Club Books, 1977; Annie Dillard, *Teaching a Stone to Talk: Expeditions and Encounters*, New York, Harper and Row, 1982; Gary Snyder, *The Practice of the Wild*, San Francisco, North Point Press, 1990; Michael Pollan, *Second Nature: A Gardener's Education*, New York, Dell, 1991. Also see Donald Worster, *The Wealth of Nature: Environmental History and the Ecological Imagination*, New York, Oxford University Press, 1993; Florence R. Krall, *Ecotone: Wayfaring on the Margins*, Albany, State University of New York Press, 1994; Andrew Szasz, *EcoPopulism: Toxic Waste and the Movement for Environmental Justice*, Minneapolis, University of Minnesota Press, 1994; John M. Meyer, *Political Nature: Environmentalism and the Interpretation of Western Thought*, Cambridge, MA, MIT Press, 2001.

83. See Anna Lorien Nelson and John S. Nelson, "Institutions in Feminist and Republican Science Fiction," *Legal Studies Forum* 22, no. 4 (1998): 641–653.

2 Rhythms of Political Satire: Postmodern Politics in Words, Musics, and Movies

1. See David Worcester, *The Art of Satire*, New York, Russell and Russell, 1940; Alan Reynolds Thompson, *The Dry Mock*, Berkeley, University of California Press, 1948; Dustin Griffin, *Satire: A Critical Reintroduction*, Lexington, University Press of Kentucky, 1994; Jane Ogborn and Peter Buckroyd, *Satire*, Cambridge, Cambridge University Press, 2001. Also see Russell L. Peterson, *Strange Bedfellows: How Late-Night Comedy Turns Democracy into a Joke*, New Brunswick, NJ, Rutgers University Press, 2008; Jonathan Gray, Jeffrey P. Jones, and Ethan Thompson, eds., *Satire TV: Politics and Comedy in the Post-Network Era*, New York, New York University Press, 2009.

2. See John S. Nelson, *Tropes of Politics: Science, Theory, Rhetoric, Action*, Madison, University of Wisconsin Press, 1998, pp. 143–147, 150–204. Also see John S. Nelson and G. R. Boynton, *Video Rhetorics: Televised Advertising in American Politics*, Urbana, University of Illinois Press, 1997, pp. 154–232.

3. See James Lull, ed., *Popular Music and Communication*, Newbury Park, CA, Sage, 1987; Simon Frith, ed., *Facing the Music*, New York, Pantheon Books, 1988; John Street, *Rebel Rock: The Politics of Popular Music*, Oxford, Basil Blackwell, 1996. Also see John Street, *Politics and Popular Culture*, Philadelphia, Temple University Press, 1997; Daniel M. Shea, *Mass Politics: The Politics of Popular Culture*, New York, St. Martin's Press/Worth, 1999.

4. See John S. Nelson and G. R. Boynton, "Making Sound Arguments: Would a Claim by Any Other Sound Mean the Same or Argue So Sweet?" in *Argument in a Time of Change*, James F. Klumpp, ed., Annandale, VA, National Communication Association, 1998, pp. 12–17.

5. See William H. McNeill, *Keeping Together in Time*, Cambridge, MA, Harvard University Press, 1995.

6. See Rick Altman, *Sound Theory, Sound Practice*, New York, Routledge, 1992; Russell Lack, *Twenty Four Frames Under: A Buried History of Film Music*, London, Quartet Books, 1997. Also see Adalaide Morris, ed., *Sound States: Innovative Poetics and Acoustical Technologies*, Chapel Hill, University of North Carolina Press, 1997.

7. See Nelson and Boynton, *Video Rhetorics*, pp. 119–153.

8. With a signal exception in Oliver Stone, the idea is implausible that Hollywood means its cinematic conspiracies literally. For a more subtle and symbolical approach, see Fredric Jameson, *The Geopolitical Aesthetic*, Bloomington, Indiana University Press, 1992, pp. 7–84.

9. See Ayn Rand, *The Fountainhead*, Indianapolis, Bobbs-Merrill, 1943; Ayn Rand, *Atlas Shrugged*, New York, Random House, 1957. Also see Jennifer Burns, *Goddess of the Market: Ayn Rand and the American Right*, New York, Oxford University Press, 2009.

10. See Beverly Merrill Kelley, "Populism in *Mr. Smith Goes to Washington*," *Reelpolitick*, Westport, CT, Praeger, 1998, pp. 7–24; Richard Maltby, *Hollywood Cinema*, Oxford, Blackwell, 1995, pp. 368–372; Dan Nimmo and James E. Combs, *Mediated Political Realities*, New York, Longman, 1983, pp. 111–112; Michael Parenti, *Make Believe Media*, New York, St. Martin's Press, 1992, pp. 6, 93.

11. Hendrik Hertzberg, "Upset Victory: *Primary Colors* Triumphs Over the Old Politics of Hollywood," *New Yorker* 74, no. 5, March 23, 1998, pp. 86–90, on pp. 86–87.

12. See Thomas Frank, *What's the Matter with Kansas? How Conservatives Won the Heart of America*, New York, Henry Holt, 2004; John Lukacs, *Democracy and Populism: Fear and Hatred*, New Haven, Yale University Press, 2005; Joe Klein, *Politics Lost: How American Democracy Was Trivialized by People Who Think You're Stupid*, New York, Doubleday, 2006; Adrian Kuzminski, *Fixing the System: A History of Populism, Ancient and Modern*, New York, Continuum, 2008.

13. See Joe Klein [Anonymous], *Primary Colors: A Novel of Politics*, New York, Warner Books, 1996.

14. Hertzberg, "Upset Victory," p. 87.

15. And it isn't exclusively American: Thomas Mann, *Reflections of an Nonpolitical Man*, Walter D. Morris, trans., New York, F. Ungar (1919), 1983.

16. See Hannah Arendt, *On Revolution*, New York, Viking Penguin, 1963; Garry Wills, *Cincinnatus: George Washington and the Enlightenment*, Garden City, NY, Doubleday, 1984.
17. Samuel R. Delany, *The Einstein Intersection*, New York, Ace Books, 1967, p. 18.
18. Peter Reiner, "Out of Time: Narcissism Drives Warren Beatty into the 'Hood," *New Times of Los Angeles*, May 14, 1998, http://www.newtimesla.com /issues/1998–05–14/film2.html.
19. See Timothy W. Luke, *Screens of Power: Ideology, Domination, and Resistance in Informational Society*, Urbana, University of Illinois Press, 1989; Benjamin R. Barber, *Jihad vs. McWorld: How Globalism and Tribalism Are Reshaping the World*, New York, Ballantine Books, 1996.
20. Reviewers of *Bulworth* like this line, but they do not hear it well. They miss the disparaging pun and put in its place a political chestnut about "an old liberal *wine* trying to pour himself into a new conservative bottle." See Mark Caro, "Truly Worthy: Warren Beatty Vents in *Bulworth*," *Chicago Tribune*, 1998, http:// metromix.com/top/1,1419,M-Metromix-Home-X!ArticleDetail-1509,00 .html?search_area=Blended&channel=Home&search_text= Bulworth; Robert Ebert, *"Bulworth,"* *Chicago Sun-Times*, 1998, http://www.suntimes.com/ ebert /ebert_reviews/1998/05/052202.html; Janet Maslin, "White Bread Senator Turns Home Boy," *New York Times*, May 15, 1998, http://www.nytimes.com /library/film/051598bulworth-film-review.html; Rainer, "Out of Time."
21. See Johann Wolfgang von Goethe, *Elective Affinities*, Elizabeth Mayer and Louise Brogan, trans., Chicago, Henry Regnery, 1963; Hayden White, *Metahistory: The Historical Imagination in Nineteenth-Century Europe*, Baltimore, Johns Hopkins University Press, 1973, pp. 29–31. Also see John S. Nelson, "Review Essay," *History and Theory* 14, no. 1 (1975): 74–91; John S. Nelson, "Tropal History and the Social Sciences," *History and Theory* 19, no. 4 (1980): 80–101; Nelson, *Tropes of Politics*, pp. 182–183.
22. See James Boyd White, *When Words Lose Their Meaning*, Chicago, University of Chicago Press, 1984; James Boyd White, *Heracles' Bow*, Madison, University of Wisconsin Press, 1985; James Boyd White, *Justice as Translation*, Chicago, University of Chicago Press, 1990; James Boyd White, *Acts of Hope*, Chicago, University of Chicago Press, 1994. Also see John S. Nelson, "When Words Gain Their Meanings: Turning Politics into Law and Back Again in Rhetoric—And What Can Happen When the Word for Law Is Literature," *Rhetoric Society Quarterly* 21, no. 3 (Summer 1991): 22–37.
23. See Hannah Arendt, *The Human Condition*, Chicago, University of Chicago Press, 1958.
24. On primary oral cultures, see Marshall McLuhan, *Understanding Media*, New York, McGraw-Hill, 1964; Eric Havelock, *The Muse Learns to Write*, New Haven, Yale University Press, 1986. On ancient politics as primary oral practices, see John S. Nelson, "Political Theory as Political Rhetoric," *What Should Political Theory Be Now?* John S. Nelson, ed., Albany, State University of New York Press, 1983, pp. 169–240. On current politics as primarily oral practices, see Nelson, *Tropes of Politics*, pp. 117–134.

25. See Lee C. McDonald, "Myth, Politics and Political Science," *Western Political Quarterly* 22, no. 1, (March 1969): 141–150.

26. See Kenneth Burke, *Counter-Statement*, Berkeley, University of California Press, 1931 (1968); Kenneth Burke, *A Grammar of Motives*, Berkeley, University of California Press, 1945; Kenneth Burke, *Language as Symbolic Action*, Berkeley, University of California Press, 1966; Kenneth Burke, *The Philosophy of Literary Form*, Berkeley, University of California Press (1941, 1967), 3rd ed., 1973. Also see Nelson and Boynton, *Video Rhetorics*, pp. 99–100, 206–208; Nelson, *Tropes of Politics*, pp. 28, 91, 137.

27. The staying power of *Network*'s satire of television news owes a great deal to the unsettling acuity of scriptwriter Paddy Chayevsky's satirical anticipations of reality programming, punditry, scandal-mongering, corporate takeovers of news divisions, stories about public-opinion polls that give the views of viewers back to them in place of events from elsewhere, substitutions of prediction and prophecy for reporting what actually has happened, and the popular cynicism for leaders cultural as well as political. See Rick Du Brow, "Fifteen Years Later, *Network* Prophecy Has Become Reality," *Des Moines Register* [*Los Angeles Times Service*], September 16, 1990, p. TV5.

28. The chorus of *Bulworth*'s endorsers include Jonathan Alter, "Beatty Goes Bonkers," *Newsweek* 131, no. 20, May 18, 1998, pp. 66–69; David Ansen, "Shock to the System," *Newsweek* 131, no. 20, May 18, 1998, pp. 70, 72; Caro, "Truly Worthy;" Mike Clark, "Beatty's *Bulworth*: Rappin' the Republic," *USA Today*, December 17, 1999, http://www.usatoday.com/life/enter /movies/lfilm129.htm; Ebert, *"Bulworth;"* Edward Guthman, "Beatty's Rap: Hilarious *Bulworth*—The Truth Sets a Senator Free," *San Francisco Chronicle*, May 22, 1998, http://www.sfgate.com/cgi-bin/article.cgi?file=/chronicle /archive/1998/05/22/DD19624.DTL; Dave Kehr, "Beatty Scores a *Bul*'s Eye: Warren's Right on Target as a Senator Who's Impolitic," *New York Daily News*, May 17, 1998, http://www.nydailynews.com/archive/98_05/051798 /new_york/57521.htm; Barbara Shulgasser, *"Bulworth,"* *San Francisco Examiner*, May 22, 1998, http://www.sfgate.com/cgi-bin/article.cgi?file=/examiner /archive/1998/05/22/WEEKEND972.dtl.

29. Caro, "Truly Worthy."

30. Shulgasser, *"Bulworth."*

31. Ebert, *"Bulworth."*

32. The ranks of *Bulworth*'s accusers include N'Gai Croal, "Same Ol' White Negro," *Newsweek* 131, no. 20, May 18, 1998, p. 72; David Edelstein, "Phat Head: Warren Beatty—White Negro, Martyr," *Slate*, May 17, 1998, http://slate.msn .com/?id=3253; Owen Gleiberman, *"Bulworth,"* *Entertainment Weekly*, May 21, 1998, http://www.ew.com/ew/review/archive/0,1683,177,00.html; Maslin, "White Bread Senator Turns Home Boy;" Charles Taylor, *"Bulworth," Salon*, May 15, 1998, http://www.salon.com/ent/movies/reviews/1998/05/cov_15review.html; Kenneth Turan, *"Bulworth*: The Horse and Buggin' Era," *Los Angeles Times*, May 15, 1998, http://www.calendarlive.com/top/1,1419,L-LATimes-Movies -X!ArticleDetail-4812,00.html?search_area=Movies&channel=Movies.

33. The *Bulworth* lyrics are said to be from Jay Bulworth, Jeremy Pikser, Gerald Baillergeau, and Victor Merritt, with the performances by Jay Bulworth, Big Yams, and Vino.

34. Turan, *"Bulworth."*

35. See Thomas Hobbes, in *Leviathan*, C. B. Macpherson, ed., New York, Penguin Books, (1651), 1968; Giambattista Vico, *The New Science*, Thomas Goddard Bergin and Max Harold Fisch, trans., Ithaca, NY, Cornell University Press (abridged from the 3rd ed., 1744; 1948), 1961; Edward W. Said, *Beginnings*, New York, Basic Books, 1975. Also see Nelson, *Ironic Politics*, pp. 63–127; Nelson, *Tropes of Politics*, pp. 99–114.

36. Taylor, *"Bulworth."*

37. Edelstein, "Phat Head."

38. Taylor, *"Bulworth."*

39. On rhetorical persuasion by ethos as the speaker's standing for the audience, see Nelson and Boynton, *Video Rhetorics*, pp. 100–118; Nelson, *Tropes of Politics*, pp. 136–141. On experiential persuasion by ethos as mood, atmosphere, or tone, see Nelson and Boynton, *Video Rhetorics*, pp. 195–232.

40. Gregory P. Dorr, "Bob Roberts: Special Edition," *The DVD Journal*, http://www.dvdjournal.com/reviews/b/bobroberts.shtml.

41. See Robert C. Elliott, *The Power of Satire*, Princeton, NJ, Princeton University Press, 1960.

42. Marjorie Baumgarten, *"Bulworth,"* *Austin Chronicle*, May 22, 1998, http://www.auschron.com/film/pages/movies/206.html. In his review of *"Bulworth,"* Turan likewise describes Amiri Baraka's character as "a shaman-type figure."

43. Shulgasser, *"Bulworth."*

44. Maitland McDonagh, "The Hollow Man," *TV Guide*, http://www.tvguide.com/movies/database/ShowMovie.asp?MI=40119.

45. See Chris Roberge, "Tim Robbins Campaigns for *Bob Roberts* and Political Change," *The Tech* 112, no. 44, September 25, 1992, p. 8; Brian Webster, *"Bob Roberts,"* *Apollo Movie Guide*, 2000, http://apolloguide.com/mov_fullrev.asp?CID=2818&RID=736.

46. On politics and music, see Mark Evan Bonds, *Wordless Rhetoric*, Cambridge, MA, Harvard University Press, 1991; Robert Walker, *Musical Beliefs*, New York, Teachers College/Columbia University Press, 1991; Laurence Berman, *The Musical Image*, Westport, CT, Greenwood Press, 1993; McNeill, *Keeping Together in Time*.

47. See Steve Perry, "Ain't No Mountain High Enough: The Politics of Crossover," in *Facing the Music*, Simon Frith, ed., New York, Pantheon Books, 1988, pp. 51–87; Mark Dery, "Black to the Future: Interviews with Samuel R. Delany, Greg Tate, and Tricia Rose," *South Atlantic Quarterly* 92, no. 4 (Fall 1993): 735–778; Richard Delgado and Jean Stefancic, *Understanding Words That Wound*, Boulder, CO, Westview Press, 2004, pp. 182–183.

48. See Murray Edelman, *From Art to Politics: How Artistic Creations Shape Political Conceptions*, Chicago, University of Chicago Press, 1995. Also see Hal Foster, *Recordings: Art, Spectacle, Cultural Politics*, Port Townsend, WA, Bay Press, 1985.

49. See John S. Nelson, "Natures and Futures for Political Theory," in *What Should Political Theory Be Now?* John S. Nelson, ed., Albany, State University of New York Press, 1983, pp. 3–24, on pp. 18–19.

50. See Robert Hariman, *Political Style: The Artistry of Power*, Chicago, University of Chicago Press, 1995; Nelson and Boynton, *Video Rhetorics*, pp. 24–25.

51. The source novel by Larry Beinhart is much more intricate, and it's well worth reading as a satire of Hollywood politics, yet it lacks the movie's superb attention to music. The first edition is *American Hero*, New York, Ballantine Books, 1993; the second is *Wag the Dog*, New York, Nation Books, 2004.

52. I thank Nicole Krassas for insisting that I learn how to listen to Public Enemy in particular.

53. See Henry Louis Gates Jr., ed., *The Classic Slave Narratives*, New York, Penguin Books, 1987.

54. Reiner, "Out of Time."

55. Taylor, "*Bulworth.*"

56. G. B. Trudeau, *Flashbacks*, Kansas City, MO, Andrews and McMeel, 1995, p. 71.

57. Ebert, "*Bulworth.*"

58. Reiner, "Out of Time."

59. Gleiberman, "*Bulworth.*"

60. See Steven Mailloux, *Rhetorical Power*, Ithaca, NY, Cornell University Press, 1989.

61. Edelstein, "Phat Head."

62. Ebert, "*Bulworth.*"

63. McDonagh, "The Hollow Man."

64. See John S. Nelson, "Stands in Politics," *Journal of Politics* 46, no. 1 (February 1984): 106–131.

65. See Dorr, "Bob Roberts."

66. Shulgasser, "*Bulworth.*"

67. See Taylor, "*Bulworth.*"

68. Turan, "*Bulworth.*"

69. On re(con)figuring politics, see Nelson, *Tropes of Politics*, especially pp. 150–204.

70. See Anton C. Zijderveld, "Parasites of Power: Court Fools during the Reign of Absolutism," *Reality in a Looking-Glass*, London, Routledge and Kegan Paul, 1982, pp. 92–130; John Southworth and Joan Southworth, *Fools and Jesters at the English Court*, Sutton, 1998; Beatrice K. Otto, *Fools Are Everywhere: Court Jesters Around the World*, Chicago, University of Chicago Press, 2001.

71. See Barbara Swain, *Fools and Folly during the Middle Ages and the Renaissance*, New York, Columbia University Press, 1932; Enid Welsford, *The Fool: His Social and Literary History*, Garden City, NY, Doubleday (1936), 1961; Zijderveld, "Into the Looking-Glass: The Spectrum of Traditional Folly," *Reality in a Looking-Glass*, pp. 8–40.

72. See Sandra Billington, *A Social History of the Fool*, New York, St. Martin's Press, 1984. Is there any tie of research or inspiration to Jay Billington Bulworth?

73. On dandies, see Susan Sontag, "Writing Itself: On Roland Barthes," *New Yorker* 58, no. 10, April 26, 1982, pp. 122–141; John Lahr, "King Cole: The Not So Merry Soul of Cole Porter," *New Yorker* 80, no. 19, July 12 and 19, 2004, pp. 100–104.

226 • Notes

74. Guthman, "Beatty's Rap."
75. Turan, "*Bulworth.*"
76. Gleiberman, "*Bulworth.*"
77. Reiner, "Out of Time."
78. See Zijderveld, *Reality in a Looking-Glass*, pp. 41–91, 156–162.
79. See Adam Gopnik, "Display Cases: The Man Who Discovered Conspicuous Consumption Is Back in Style," *New Yorker* 75, nos. 9–10, April 26 and May 3, 1999, pp. 176–184.
80. See John S. Nelson, "Politics and Truth: Arendt's Problematic," *American Journal of Political Science* 22, no. 2 (May 1978): 270–301; John S. Nelson, "Argument without Truth: Hannah Arendt on Political Judgment and Public Persuasion," in *Argument in a Time of Change*, James F. Klumpp, ed., Annandale, VA, National Communication Association, 1998, pp. 40–45.
81. See John S. Nelson, "Political Foundations for Rhetoric of Inquiry," in *The Rhetorical Turn: Invention and Persuasion in the Conduct of Inquiry*, Herbert W. Simons, ed., Chicago, University of Chicago Press, 1990, pp. 258–289.
82. Turan, "*Bulworth.*"
83. Edelstein, "Phat Head."
84. McDonagh, "The Hollow Man."
85. Croal, "Same Ol' White Negro," p. 72.
86. Shulgasser, "*Bulworth.*"
87. Maslin, "White Bread Senator Turns Home Boy."
88. Guthman, "Beatty's Rap."
89. Ebert, "*Bulworth.*"
90. Taylor, "*Bulworth.*"
91. Ansen, "*Bulworth.*"
92. Taylor, "*Bulworth.*"
93. Reiner, "Out of Time."
94. Shulgasser, "*Bulworth.*"
95. On the rhetorical power and political substance of delivery, see Nelson and Boynton, *Video Rhetorics*, pp. 87–118.

3 Realism as a Political Style: Noir Insights

1. Nicholas Lemann, "Conflict of Interests," *New Yorker* 84, no. 24, August 11 and 19, 2008, pp. 86–92, p. 87.
2. Ryan Lizza, "Making It: How Chicago Shaped Obama," *New Yorker* 84, no. 23, July 21, 2008, pp. 48–65, on pp. 58, 62, and 65.
3. See Niccolò Machiavelli, in *The Prince*, Robert M. Adams, ed. and trans., New York, Norton (1975), 2nd ed., 1992. Also see Christopher Matthews, *Hardball*, New York, HarperCollins, 1988; Christopher Matthews, *Life's a Campaign*, New York, Random House, 2007.
4. See John S. Nelson, "The Ideological Connection: Or, Smuggling in the Goods, Parts I–II," *Theory and Society* 4, nos. 3–4 (Fall–Winter 1977): 421–448, 573–590; John S. Nelson, "Ashcraft's Problem of Ideology," *Journal of Politics* 42,

no. 3 (August 1980): 709–715; John S. Nelson, "Stands in Politics," *Journal of Politics* 46, no. 1 (February 1984): 106–131.

5. See Roland Barthes, *Mythologies*, Annette Lavers, trans., New York, Hill and Wang, 1972; Henry Tudor, *Political Myth*, New York, Praeger, 1972; H. Mark Roelofs, *Ideology and Myth in American Politics*, Boston, Little, Brown, 1976; James Oliver Robertson, *American Myth, American Reality*, New York, Hill and Wang, 1980; Robert Ellwood, *The Politics of Myth*, Albany, State University of New York, Press, 1999. Also see John S. Nelson, "Orwell's Political Myths and Ours," in *The Orwellian Moment*, Robert L. Savage, James E. Combs, and Dan D. Nimmo, eds., Fayetteville, University of Arkansas Press, 1989, pp. 11–44; John S. Nelson, "Political Mythmaking for Postmoderns," in *Spheres of Argument*, Bruce E. Gronbeck, ed., Annandale, VA, Speech Communication Association, 1989, pp. 175–183. And see John S. Nelson and G. R. Boynton, *Video Rhetorics: Televised Advertising in American Politics*, Urbana, University of Illinois Press, 1997.

6. See John S. Nelson, *Tropes of Politics: Science, Theory, Rhetoric, Action*, Madison, University of Wisconsin Press, 1998.

7. Kenneth Tynan, "The Third Act: Entries from Kenneth Tynan's Journals, 1975–78," *New Yorker* 76, no. 23, August 14, 2000, pp. 60–71, entry from October 19, 1975 on pp. 64–65. Also see Bruno Bettelheim, "The Art of Moving Pictures: Man, Superman, and Myth," *Harper's Magazine* 263, no. 1577, October 1981, pp. 80–83; Garry Wills, *Reagan's America: Innocents At Home*, New York, Penguin Books (1987), 2nd ed., 1988; Garry Wills, *John Wayne's America: The Politics of Celebrity*, New York, Simon and Schuster, 1997.

8. Marge Piercy, *He, She and It*, New York, Fawcett Crest, 1991, p. 25.

9. See Foster Hirsch, *Detours and Lost Highways: A Map of Neo-Noir*, New York, Limelight Editions, 1999, pp. 67–107; Andrew Spicer, *Film Noir*, London, Pearson Education, 2002, pp. 14–16.

10. See J. P. Telotte, *Voices in the Dark: The Narrative Patterns of Film Noir*, Urbana, University of Illinois Press, 1989, pp. 22–26, 134–178.

11. On expressionism (and expressivism) in noir, see Telotte, *Voices in the Dark*, pp. 17–22, 32–36, 93–104; Frank Krutnik, *In a Lonely Street: Film Noir, Genre, Masculinity*, London, Routledge, 1991, pp. 20–27, 46–50; R. Barton Palmer, *Hollywood's Dark Cinema: The American Film Noir*, New York, Twayne, 1994, pp. 32–70; Spicer, *Film Noir*, pp. 11–13. On existentialism in neo noir, see Spicer, *Film Noir*, pp. 22–24; Mark T. Conard, ed., *The Philosophy of Neo-Noir*, Lexington, University Press of Kentucky, 2007.

12. Oddly a third neo-noir film that features stage magic appeared only a year later, in 2007: *Death Defying Acts* is another provocative movie with more than a few connections to its two predecessors.

13. See Hannah Arendt, "Thinking and Moral Considerations," *Social Research* 38, no. 3 (Autumn 1971): 417–446.

14. The trilogy was unfinished at her death. See Hannah Arendt, *The Life of the Mind*, New York, Harcourt Brace Jovanovich: *Thinking*, 1978; *Willing*, 1978.

15. See John S. Nelson, "Commerce among the Archipelagos: Rhetoric of Inquiry as a Practice of Coherent Education," in *The Core and the Canon*, L. Robert

Stevens, G. L. Seligmann, and Julian Long, eds., Denton, TX, University of North Texas Press, 1993, pp. 78–100.

16. See Pierre Bourdieu, *Distinction: A Social Critique of the Judgment of Taste*, London, Routledge and Kegan Paul, 1984. Also see Erin Manning, *Politics of Touch: Sense, Movement, Sovereignty*, Minneapolis, University of Minnesota Press, 2007.

17. See Dick Hebdige, *Subculture: The Meaning of Style*, London, Routledge, 1979; Barry Brummett, *A Rhetoric of Style*, Carbondale, Southern Illinois University, 2008.

18. Robert Hariman, *Political Style: The Artistry of Power*, Chicago, University of Chicago Press, 1995, p. 4.

19. Hariman, *Political Style*, p. 3.

20. Kim Stanley Robinson, *A Short, Sharp Shock*, New York, Bantam Books, 1990, pp. 15–16.

21. On performance, see Ferdinand Mount, *The Theatre of Politics*, New York, Schocken Books, 1972; Sue-Ellen Case and Janelle Reinelt, eds., *The Performance of Power: Theatrical Discourse and Politics*, Iowa City, University of Iowa Press, 1991; Mady Schutzman, *The Real Thing: Performance, Hysteria, and Advertising*, Hanover, NH, Wesleyan University Press, 1999.

22. See Raymond Seidelman, *Disenchanted Realists*, Albany, State University of New York Press, 1985. Also see Nelson, *Tropes of Politics*, pp. 99–114.

23. See Foster Hirsch, *The Dark Side of the Screen: Film Noir*, London, Da Capo Press, (1981), 2nd ed., 2001; Palmer, *Hollywood's Dark Cinema*; Nicholas Christopher, *Somewhere in the Night: Film Noir and the American City*, New York, Henry Holt, 1997; Hirsch, *Detours and Lost Highways*; Alain Silver and James Ursini, *The Noir Style*, Woodstock, NY, Overlook Press, 1999; Ronald Schwartz, *Neo-Noir: The New Film Noir Style from Psycho to Collateral*, Lanham, MD, Rowman and Littlefield, 2005; Mike Chopra-Gant, *Hollywood Genres and Postwar America: Masculinity, Family and Nation in Popular Movies and Film Noir*, New York, I. B. Tauris, 2006.

24. See John S. Nelson, "John le Carré and the Postmodern Myth of the State," *Finnish Yearbook of Political Thought* 3 (1999): 100–131; John S. Nelson, "Four Forms for Terrorism: Horror, Dystopia, Thriller, and Noir," in *Transnational Cinema: The Film Reader*, Elizabeth Ezra and Terry Rowden, eds., New York, Routledge, 2006, pp. 181–195.

25. Hariman, *Political Style*, p. 13.

26. Ibid. p. 4.

27. Ibid. pp. 25–26.

28. Ibid. pp. 13–49.

29. See Sheldon S. Wolin, "Machiavelli: Politics and the Economy of Violence," *Politics and Vision*, Princeton, NJ, Princeton University Press (1960), expanded edition, 2004, pp. 175–213.

30. See Hans J. Morgenthau, *Scientific Man versus Power Politics*, Chicago, University of Chicago Press, 1946; Hans J. Morgenthau, *In Defense of the National Interest*, New York, Knopf, 1951; Hans J. Morgenthau, *Politics among*

Nations, New York, Knopf, 1954; Hans J. Morgenthau, *Truth and Power*, New York, Praeger, 1970. Also see Henry A. Kissinger, *The Necessity for Choice*, New York, Harper and Row, 1961; Henry A. Kissinger, *American Foreign Policy*, New York, Norton, 1974; Henry A. Kissinger, *Diplomacy*, New York, Simon and Schuster, 1994; Henry A. Kissinger, *Does America Need a Foreign Policy?* New York, Simon and Schuster, 2001.

31. Hariman, *Political Style*, p. 73.
32. See John S. Nelson, "Orwell's Political Myths and Ours," in *The Orwellian Moment*, Robert L. Savage, James E. Combs, and Dan D. Nimmo, eds., Fayetteville, University of Arkansas Press, 1989, pp. 11–44; John S. Nelson, "Political Mythmaking for Postmoderns," in *Spheres of Argument*, Bruce E. Gronbeck, ed., Annandale, VA, Speech Communication Association, 1989, pp. 175–183. Also see Nelson, *Video Rhetorics* and Nelson, *Tropes of Politics*.
33. Machiavelli, *The Prince*, p. 42.
34. See Hanna Fenichel Pitkin, *Fortune Is a Woman: Gender and Politics in the Thought of Niccolò Machiavelli*, Chicago, University of Chicago Press (1984) 1999.
35. Keen attention to the sapping power of disappointment helps make the "dismal science" of economics into a realist discipline. See Albert O. Hirschman, *Shifting Involvements*, Princeton, NJ, Princeton University Press, 2002.
36. See Matthews, *Hardball*, pp. 107–116.
37. See Bram Stoker, *Dracula*, New York, Signet Books (1897), with scenes from the Francis Ford Coppola film (1992).
38. See William Shakespeare, *The Tragedy of Hamlet, Prince of Denmark*, New York, Dover, 1602.
39. See Antoine de Saint-Exupéry, *The Little Prince*, Katherine Woods, trans., Harcourt, Brace and World, 1943, especially pp. 64–71. Also see Edmund Burke, *Reflections on the Revolution in France*, Garden City, NY, Doubleday, 1961
40. See Jacob Grimm and Wilhelm Grimm, "The Frog King, or Iron Heinreich," *The Complete Fairy Tales of the Brothers Grimm*, Jack Zipes, trans., New York, Bantam Books, 3rd ed., 2003, pp. 1–2; Hans Christian Andersen, "The Princess and the Pea," *The Complete Fairy Tales and Stories*, Erik Christian Haugaard, trans., New York, Random House, pp. 20–21; Frances Hodgson Burnett, *A Little Princess*, Baltimore, Penguin Books, 1963; J. K. Rowling, *The Half-Blood Prince*, New York, Scholastic Press, 2005. On Diana as the People's Princess, see *The Queen* (2006). And on the Joker as the Clown Prince of Crime, see Mark D. White and Robert Arp, eds., *Batman and Philosophy: The Dark Knight of the Soul*, New York, Wiley, 2008.
41. See Matthews, *Hardball*, pp. 153–226; Matthews, *Life's a Campaign*, pp. 127–167.
42. See Bernard Williams, *Utilitarianism and Beyond*, New York, Cambridge University Press, 1982; Bernard Williams, *In the Beginning Was the Deed: Realism and Moralism in Political Argument*, Princeton, NJ, Princeton University Press, 2005.

43. See John S. Nelson, "Prudence as Republican Politics in American Popular Culture," in *Prudence Classical Virtue, Postmodern Practice*, Robert Hariman, ed., University Park, Pennsylvania State University Press, 2003, pp. 229–257.
44. See Hariman, *Political Style*, pp. 30–35.
45. See Francis A. Beer and Robert Hariman, eds., *Post-Realism*, East Lansing, Michigan State University Press, 1996, pp. 31–165.
46. See Arthur F. Bentley, *The Process of Government*, Cambridge, MA, Harvard University Press (1908), 1967; David B. Truman, *The Governmental Process*, New York, Knopf, 1951. Also see Robert A. Dahl, *A Preface to Democratic Theory*, Chicago, University of Chicago Press, 1956; Robert A. Dahl, *Pluralist Democracy in the United States*, Chicago, Rand McNally, 1967; Robert A. Dahl, *Polyarchy*, New Haven, Yale University Press, 1971; Robert A. Dahl, *Dilemmas of Pluralist Democracy*, New Haven, Yale University Press, 1982.
47. William Galston, "The Obligation to Play Political Hardball," *Philosophy and Public Policy* 9, no. 1 (Winter 1989): 6–9.
48. See Reinhold Niebuhr, *Christianity and Power Politics*, Hamden, CT, Archon Books (1940), 1969; Reinhold Niebuhr, *Christian Realism and Political Problems*, Fairfield, New York, Scribner, 1953; Reinhold Niebuhr, *Moral Man and Immoral Society*, New York, Scribner, 1960; Reinhold Niebuhr, *The Children of Light and the Children of Darkness*, New York, Scribner, 1960. Also see Beverly Merrill Kelley, *Reelpolitick: Political Ideologies in '30s and '40s Films*, Westport, CT, Praeger, 1989.
49. See Thomas Hobbes, in *Leviathan*, C. B. Macpherson, ed., New York, Penguin Books (1651), 1968; John Locke, in *Two Treatises of Government*, Peter Laslett, ed., New York, New American Library, 1963. And yes, the political aesthetics of *Hero* as an epic are idealist; yet the political lessons of *Hero* are in the end realist: a fascinating meld reminiscent of Hobbes.
50. See Michael Walzer, "Political Action: The Problem of Dirty Hands," *Philosophy and Public Affairs* 2, no. 2 (Winter 1973): 160–180; Jane Mayer, "Whatever It Takes: The Politics of the Man Behind *24*," *New Yorker* 81, no. 50 (February 19, 2007).
51. See James Ellroy, *L. A. Confidential*, New York, Warner Books, 1990.
52. Al McGuire, "Introduction" to John Feinstein, *A Season on the Brink: A Year with Bobby Knight and the Indiana Hoosiers*, New York, Simon and Schuster, 1986, pp. ix–xiv, on p. xi.
53. See Alain Silver and James Ursini, eds., *Film Noir Reader*, New York, Limelight Editions, 1996, pp. 3–10; Mark T. Conrad, ed., *The Philosophy of Neo-Noir*, Lexington, University Press of Kentucky, 2007, pp. 1–4. Also see Krutnik, *In a Lonely Street*, pp. 15–29; Palmer, *Hollywood's Dark Cinema*, pp. ix–31; Hirsch, *Detours and Lost Highways*, pp. 1–6; Spicer, *Film Noir*, pp. 105.
54. Spicer, *Film Noir*, p. 2.
55. Also neo noir, if less obviously so, is Nolan's *Inception* (2010), the film he directed between *The Dark Knight* and that trilogy's conclusion in *The Dark Knight Rises* (2012).

56. Nolan based his film on Christopher Priest, *The Prestige*, New York, Tom Doherty Associates, 1995. But the novel is neither noirish nor focused on politics of realism.

57. See William Shakespeare, *The Tragedy of Hamlet, Prince of Denmark*, New York, Dover, 1602.

58. See Johann Wolfgang von Goethe, *Faust*, Walter Kaufmann, trans., Garden City, NY, Doubleday, 1961; Marshall Berman, "Goethe's *Faust*: The Tragedy of Development," *All That Is Solid Melts into Air*, New York, Simon and Schuster, 1982, pp. 37–86; Harry Redner, *In the Beginning Was the Deed*, University of California Press, 1982. Also see Thomas Mann, *Doctor Faustus*, H. T. Lowe-Porter, trans., New York, Random House, 1948. Also see John S. Nelson, "Toltechs, Aztechs, and the Art of the Possible," *Polity* 8, no. 1 (Fall 1975): 80–116.

59. See Miguel de Cervantes Saavedra, *Don Quixote*, James H. Montgomery, trans., Indianapolis, Hackett (1605), 2009.

60. Directed by Roman Polanski, *Chinatown* (1974) won an Oscar only for Robert Towne's original screenplay, yet it garnered an additional ten nominations.

61. See Jean-Paul Sartre, *No Exit, and Three Other Plays*, Stuart Gilbert and Lionel Abel, trans., New York, Random House (1943, 1945, 1947, 1948), 1946, 1948, 1949; Robert Porfirio, "No Way Out: Existential Motifs in the *Film Noir* (1976)," in *Film Noir Reader*, Alain Silver and James Ursini, eds., New York, Limelight Editions, 1996, pp. 77–93.

62. See Susan Jacoby, *Wild Justice: The Evolution of Revenge*, New York, Harper and Row, 1983; Peter A. French, *The Virtues of Vengeance*, Lawrence, University Press of Kansas, 2001.

63. See Roberta E. Pearson and William Uricchio, eds., *The Many Lives of the Batman: Critical Approaches to a Superhero and His Media*, New York, Routledge, 1991; Tom Morris and Matt Morris, eds., *Superheroes and Philosophy: Truth, Justice, and the Socratic Way*, Chicago, Open Court, 2005; Mark D. White, ed., *Watchmen and Philosophy: A Rorschach Test*, New York, Wiley, 2009.

64. On "crafts," see Plato, *Republic*, G. M. A. Grube and C. D. C. Reeve, trans., Indianapolis, Hackett, 1992, 332c–374c. On "styles," see Plato, *Republic*, 394e–398b.

65. People who seem to want their politics mostly realist, literalist, fundamentalist, and foolish—hence strangely antiscientific too—have become harsh critics of college curricula that require the arts and humanities, but they are wrong for many reasons, this one included. See Gerald Graff, *Professing Literature: An Institutional History*, Chicago, University of Chicago Press, 1987; Wayne C. Booth, *The Company We Keep: An Ethics of Fiction*, Berkeley, University of California Press, 1988; Wayne C. Booth, *The Vocation of a Teacher*, Chicago, University of Chicago Press, 1988, pp. 101–150; Louis Menand, *The Marketplace of Ideas: Reform and Resistance in the American University*, New York, Norton, 2010; Martha C. Nussbaum, *Not for Profit: Why Democracy Needs the Humanities*, Princeton, NJ, Princeton University Press, 2010.

66. See Hariman, *Prudence*.

67. See Peter L. Berger and Thomas Luckmann, *The Social Construction of Reality*, Garden City, NY, Doubleday, 1966; John S. Nelson, "Destroying Political Theory in Order to Save It (Or, John Gunnell Turns on the Western Tradition)," in *Tradition, Interpretation, and Science: Political Theory in the American Academy*, John S. Nelson, ed., Albany, State University of New York Press, 1986, pp. 281–318.

68. See Friedrich Nietzsche, "On Truth and Falsity in Their Extramoral Sense," in *Essays on Metaphor*, Warren Shibles, ed., Whitewater, WI, Language Press, 1972, pp. 1–13. Also see Daniel W. Conway, *Nietzsche and the Politics*, London, Routledge, 1997, pp. 130–138; Steven D. Hales and Rex Welshon, *Nietzsche's Perspectivism*, Urbana, University of Illinois Press, 2000.

69. See Robert Hariman, "A Boarder in one's Own Home: Franz Kafka's Parable of the Bureaucratic Style," *Political Style: The Artistry of Power*, Chicago, University of Chicago Press, 1995, pp. 141–176.

70. Hariman, *Political Style*, p. 194.

71. See Hannah Arendt, *The Human Condition: A Study of the Central Dilemmas Facing Modern Man*, Chicago, University of Chicago Press, 1958; Hannah Arendt, *On Revolution*, New York, Viking Press, 1963; Hannah Arendt, *Between Past and Future: Eight Exercises in Political Thought*, New York, Viking Press, (1963), enlarged edition, 1968; Hannah Arendt, *Crises of the Republic*, New York, Harcourt Brace Jovanovich, 1972; Hannah Arendt, "Home to Roost: A Bicentennial Address," *New York Review of Books* 22, no. 11, June 26, 1975, pp. 3–6. Also see Margaret Canovan, *Hannah Arendt: A Reinterpretation of Her Political Thought*, Cambridge, Cambridge University Press, 1992; Bonnie Honig, *Political Theory and the Displacement of Politics*, Ithaca, NY, Cornell University Press, 1993; Dana R. Villa, *Politics, Philosophy, Terror: Essays on the Thought of Hannah Arendt*, Princeton, NJ, Princeton University Press, 1999, pp. 128–179; Elisabeth Young-Bruehl, *Why Arendt Matters*, New Haven, Yale University Press, 2006.

72. See Melvin Tumin, "Pie in the Sky...," *Dissent* 6, no. 1, Winter 1959, pp. 65–71; Benjamin I. Schwartz, "The Religion of Politics," *Dissent* 17, no. 2, March–April 1970, pp. 144–161. Also see Margaret Canovan, *The Political Thought of Hannah Arendt*, New York, Harcourt Brace Jovanovich, 1974; Lisa Jane Disch, *Hannah Arendt and the Limits of Philosophy*, Ithaca, NY, Cornell University Press, 1994; Dana R. Villa, *Arendt and Heidegger: The Fate of the Political*, Princeton, NJ, Princeton University Press, 1996.

73. See Arendt, *On Revolution*, pp. 81–82. Also see Hannah Arendt, "A Reply [to Eric Voegelin]," *Review of Politics* 15, no. 1 (January 1953): 76–85, on p. 81.

74. See Jürgen Habermas, "Hannah Arendt's Communications Concept of Power," Thomas McCarthy, trans., *Social Research* 44, no. 1 (Spring 1977): 3–24.

4   Noir in Paradise: Testing and Twisting Realist Politics

1. See John S. Nelson and G. R. Boynton, *Video Rhetorics: Televised Advertising in American Politics*, Urbana, University of Illinois Press, 1997; G. R. Boynton

and John S. Nelson, *Hot Spots: Multimedia Analyses of Political Ads,* Urbana, University of Illinois Press, 1997, videocassette.

2. See John S. Nelson, "The Ideological Connection: Or, Smuggling in the Goods, Part I–II," *Theory and Society* 4, nos. 3–4 (Fall–Winter 1977): 421–448, 573–590.

3. See Foster Hirsch, *Detours and Lost Highways: A Map of Neo-Noir,* New York, Limelight Editions, 1999; Mark T. Conard, ed., *The Philosophy of Neo-Noir,* Lexington, University Press of Kentucky, 2007; Mark Bould, Kathrina Glitre, and Greg Tuck, eds., *Neo-Noir,* New York, Wallflower Press, 2009.

4. See Mike Davis, *City of Quartz: Excavating the Future in Los Angeles,* New York, Random House, 1990.

5. See J. P. Telotte, *Voices in the Dark: The Narrative Patterns of Film Noir,* Urbana, University of Illinois Press, 1989; R. Barton Palmer, *Hollywood's Dark Cinema: The American Film Noir,* New York, Twayne, 1994; Alain Silver and James Ursini, *The Noir Style,* Woodstock, NY, Overlook Press, 1999; Sheri Chinen Biesen, *Blackout: World War II and the Origins of Film Noir,* Baltimore, Johns Hopkins University Press, 2005; Eddie Robson, *Film Noir,* London, Virgin Books, 2005; Ronald Schwartz, *Neo-Noir: The New Film Noir Style from Psycho to Collateral,* Lanham, MD, Rowman and Littlefield, 2005; Mark T. Conrad, ed., *The Philosophy of Film Noir,* Lexington, University Press of Kentucky, 2006; William Luhr, *Film Noir,* Malden, MA, Wiley-Blackwell, 2012.

6. See Raymond Chandler, *The Simple Art of Murder,* New York, Random House, 1939; Ernest Mandel, *Delightful Murder: A Social History of the Crime Story,* Minneapolis, University of Minnesota Press, 1984; Cynthia S. Hamilton, *Western and Hard-Boiled Detective Fiction in America: From High Noon to Midnight,* Iowa City, University of Iowa Press, 1987; Tony Hilfer, *The Crime Novel: A Deviant Genre,* Austin, University of Texas Press, 1990; Marcus Klein, *Easterns, Westerns, and Private Eyes: American Matters, 1970–1900,* Madison, University of Wisconsin Press, 1994; William Marling, *The American Roman Noir: Hammett, Cain, and Chandler,* Athens, University of Georgia Press, 1995; Stephen F. Soitos, *The Blues Detective: A Study of African American Detective Fiction,* Amherst, University of Massachusetts Press, 1996; John T. Irwin, *Unless the Threat of Death Is Behind Them: Hard-Boiled Fiction and Film Noir,* Baltimore, Johns Hopkins University Press, 2006.

7. See David E. Ruth, *Inventing the Public Enemy: The Gangster in American Culture, 1918–1934,* Chicago, University of Chicago Press, 1996; Alain Silver and James Ursini, eds., *Gangster Film Reader,* New York, Limelight Editions, 2007.

8. See E. Ann Kaplan, ed., *Women in Film Noir,* London, British Film Institute (1978), 2nd ed., 1980; Mary Ann Doane, *Femmes Fatales: Feminism, Film Theory, Psychoanalysis,* New York, Routledge, 1991; Eddie Muller, *Dark City Dames: The Wicked Women of Film Noir,* New York, HarperCollins, 2001; Jans B. Wager, *Dames in the Driver's Seat: Rereading Film Noir,* Austin, University of Texas Press, 2005. Also see Frank Krutnik, *In a Lonely Street: Film Noir, Genre, Masculinity,* London, Routledge, 1991; Mike Chopra-Gant, *Hollywood Genres*

and Postwar America: Masculinity, Family and Nation in Popular Movies and Film Noir, New York, I. B. Tauris, 2006.

9. See Foster Hirsch, *The Dark Side of the Screen: Film Noir*, London, Da Capo Press (1981), 2nd ed., 2001; Silver and Ursini, eds., *Film Noir Reader*.
10. See Andrew Spicer, *Film Noir*, London, Pearson Education, 2002.
11. See John S. Nelson, "Four Forms for Terrorism: Horror, Dystopia, Thriller, and Noir," in *Transnational Cinema: The Film Reader*, Elizabeth Ezra and Terry Rowden, eds., New York, Routledge, 2006, pp. 181–195.
12. On made-for-TV movies, see Todd Gitlin, "Movies of the Week," *Inside Prime Time*, New York, Random House, 1983, pp. 157–200.
13. For example, I am yet to see David Fincher's *House of Cards* (2013–) from Netflix, which has been claimed as noir by Emily Nussbaum, "Shark Week: House of Cards, Scandal, and the Political Game," *New Yorker* 89, no. 2 February 25, 2013, pp. 74–76.
14. For something close to a counterargument, but not quite, see Jeremy G. Butler, "Miami Vice: The Legacy of *Film Noir*," Silver and Ursini, eds., *Film Noir Reader*, pp. 289–305.
15. See Stieg Larsson, *Millennium Trilogy*, Reg Keeland, trans., New York, Knopf: *The Girl with the Dragon Tattoo* (2005), 2008; *The Girl Who Played with Fire* (2006), 2009; *The Girl Who Kicked the Hornet's Nest* (2007), 2009. For film adaptations to date, see *The Girl with the Dragon Tattoo* (2009, 2011), *The Girl Who Played with Fire* (2009), and *The Girl Who Kicked the Hornet's Nest* (2009). On *Forbrydelsen* and *The Killing*, see Nancy Franklin, "Northwest Noir: Dial AMC for Murder," *New Yorker* 87, no. 12 May 9, 2011, pp. 82–83; Lauren Collins, "Danish Postmodern: Why Are So Many People Fans of Scandinavian TV?" *New Yorker* 88, no. 42 January 7, 2013, pp. 22–30.
16. See Robert B. Parker, New York, Berkley Books: *Trouble in Paradise*, 1999; *Night Passage*, 2001; *Death in Paradise*, 2002; *Stone Cold*, 2004; *Sea Change*, 2007; *High Profile*, 2008; *Stranger in Paradise*, 2009; *Night and Day*, 2009; *Split Image*, 2011.
17. Michael Brandman has written two further novels in the Jesse Stone series, New York, Putnam: *Robert B. Parker's Killing the Blues*, 2011; *Robert B. Parker's Fool Me Twice*, 2012.
18. See Nelson and Boynton, *Video Rhetorics*, pp. 27–86; Rick Altman, *Film/Genre*, London, British Film Institute, 1999.
19. But yes, there are some categorically harder cases, even in neo noirs: see Porter (Mel Gibson) in *Payback* (1999) and Chev Chelios (Jason Statham) in *Crank* (2006).
20. See Hannah Arendt, *The Origins of Totalitarianism*, New York, Harcourt Brace Jovanovich (1951), 4th ed., 1973; Hannah Arendt, *The Human Condition*, Chicago, University of Chicago Press, 1958; Peter Berger and Thomas Luckmann, *The Social Construction of Reality*, Garden City, NY, Doubleday, 1966; Peter Berger, Brigitte Berger, and Hansfried Kellner, *The Homeless Mind*, New York, Random House, 1973; Michel Foucault, *The Archeology of Knowledge*, A. M. Sheridan Smith, trans., New York, Random House (1969),

1972; Michel Foucault, *Discipline and Punish*, Alan Sheridan, trans., New York, Random House (1975), 1977; Erving Goffman, *Asylums*, Garden City, NY, Doubleday, 1961; Erving Goffman, *Frame Analysis*, New Yorker, Harper and Row, 1974; Maurice Merleau-Ponty, *Phenomenology of Perception*, Colin Smith, trans., New York, Humanities Press, 1962; Maurice Merleau-Ponty, *Signs*, Richard C. McCleary, trans., Evanston, IL, Northwestern University Press, 1964; Jean-Paul Sartre, *Being and Nothingness*, Hazel E. Barnes, trans., New York, Washington Square Press (1953), 1966; Jean-Paul Sartre, *Situations*, Benita Eisler, trans., New York, George Braziller (1958), 1965.

21. On polymorphous perversity, see Norman O. Brown, *Life against Death*, Middletown, CT, Wesleyan University Press, 1959; Herbert Marcuse, *Eros and Civilization*, New York, Random House, 1955. On boredom, see Saul Bellow, "On Boredom," *New York Review of Books* 22, no. 13, August 7, 1975, p. 22; Haskell E. Bernstein, "Boredom and the Ready-Made Life," *Social Research* 42, no. 3 (Autumn 1975): 512–537; Patricia Meyer Spacks, *Boredom: The Literary History of a State of Mind*, Chicago, University of Chicago Press, 1995. Also see Nina Eliasoph, *Avoiding Politics: How Americans Produce Apathy in Everyday Life*, New York, Cambridge University Press, 1998.

22. See John S. Nelson, "Conspiracy as a Hollywood Trope for System," *Political Communication* 20, no. 4 (October–December 2003): 499–503.

23. See George V. Higgins, *The Friends of Eddie Coyle*, New York, Henry Holt, 1970; George V. Higgins, *Killing Them Softly*, New York, Random House, 1974; George V. Higgins, *At End of Day*, New York, Harcourt Brace Jovanovich, 2000. Also see Elmore Leonard, *52 Pickup*, New York, HarperCollins, 1974; Elmore Leonard, *Glitz*, New York, William Morrow, 1983; Elmore Leonard, *Tishomingo Blues*, New York, HarperCollins, 2002.

24. See *Hamlet*, I.v.211–212: "The time is out of joint; O cursed spite!/That ever I was born to set it right!" Several neo noirs evoke Shakespeare's Hamlet as the genre's originary plot: among them, *The Glass House* (2001), *Mulholland Dr.* (2001), and *Savages* (2012). Also see Samuel A. Chambers, *Untimely Politics*, New York, New York University Press, 2003.

25. See Marcello Truzzi and Scot Morris, "Sherlock Holmes as a Social Scientist," *Psychology Today* 5, no. 7, December 1971, pp. 62–65, 85–86.

26. See Frederik Pohl, *Syzygy*, New York, Bantam, 1981; Barbara J. Hill and John S. Nelson, "Facing the Holocaust: Robert Arneson's Ceramic Myth of Postmodern Catastrophe," *Human Rights/Human Wrongs: Art and Social Change*, Seattle, University of Washington Press, 1986, pp. 189–209.

27. See Harold Bloom, "Hamlet," *Shakespeare: The Invention of the Human*, New York, Riverhead Books, 1998, pp. 383–431.

28. See Johann Wolfgang von Goethe, *Faust*: Louis MacNeice, trans., New York, Oxford University Press, 1951; Walter Kaufmann, trans., Garden City, NY, Doubleday, 1961. Also see John S. Nelson, "Toltechs, Aztechs, and the Art of the Possible: Parenthetic Comments on the Political Through Language and Aesthetics," *Polity* 8, no. 1 (Fall 1975): 80–116; Marshall Berman, "Goethe's *Faust*: The Tragedy of Development," *All That Is Solid Melts into Air*, New

York, Simon and Schuster, 1982, pp. 37–86; Harry Redner, *In the Beginning Was the Deed*, Berkeley, University of California Press, 1982.

29. See Peter A. French, *The Virtues of Vengeance*, Lawrence, University Press of Kansas, 2001.

30. See Jean-Paul Sartre, *No Exit, and Three Other Plays*, Stuart Gilbert and Lionel Abel, trans., New York, Random House (1943, 1945, 1947, 1948), 1946, 1948, 1949; Robert Porfirio, "No Way Out: Existential Motifs in the *Film Noir* (1976)," Silver and Ursini, eds., *Film Noir Reader*, pp. 77–93. Also see John S. Nelson, "Stands in Politics," *Journal of Politics* 46, no. 1 (February 1984): 106–131.

31. See Miguel de Cervantes Saavedra, *Don Quixote*, James H. Montgomery, trans., Indianapolis, Hackett (1605), 2009.

32. On realism as a political style, see Christopher Matthews, *Hardball*, New York, Harper and Row, 1988; Robert Hariman, "No Superficial Attractions and Ornaments: The Invention of Modernity in Machiavelli's Realist Style," *Political Style: The Artistry of Power*, Chicago, University of Chicago Press, 1995, pp. 13–49.

33. See Nelson and Boynton, *Video Rhetorics*, pp. 33–56; Nelson and Boynton, "Paradigms of Politics," *Hot Spots*, first video.

34. See Henry Tudor, *Political Myth*, New York, Praeger, 1972; H. Mark Roelofs, *Ideology and Myth in American Politics*, Boston, Little, Brown, 1976; James Oliver Robertson, *American Myth, American Reality*, New York, Hill and Wang, 1980.

35. See Garry Wills, *John Wayne's America*, New York, Simon and Schuster, 1997; John S. Nelson, *Tropes of Politics: Science, Theory, Rhetoric, Action*, Madison, University of Wisconsin Press, 1998; John Izod, *Myth, Mind and the Screen*, Cambridge, Cambridge University Press, 2001.

36. See M. M. Bakhtin, "Epic and Novel," in *The Dialogic Imagination: Four Essays*, Michael Holquist, ed., Caryl Emerson and Michael Holquist, trans., Austin, University of Texas Press, 1981; Larry Allums, ed., *The Epic Cosmos*, Dallas, Dallas Institute of Humanities and Culture, 1992; Franco Moretti, *Modern Epic: The World System from Goethe to García Márquez*, Quintin Hoare, trans., London, Verso (1994), 1996; Margaret Beissinger, Jane Tylus, and Susanne Wofford, eds., *Epic Traditions in the Contemporary World: The Poetics of Community*, Berkeley, University of California Press, 1999; Dean A. Miller, *The Epic Hero*, Baltimore, Johns Hopkins University Press, 2000.

37. See Marshall McLuhan, *The Gutenberg Galaxy*, Toronto, University of Toronto Press, 1962; George Steiner, *In Bluebeard's Castle*, New Haven, Yale University Press, 1971; Richard Bauman, *Verbal Art as Performance*, Rowley, MO, Newbury House, 1977; Jack Goody, *The Domestication of the Savage Mind*, Cambridge, Cambridge University Press, 1977; Eric Havelock, *The Muse Learns to Write*, New Haven, Yale University Press, 1986; Eric Havelock, *The Literate Revolution in Greece and Its Cultural Consequences*, Princeton, NJ, Princeton University Press, 1982; Walter J. Ong, *Orality and Literacy*, New York, Methuen, 1982.

38. See Lee C. McDonald, "Myth, Politics, and Political Science," *Western Political Quarterly* 22, no. 1 (March 1969): 141–150.

39. See George R. R. Martin, *A Song of Ice and Fire*, New York, Bantam Books: *A Game of Thrones*, 1997; *A Clash of Kings*, 1999; *A Storm of Swords*, 2000; *A Feast of Crows*, 2005; *A Dance of Dragons*, 2011.

40. See Nicholas Christopher, *Somewhere in the Night: Film Noir and the American City*, New York, Henry Holt, 1997; Eddie Muller, *Dark City: The Lost World of Film Noir*, New York, St. Martin's Press, 1998; Edward Dimendberg, *Film Noir and the Spaces of Modernity*, Cambridge, MA, Harvard University Press, 2004; Alain Silver and James Ursini, *L. A. Noir: The City as Character*, Santa Monica, CA, Santa Monica Press, 2005; Gyan Prakash, *Noir Urbanisms: Dystopic Images of the Modern City*, Princeton, NJ, Princeton University Press, 2010.

41. See Alasdair MacIntyre, *After Virtue*, Notre Dame, IN, University of Notre Dame Press (1981), enlarged edition, 1984.

42. See Georg Simmel, "The Stranger," in *The Sociology of Georg Simmel*, Kurt H. Wolff, ed. and trans., New York, Free Press, 1950, pp. 402–408.

43. See Teresa de Lauretis, *Alice Doesn't: Feminism, Semiotics, Cinema*, Bloomington, Indiana University Press, 1984; Teresa de Lauretis, *Technologies of Gender: Essays on Theory, Film and Fiction*, Bloomington, Indiana University Press, 1987.

44. See Robert D. Kaplan, *Warrior Politics: Why Leadership Demands a Pagan Ethos*, New York, Random House, 2002.

45. See Robert Hariman, "No One Is in Charge Here: Ryszard Kapuscinski's Anatomy of the Courtly Style," *Political Style: The Artistry of Power*, Chicago, University of Chicago Press, 1995, pp. 51–94.

46. See Niccolò Machiavelli, in *The Prince*, Robert M. Adams, ed. and trans., New York, Norton (1977), 2nd ed., 1992. Also see Matthews, *Hardball*; Christopher Matthews, *Life's a Campaign*, New York, Random House, 2007.

47. See Nelson, *Tropes of Politics*, pp. 150–179.

48. See Hariman, "No One Is In Charge Here," pp. 51–94.

49. See Kiku Adatto, "The Maverick Hero in American Movies," *Picture Perfect*, New York, Random House, 1993, pp. 124–166.

50. I thank Anna Lorien Nelson for the *Scrubs* example and Connie Nelson for calling attention to *Places in the Heart*.

51. See Carl G. Jung, in *Psyche and Symbol*, Violet S. deLaszlo, ed., Garden City, NY, Doubleday, 1958; Carl G. Jung, in *The Portable Jung*, Joseph Campbell, ed., R. F. C. Hull, trans., New York, Viking Press, 1971. Also see Joseph Campbell, *The Hero with a Thousand Faces*, New York, World, 1949.

52. See Robin Morgan, ed., *Sisterhood Is Powerful*, New York, Random House, 1970; Robin Morgan, ed., *Sisterhood Is Forever*, New York, Washington Square Press, 2003.

53. See John S. Nelson, "Orwell's Political Myths and Ours," in *The Orwellian Moment*, Robert L. Savage, James E. Combs, and Dan D. Nimmo, eds., Fayetteville, University of Arkansas Press, 1989, pp. 11–44; Nelson and Boynton, *Video Rhetorics*, pp. 195–222; Nelson, *Tropes of Politics*, pp. 115–230.

54. See Dan Nimmo and James E. Combs, *Subliminal Politics*, Englewood Cliffs, NJ, Prentice-Hall, 1980; Dan Nimmo and James E. Combs, *Mediated Political Realities*, New York, Longman (1983), 2nd ed., 1990; Tania Modleski, ed.,

Studies in Entertainment, Bloomington, Indiana University Press, 1986; Jim Collins, *Uncommon Cultures*, New York, Routledge, 1989; Patricia Mellencamp, ed., *Logics of Television: Essays in Cultural Criticism*, Bloomington, Indiana University Press, 1990; Michael Parenti, *Make-Believe Media*, New York, St. Martin's Press, 1992; Michael Parenti, *Land of Idols*, New York, St. Martin's Press, 1994. Keep in mind, though, that the notions of "entertainment" and "mass media" can mislead.

55. See Walter R. Fisher, "Narration as a Human Communication Paradigm," *Communication Monographs* 51, no. 1 (1984): 1–22; Walter R. Fisher, *Human Communication as Narration: Toward a Philosophy of Reason, Value, and Action*, Columbia, University of South Carolina Press, 1987. Also see W. J. T. Mitchell, ed., *On Narrative*, Chicago, University of Chicago Press, 1981; Murray Jardine, *Speech and Political Practice: Recovering the Place of Human Responsibility*, Albany, State University of New York Press, 1998; Rick Altman, *A Theory of Narrative*, New York, Columbia University Press, 2008.

56. See Nussbaum, "Shark Week." As Nussbaum hints, the first Netflix series, *House of Cards* (2013) with Kevin Spacey, works differently. Its first appearance is as an entire season of episodes for viewing all at once, more or less, on DVD. Not so incidentally, Nussbaum thinks of this series as noir—leading me to add that it is therefore (likely to be) more realist in political style than most dramas on American television. But as Nussbaum knows, a lot of viewers have been waiting to see whole seasons of dramas for the first time in a format that becomes one show after another from DVD or cable-cast weekend "marathons."

57. See Richard E. Peck, "Films, Television, and Tennis," in *Man and the Movies*, W. R. Robinson, ed., Baton Rouge, Louisiana State University Press, 1967, pp. 97–111; Raymond Williams, *Television: Technology and Cultural Form*, Hanover, NJ, Wesleyan University Press (1974), 2nd ed., 1992; John Fiske and John Hartley, *Reading Television*, London, Routledge, 1978; Todd Gitlin, ed., *Watching Television*, New York, Random House, 1986; Cynthia Schneider and Brian Wallis, eds., *Global Television*, Cambridge, MA, MIT Press, 1988; Samuel A. Chambers, *The Queer Politics of Television*, London, I. B. Tauris, 2009.

58. See Emily Nussbaum, "Trigger Happy: *Justified* and the Dangers of Charm," *New Yorker* 88, no. 44 January 21, 2013, pp. 76–77.

59. See John Hartley, *Tele-ology: Studies in Television*, London, Routledge, 1992.

60. See J. R. R. Tolkien, *The Lord of the Rings*, New York, Ballantine Books, 1965: *The Fellowship of the Ring*, *The Two Towers*, and *The Return of the King*.

61. See Hannah Arendt, "Thinking and Moral Considerations," *Social Research* 38, no. 3 (Autumn 1971): 417–446.

62. See Jason Jacobs, "Al Swearengen, Philosopher King," in *Reading Deadwood*, David Laverty, ed., New York, I. B. Taurus, 2006, pp. 11–21; Kim Akass, "You Motherfucker: Al Swearengen's Oedipal Dilemma," in *Reading Deadwood*, David Laverty, ed., New York, I. B. Taurus, 2006, pp. 23–32; Paul A. Cantor, "The Deadwood Dilemma: Freedom versus Law," in *Damned If You Do: Dilemmas of Action in Literature and Popular Culture*, Margaret S. Hrezo and John M. Parrish, eds., Lanham, MD, Lexington Books, 2010, pp. 21–39.

63. On what "everybody knows," see Nelson, *Tropes of Politics*, pp. 135–136.
64. NBC's *Hannibal* (2013–) series bears the title of the film made from the third Lecter novel by Thomas Harris: *Hannibal*, New York, Dell Books, 1999. And like that novel, it features the character of Hannibal Lecter (Mads Mikkelsen). But even though Ridley Scott's film (2001) of that novel is neo noir as well as horror, the television series so far is based instead on the first Lecter novel by Thomas Harris: *Red Dragon*, New York, St. Martin's Press, 1981. As in that first book, the other focal character is Will Graham (Hugh Dancy), not Clarice Starling as in the next two novels. Neither film version of the first Lecter novel—not *Manhunter* (1986) or *Red Dragon* (2002) —is neo noir in the least, and the TV series follows suit as psychological horror instead.
65. Neither of the *Blade* sequels—*Blade II* (2002) or *Blade: Trinity* (2004)—shows much commitment to neo noir, even though David S. Goyer wrote the scripts for all three films and even directed the third.
66. Both movies were conceived and directed by Luc Besson, but *La Femme Nikita* is in French, so, although widely viewed in the United States, it does not appear in the counts for neo-noir films in English. As an early example of feminist noir, it seems to have been highly influential in America.
67. The television series was such a sensation as to spur a theatrical release, but *Twin Peaks: Fire Walk with Me* (1992) seems to be horror inflected by thriller conventions rather than neo noir.
68. See Ellen Seiter, Hans Borchers, Gabriele Kreutzner, and Eva-Maria Warth, eds., *Remote Control: Television, Audience and Cultural Power*, London, Routledge, 1989.

Conclusion   Unsettling Idealism versus Realism: Perfectionism in Two Classics of Neo Noir

1. Sidney Pollack on TCM's *Elvis Mitchell: Under the Influence,* season 1, episode 1, July 7, 2008.
2. See Michael Parenti, *Land of Idols: Political Mythology in America*, New York, St. Martin's Press, 1994; Adrienne L. McLean, ed., *Glamour in a Golden Age: Movies Stars of the 1930s*, New Brunswick, NJ, Rutgers University Press, 2011.
3. See Tejaswini Ganti, *Bollywood: A Guidebook to Popular Hindi Cinema*, New York, Routledge (2004), 2nd ed., 2013; Ajay Gehlawat, *Reframing Bollywood: Theories of Popular Hindi Cinema*, Thousand Oaks, CA, Sage, 2010.
4. See Ralph Waldo Emerson, in *Essays and Lectures*, Joel Porte, ed., New York, Library of America, 1983. Also see Friedrich Nietzsche, in *The Portable Nietzsche*, Walter Kaufmann, ed. and trans., New York, Viking Press, 1954; Friedrich Nietzsche, *The Birth of Tragedy* and *The Genealogy of Morals*, Francis Golffing, trans., Garden City, NY, Doubleday, 1956; Friedrich Nietzsche, in *A Nietzsche Reader*, R. J. Hollingdale, ed. and trans., New York, Penguin Books, 1977; Friedrich Nietzsche, in *Friedrich Nietzsche on Rhetoric and Language*, Sander L. Gilman, Carole Blair, and David J. Parent, eds. and trans., New York, Oxford University Press, 1979; Friedrich Nietzsche, *Daybreak*, R. J. Hollingdale, trans.,

Cambridge, Cambridge University Press, 1982. And see Stanley Cavell, *This New Yet Unapproachable America: Lectures after Emerson after Wittgenstein*, Albuquerque, NM, Living Batch Press, 1989; Stanley Cavell, *Conditions Handsome and Unhandsome: The Constitution of Emersonian Perfectionism*, Chicago, University of Chicago Press, 1990; Stanley Cavell, *Philosophical Passages: Wittgenstein, Emerson, Austin, Derrida*, Cambridge, MA, Blackwell, 1995; Stanley Cavell, in *Emerson's Transcendental Etudes*, David Justin Hodge, ed., Stanford, CA, Stanford University Press, 2003.

5. See John S. Nelson, "Orwell's Political Myths and Ours," in *The Orwellian Moment: Hindsight and Foresight in the Post-1984 World*, Robert L. Savage, James E. Combs, and Dan D. Nimmo, eds., Fayetteville, University of Arkansas Press, 1989, pp. 11–44.

6. See Friedrich Nietzsche, in *The Will to Power*, Walter Kaufmann, ed., Walter Kaufmann and R. J. Hollingdale, trans., New York, Random House, 1967; Friedrich Nietzsche, *Twilight of the Idols* and *The Antichrist*, R. J. Hollingdale, trans., New York, Penguin Books (1889 and 1885), 1968; Friedrich Nietzsche, *Human All Too Human*, Gary Handwerk, trans., Stanford, CA, Stanford University Press, 1995; Friedrich Nietzsche, *On the Advantage and Disadvantage of History for Life*, Peter Preuss, trans., Indianapolis, Hackett, 1982.

7. See Robert Goldman and Stephen Papson, *Nike Culture: The Sign of the Swoosh*, Thousand Oaks, CA, Sage, 1998.

8. See Tracy B. Strong, *Friedrich Nietzsche and the Politics of Transformation*, Berkeley, University of California Press, 1975; Mark E. Warren, *Nietzsche and Political Thought*, Cambridge, MA, MIT Press, 1988; Daniel Conway, *Nietzsche and the Political*, New York, Routledge, 1997.

9. See Max Weber, "Politics as a Vocation," in *From Max Weber*, H. H. Gerth and C. Wright Mills, eds., New York, Oxford University Press, 1946, pp. 77–128. Also see John S. Nelson, *Tropes of Politics: Science, Theory, Rhetoric, Action*, Madison, University of Wisconsin Press, 1998, pp. 205–230.

10. See Albert Camus, *Caligula, and Three Other Plays*, Stuart Gilbert, trans., New York, Random House, 1958.

11. See Hannah Arendt, *The Origins of Totalitarianism*, New York, Harcourt Brace Jovanovich (1951, 1958), 4th ed., 1973; Hannah Arendt, *Eichmann in Jerusalem: A Report on the Banality of Evil*, New York, Viking Press (1963), enlarged edition, 1964.

12. See Isadore Traschen, "Pure and Ironic Idealism," *South Atlantic Quarterly* 59, no. 2 (Spring 1960): 163–170.

13. The novels about Hannibal Lecter are by Thomas Harris: *Red Dragon*, New York, St. Martin's Press, 1981; *The Silence of the Lambs*, New York, St. Martin's Press, 1988; *Hannibal*, New York, Dell Books, 1999; *Hannibal Rising*, New York, Delacorte Press, 2006.

14. The Lecter novels, movies, and now the *Hannibal* (2013–) television series spill over with name symbolism, but the present analysis needs to leave most of that for another occasion. The same goes for the recognition that, as a character of horror, Hannibal is more a vampire than a cannibal: see Harris, *Hannibal*, p. 324.

15. See Cormac McCarthy, *No Country for Old Men*, New York, Random House, 2005.
16. See Josh Levine, *The Coen Brothers: The Story of Two American Filmmakers*, Toronto, ECW Press, 2000.
17. See Lee Clark Mitchell, *Westerns*, Chicago, University of Chicago Press, 1996, pp. 28–54.
18. *Star Trek Into Darkness* (2013) identifies its principal villain, Kahn, as a perfectionist Overman, and it has him complain that Admiral Marcus as a realist "wanted to exploit my savagery."
19. On p. 153 of *No Country for Old Men*, McCarthy has Moss ask Wells, "What is [Chigurh] supposed to be, the ultimate bad-ass?" But Moss doesn't understand the answer: "I don't think that's how I would describe him . . . I guess I'd say that he doesn't have a sense of humor."
20. McCarthy, *No Country for Old Men*, p. 218.
21. The novel's version differs only a little: see McCarthy, *No Country for Old Men*, pp. 3–4.
22. Again the novel's take is much the same: see McCarthy, *No Country for Old Men*, p. 309.
23. McCarthy, *No Country for Old Men*, p. 253.
24. See Norman Spinrad, *Agent of Chaos*, New York, Popular Press, 1967.
25. See Harris, *Red Dragon, The Silence of the Lambs, Hannibal, Hannibal Rising*. And see *Manhunter* (1996) and *Hannibal Rising* (2007).
26. McCarthy, *No Country for Old Men*, p. 256. See Georg Wilhelm Friedrich Hegel on "the Cunning of Reason" and how "whatever is, is right" in such works as: *Phenomenology of Spirit*, A. V. Miller, trans., New York, Oxford University Press, 1977; *Philosophy of Right*, T. M. Knox, trans., New York, Oxford University Press, 1952; *Reason in History*, Robert S. Hartman, trans., Indianapolis, Bobbs-Merrill, 1953; *The Philosophy of History*, J. Sibree, trans., New York, Dover, 1956.
27. McCarthy, *No Country for Old Men*, p. 153.
28. Ibid. p. 259.
29. See Albert Camus, *The Stranger*, Stuart Gilbert, trans., New York, Random House, 1946.
30. McCarthy, *No Country for Old Men*, p. 256.
31. Ibid.
32. Ibid. p. 257.
33. Ibid. pp. 258–259.
34. Ibid. p. 260.
35. Ibid. p. 257.
36. This is what the title character (Tom Selleck) brands Alan Garner (Todd Hofley) in *Jesse Stone: No Remorse* (2010).
37. See Marshall McLuhan, *Understanding Media: The Extensions of Man*, New York, McGraw-Hill, 1964; Jim Collins: *Uncommon Cultures*, New York, Routledge, 1989.
38. See Stanley Cavell, *The Claim of Reason: Wittgenstein, Skepticism, Morality, and Tragedy*, New York, Oxford University Press, 1979.

39. See Hayden White, *Metahistory: The Historical Imaginatiion in Nineteenth-Century Europe*, Baltimore, Johns Hopkins University Press, 1973; Hayden White, *Tropics of Discourse: Essays in Cultural Criticism*, Baltimore, Johns Hopkins University Press, 1978. Also see John S. Nelson, "Review Essay," *History and Theory* 14, no. 1 (1975): 74–91; John S. Nelson, "Tropal History and the Social Sciences," *History and Theory* 19, no. 4 (1980): 80–101

40. See Hannah Arendt, *On Revolution*, New York, Viking Press, 1963, pp. 83–110; Lionel Trilling, *Sincerity and Authenticity*, Cambridge, MA, Harvard University Press, 1971.

41. See Immanuel Kant, *Groundwork of the Metaphysic of Morals*, H. J. Paton, trans., New York, Harper and Row, 1948; Immanuel Kant, *Critique of Pure Reason*, Norman Kemp Smith, trans., New York, St. Martin's Press, 1929; Immanuel Kant, *Critique of Practical Reason*, Lewis White Beck, trans., Indianapolis, Bobbs-Merrill, 1956.

42. See Ernst Cassirer, *The Philosophy of Symbolic Forms*, Ralph Manheim, trans., New Haven, Yale University Press, in three volumes: *Language*, 1953; *Mythical Thought*, 1955; *The Phenomenology of Knowledge*, 1957. Also see Ernst Cassirer, *An Essay on Man*, New Haven, Yale University Press, 1944; Ernst Cassirer, *The Myth of the State*, New Haven, Yale University Press, 1946; Ernst Cassirer, *Language and Myth*, Susanne K. Langer, trans., New York, Dover, 1946; Ernst Cassirer, *The Logic of the Humanities*, Clarence Smith Howe, trans., New Haven, Yale University Press, 1960.

43. See Kenneth Burke, *The Philosophy of Literary Form*, Berkeley, University of California Press (1941, 1967), 3rd ed., 1973.

44. See Northrop Frye, *Anatomy of Criticism: Four Essays*, Princeton, NJ, Princeton University Press, 1957; Kenneth Burke, "Four Master Tropes," *A Grammar of Motives*, Berkeley, University of California Press (1945), 1969, pp. 503–517; Karl Mannheim, *Ideology and Utopia*, Louis Wirth and Edward Shils, trans., New York, Harcourt, Brace and World, 1936.

45. See Ludwig Wittgenstein, *The Blue and Brown Books: Preliminary Studies for the Philosophical Investigations*, New York, Harper and Row, 1958; Ludwig Wittgenstein, *Philosophical Investigations*, G. E. M. Anscombe, trans., New York, Macmillan, 3rd ed., 1958.

46. See John S. Nelson, *Tropes of Politics: Science, Theory, Rhetoric, Action*, Madison, University of Wisconsin Press, 1998.

Index

CPSIA information can be obtained at www.ICGtesting.com
Printed in the USA
LVOW04*2106080715

445474LV00007B/195/P